Executive Dominance in Times of Crisis

In recent times, there has been a growing dominance of executives centered on the figure of a central leader, while parliaments, which should be the focus of political power, are being marginalized. This development reflects a historical process that has only worsened with the COVID-19 emergency. This book argues that the frequent use of unilateral acts by the executive, exacerbated in times of emergency, can lead to a process of serious democratic erosion. It holds that the unlimited expansion of unilateral action is incompatible with the principle of separation of powers and the basic elements of a constitutional democracy. The judicial and legislative branches, especially in times of crisis, must exercise firm control over executive acts. It puts forward the case that they should limit abuses and risks to democracy based on parameters that are attentive to democratic principles, institutional capacities, and the protection of fundamental rights. In this scenario, the book offers a contemporary analysis of executive dominance in Brazil, Italy, and Germany, particularly in the context of the COVID-19 pandemic. It engages with traditional literature on the subject while providing a novel perspective, particularly in relation to the Global South. The book will be of interest to academics and researchers working in the areas of constitutional law and politics, administrative law, and international and comparative law.

Camila Almeida Porfiro holds a PhD in public law from the University of Rome Tor Vergata and a master's degree in public law from the State University of Rio de Janeiro (UERJ). She has served as a law clerk at the Brazilian Supreme Court and has been a visiting researcher at Ludwig Maximilian University of Munich (LMU). Additionally, she was a visiting fellow at the Human Rights Center of the University of Essex.

Routledge Research in Public Law

Available titles in this series include:

Rule of Law in Crisis
Constitutionalism in a State of Flux
Edited by Martin Belov

Lawfare and Judicial Legitimacy
The Judicialisation of Politics in the case of South Africa
Kate Dent

Public Administration and Expertise in Democratic Governments
Comparative Public Law in the Twenty-First Century
Edited by Susan Rose-Ackerman

Comparative Administrative Law
Perspectives from Central and Eastern Europe
Edited by Ieva Deviatnikovaitė

The Equilibrium of Parliamentary Law-making
Comparative Perspectives on the Role of Courts in a Democracy
Viktor Kazai

Executive Dominance in Times of Crisis
Governing by Decree and the Pandemic
Camila Almeida Porfiro

For more information about this series, please visit: https://www.routledge.com/Routledge-Research-in-Public-Law/book-series/RRIPL

Executive Dominance in Times of Crisis

Governing by Decree and the Pandemic

Camila Almeida Porfiro

Routledge
Taylor & Francis Group
LONDON AND NEW YORK

First published 2025
by Routledge
4 Park Square, Milton Park, Abingdon, Oxon OX14 4RN

and by Routledge
605 Third Avenue, New York, NY 10158

Routledge is an imprint of the Taylor & Francis Group, an informa business

British Library Cataloguing-in-Publication Data
A catalogue record for this book is available from the British Library

Library of Congress Cataloging-in-Publication Data
Names: Porfiro, Camila Almeida, author.
Title: Executive dominance in times of crisis : governing by decree and the pandemic / Camila Almeida Porfiro.
Description: Abingdon, Oxon [UK] ; New York, NY : Routledge, 2025. | Series: Routledge research in public law | Includes bibliographical references and index.
Identifiers: LCCN 2025003066 | ISBN 9781041006213 (hardback) | ISBN 9781041006220 (paperback) | ISBN 9781003610816 (ebook)
Subjects: LCSH: Legislative bodies. | Parliamentary practice. | Legislative power. | COVID-19 Pandemic, 2020-2023. | Executive power. | Constitutional law.
Classification: LCC K3312 .P67 2025 | DDC 342/.062—dc23/eng/20250128
LC record available at https://lccn.loc.gov/2025003066

ISBN: 978-1-041-00621-3 (hbk)
ISBN: 978-1-041-00622-0 (pbk)
ISBN: 978-1-003-61081-6 (ebk)

DOI: 10.4324/9781003610816

Typeset in Galliard
by Apex CoVantage, LLC

Contents

Introduction 1

1 The executive dominance and the marginalization of parliaments: governing by decree 15

1.1 The (im)balance between the branches of government: the imperial executive 16
1.2 Deficiencies in legislative oversight of the executive branch 19
1.3 Deficiencies in judicial oversight of the executive branch 23
1.4 The judiciary, the executive, and the public opinion 26

2 When do presidents and prime ministers rule by decree? 31

2.1 The party composition of the Congress 33
2.2 Popularity ratings 35
2.3 Start or end of term 36
2.4 Crisis scenarios 37
2.5 Institutional and political limits to unilateral power 39

3 Justifying unilateral executive action 42

3.1 Celerity 43
3.2 Expertise 43
3.3 Flexibility 46
3.4 Escaping the formal legislative process 48
3.5 Instruments of legislative interpretation 49
3.6 Filling regulatory gaps 50
3.7 The symbolic role of decrees 51
3.8 Decrees shift the political burden from the legislature to the executive 52

4 Unilateral executive action in times of crisis 55

4.1 Should the other branches of government be deferential to the executive in emergencies? 55
4.2 Authoritarian infra-legalism, abusive constitutionalism, and "constitutional hardball" 59
4.3 Decrees and the democratic principle 61
4.4 Executive underreach in a crisis 63
4.5 The different types of crises and levels of control 65

5 Checks and balances during the COVID-19 pandemic 69

5.1 Executive dominance, democratic backlash, and autocratic populism 69
5.2 Good examples of judicial, legislative, and subnational checks on the executive 71
5.3 Strategies for legislative oversight of the executive branch during the pandemic 72
5.4 Strategies for judicial oversight of the executive branch during the pandemic 76
5.5 Supervision and oversight by subnational governments 79
5.6 Deliberative democracy and social participation 81

6 Constitutional limits of decrees in times of emergency 85

6.1 What does the "faithful execution" of laws mean? 86
6.2 Restrictions on fundamental rights by normative acts of the executive branch 93

7 The legal responses to COVID-19 in Italy, Brazil, and Germany 102

7.1 Italy: "weak-form review" 103
7.1.1 Criticism of the use of prime minister's decrees (DPCM) during the pandemic: violation of the principle of legality and the democratic principle 106
7.1.2 Prime minister's decrees (DPCMs) versus decree-laws 108
7.1.3 Is the broad delegation of normative power to the Italian prime minister constitutional? 110

7.1.4 *Criticism of the decision of the Italian Constitutional Court n. 198 of October 22, 2021* 113
7.1.5 *The Italian Constitutional Court during the pandemic* 119
7.1.6 *The concentration of power in the hands of the prime minister: the personalization of politics in Italy* 120
7.1.7 *The normative authority of the minister of health. A third-degree delegation?* 123
7.2 *Brazil: "mid-term review"* 125
7.2.1 *The role of the National Congress in managing the crisis* 126
7.2.2 *Local governments and the pandemic: regulatory chaos and lack of coordination* 129
7.2.3 *Judicial oversight of executive actions* 132
7.3 *Germany: "strong-form" review* 134
7.3.1 *German federalism and the role of subnational governments* 135
7.3.2 *Coordination and decentralization* 137
7.3.3 *Delegated legislation: predefinition of the content, object, and scope of executive regulations* 139
7.3.4 *Judicial oversight during the pandemic: balancing fundamental rights* 143

Conclusions 149

Index 154

Introduction

In his first year in office, Brazil's former president, Jair Bolsonaro, issued 536[1] presidential decrees and said he had more power than the president of the Chamber of Deputies because of his authority to issue decrees with the stroke of a pen.[2-3] Bolsonaro has used his decree power to relax the Brazilian regulations on the carrying of guns and ammunition;[4] to abolish the "National Policy for Social Participation" and hundreds of collegial bodies of the federal administration created to allow the participation of civil society in the formulation of public policies;[5] to modify the Law of Access to Information, which guarantees access to local, state, and federal government records;[6] to relax

1 Brazilian Legislation Official Website. *Decrees.* Available at: http://www4.planalto.gov.br/legislacao/portal-legis/legislacao-1/decretos1/decretos-1.

2 Folha de São Paulo (Brazilian Newsaper). *Bolsonaro says he has more power than Maia because he has a 'pen to sign decrees'.* May 28, 2020. Available at: https://www1.folha.uol.com.br/poder/2019/05/bolsonaro-diz-ter-mais-poder-que-maia-por-ter-caneta-para-editar-decretos.shtml.

3 In Brazil, presidents may issue executive decrees to ensure the faithful execution of laws and to manage the operations of the federal bureaucracy. Decrees are considered secondary legislation and can be issued without the involvement of the legislative branch of government. *See* Constitution of the Federative Republic of Brazil.

> Article 84. The President of the Republic shall have the exclusive power to: IV – sanction, promulgate and order the publication of laws, as well as to issue decrees and regulations for the true enforcement thereof; (. . .) VI – provide for the following, by means of a decree: a) organization and operation of federal government services, whenever no augmentation of expenditures or creation or abolishment of government bodies is involved; b) abolishment of public positions or posts, if vacant.

4 Brazil. Presidential Decree n. 9.847/2019. Available at: https://www4.planalto.gov.br/legislacao/portal-legis/legislacao-1/decretos1/2019-decretos. *See also* CNN. *Brazil's Bolsonaro signs executive order easing gun rules.* May 8, 2019. Available at: https://edition.cnn.com/2019/05/08/americas/bolsonaro-brazil-gun-laws-intl/index.html.

5 Brazil. Presidential Decrees n. 9.759/2019 and 9.812/2019. Available at: https://www4.planalto.gov.br/legislacao/portal-legis/legislacao-1/decretos1/2019-decretos.

6 Brazil. Presidential Decree n. 9.690/2019. Available at: https://www4.planalto.gov.br/legislacao/portal-legis/legislacao-1/decretos1/2019-decretos.

DOI: 10.4324/9781003610816-1

environmental laws;[7] to modify the authority responsible for forest concession policies;[8] and to classify "beauty salons and gyms" as "essential activities" during the COVID-19 pandemic.[9] The Brazilian president has issued decrees in the face of congressional opposition to implement campaign promises and speed up changes that, in theory, should be approved by the Chamber of Deputies and the Senate.

However, Brazil is not the only country where decrees are used to change the meaning of laws and promote political reforms without parliament. In the United States, in his first term, President Donald Trump faced criticism for issuing a large number of executive orders for various purposes, including building a wall on the border with Mexico,[10] making it easier to fire federal government employees, and weakening the unions that represent them.[11] In 2017, Trump also signed an executive order known as Buy American, Hire American to "strictly enforce" immigration laws and control the granting of work visas to foreigners.[12]

Recently, Argentine President Javier Milei promoted the phenomenon known as *decretazo*[13] by issuing a record number of "decrees of necessity and urgency"[14] to implement radical changes in various economic sectors

7 Brazil. Presidential Decree n. 9.760/2019. Available at: https://www4.planalto.gov.br/legislacao/portal-legis/legislacao-1/decretos1/2019-decretos.

8 Brazil. Presidential Decree n. 10.347/2020. Available at: https://www4.planalto.gov.br/legislacao/portal-legis/legislacao-1/decretos1/2020-decretos.

9 Brazil. Presidential Decree n. 10.344/2020. Available at: https://www4.planalto.gov.br/legislacao/portal-legis/legislacao-1/decretos1/2020-decretos.

10 BBC News. *Trump orders wall to be built on Mexico border*. January 26, 2017. Available at: https://www.bbc.com/news/world-us-canada-38740717.

11 The New York Times. *Trump moves to ease the firing of federal workers*. May 25, 2018. Available at: https://www.nytimes.com/2018/05/25/business/economy/trump-federal-workers.html.

12 United States of America. White House Official Website. *Presidential executive order on buy American and hire American*. Available at: https://www.whitehouse.gov/presidential-actions/presidential-executive-order-buy-american-hire-american/.

13 BBC News. *En qué consiste el polémico Decreto de Necesidad y Urgencia presentado por Milei en Argentina para liberalizar la economía del país*. December 21, 2023. Available at: https://www.bbc.com/mundo/articles/c6p17951dwno#:~:text=El%20decreto%20de%20Milei%20autoriza,de%20promoci%C3%B3n%20comercial%2C%20entre%20otras.

14 In Argentina, the "decrees of necessity and urgency" have the force of law. They can introduce or modify primary legislation. *See* Constitution of Argentina.

> Article 99 – The President of the Nation has the following powers: (. . .) 3. He participates in the enactment of the laws according to the Constitution, promulgates them, and has them published. The Executive Power may not issue dispositions of a legislative nature in any case whatsoever, under penalty of their absolute and incurable nullity. Only when exceptional circumstances make it impossible to follow the regular procedures provided by this Constitution for the passing of laws, and the situation does not involve rules that regulate criminal, tax, or electoral matters or the regime governing political parties, may [the President] dictate decrees by reason of necessity and urgency, which are to be decided at a general meeting of Ministers, who must endorse them, together with the Chief of the Cabinet of Ministers. The Chief of the Cabinet of Ministers, personally and within ten days, shall submit the measure for the consideration of the Standing Bicameral Committee, whose membership must

and to reform labor regulations.[15] Decades earlier, the former president of Argentina, Carlos Menem, also promoted a *decretazo*[16] in the 1990s, issuing decrees to promote privatizations and the deregulation of the economy in an attempt to overcome the severe economic crisis that plagued the country. According to Menem, the large number of these acts was justified by the emergency scenario, which did not allow waiting for the outcome of political obstacles and the legislative process.[17]

Also, in Paraguay, during the politically unstable administrations of Juan Carlos María Wasmosy Monti (1993–1998) and Fernando Lugo (2008–2012), there were a record number of decrees, while in Peru there was an increasing number of these unilateral acts during the authoritarian period of Alberto Fujimori (1990–2000).[18] Moreover, in post-socialist European states, such as Ukraine, the economic and political reforms of the early 1990s were also carried out through unilateral normative acts issued by the heads of the executive.[19]

It can be observed that, over several decades, the power and decision-making authority of the parliament has been transferred to the chief executive in a highly concentrated and centralizing manner.[20] The growing strength of populist

---

reflect the proportion of the political representation of each Chamber. This Committee shall forward its report within ten days to a plenary session of each Chamber for its express treatment, which the Chambers shall consider immediately. A special law approved by an absolute majority of the totality of the members of each Chamber shall regulate the procedure and the scope of the intervention of Congress.

15 On January 4, 2024, the Argentine Labor Court suspended part of the decrees on the grounds that there is no proven need or urgency for the executive branch to bypass the National Congress. *See El País*. Argentine justice system halts President Javier Milei's labor reforms. January 4, 2024. Available at: https://english.elpais.com/international/2024-01-04/argentine-justice-system-halts-president-javier-mileis-labor-reforms.html.

16 Rubio, Delia Ferreira; Goretti, Matteo. Cuando el presidente gobierna solo. Menem y los decretos de necesidad y urgencia hasta la reforma constitucional (julio 1989–agosto 1994). *Desarrollo Económico*, v. 36, n. 141, 1996, p. 443–474.

17 Rubio, Delia Ferreira; Goretti, Matteo. Cuando el presidente gobierna solo. Menem y los decretos de necesidad y urgencia hasta la reforma constitucional (julio 1989–agosto 1994). *Op. cit.*

18 Inácio, Magna; Llanos, Mariana. The institutional presidency in Latin America: A comparative analysis. *Presidential Studies Quarterly*, v. 46, n. 3, 2016, p. 531–549.

19 Kubicek, Paul. Delegative democracy in Russia and Ukraine. *Communist and Post-Communist Studies*, v. 27, n. 4, 1994, *passim*.

20 *See, e.g.*, Elgie, Robert; Passarelli, Gianluca. The presidentialization of political executives. In: *The Oxford handbook of political executives*. Oxford: Oxford University Press, 2020, p. 359–381; Poguntke, Thomas; Webb, Paul. The presidentialization of politics in democratic societies: A framework for analysis. In: Poguntke, Thomas; Webb, Paul (Eds.). *The presidentialization of politics: A comparative study of modern democracies*, v. 1. Oxford University Press, 2005, p. 1–25; Blondel, Jean. *The presidential republic*. London: Palgrave Macmillan London, 2015, p. 23–41; Howell, William G. Unilateral powers: A brief overview. *Presidential Stud. Q.*, v. 35, 2005, p. 417; Posner, Eric A.; Vermeule, Adrian. *The executive unbound: After the Madisonian republic*. Oxford: Oxford University Press, 2011, *passim*; Ackerman, Bruce. Good-bye, montesquieu. In: Rose-Ackerman, Susan; Lindseth, Peter L. (Eds.). *Comparative administrative law*. Cheltenham: Edward Elgar Publishing, 2010, p. 128–133; Ackerman, Bruce. The new separation of powers. In: *The rule of law and the separation of powers*. New York:

presidents and prime ministers has revealed a revolution in contemporary real-world politics: the ***pendulum*** of power has shifted toward the executive and away from parliament. There is a growing dominance of executives centered on the figure of a central leader, while parliaments, which should be the *focus* of political power, are being marginalized. And this phenomenon occurs even in parliamentary systems.[21] Political scientists and legal scholars have denounced the contemporary trend toward the "presidentialization of politics", a process by which parliamentary regimes acquire the characteristics of presidential systems without any formalized constitutional change.[22] Also, these *presidentializing* and *personalizing* tendencies are not just the spectacle of a specific, one-off election campaign. They reflect a historical process that has only worsened with the COVID-19 emergency.[23]

Indeed, the pandemic has exacerbated this phenomenon of executive dominance and overproduction of regulations. In many countries, restrictive measures such as lockdowns and curfews have been authorized by executive decrees with minimal parliamentary involvement.[24] Even consolidated democracies such as the United States and Italy have relied on secondary legislation to enact restrictions on freedom of movement, assembly, and political and religious expression. All this with a minimal and extremely vague legislative delegation that did not provide sufficient parameters and other details for administrative action. Many of the measures did not have a clear legal basis. In Italy, for example, the crisis was mainly addressed through decrees of the President of the Council of Ministers (DPCM) and regulations of the minister of health, which, among other measures, led to the prohibition of movement in entire Italian regions. These instruments do not represent primary legislation and are the product of an excessively vague and

---

Routledge, 2017, p. 395–490; Ackerman, Bruce. The emergency constitution. *Yale Law Journal*, v. 113, 2003, p. 1.029.

21 Rullo, Luigi. The COVID-19 pandemic crisis and the personalization of the government in Italy. *Internationsal Journal of Public Leadership*, v. 17, n. 2, 2021, p. 196–207.

22 Calise, Mauro. Personalization of politics. In: Badie, Bertrand; Berg-Schlosser, Dirk; Morlino, Leonardo (Eds.). *International encyclopedia of political science*. London: Sage, 2011, p. 1.858–1.861.

23 The global COVID-19 pandemic caused by the new SARS-CoV-2 coronavirus was declared a global health emergency by the World Health Organization on January 30, 2020. As infection rates grew exponentially around the world, the restrictions on individual liberty, movement, assembly, worship, education, and commerce, as well as elections, parliaments, and courts, became the most restrictive in contemporary history. *See* World Health Organization (WHO). *Coronavirus disease (COVID-19) pandemic*. Available at: https://www.who.int/emergencies/diseases/novel-coronavirus-2019. *See also* Grogan, Joelle. Analysing global use of emergency powers in response to COVID-19. *European Journal of Law Reform*, v. 4, 2020, p. 338.

24 *See, e.g.*, Ginsburg, Tom; Versteeg, Mila. The bound executive: Emergency powers during the pandemic. *International Journal of Constitutional Law*, v. 19, n. 5, December 2021, p. 1498–1535; Deere, Kelly J. Governing by executive order during the COVID-19 pandemic: Preliminary observations concerning the proper balance between executive orders and more formal rule making. *Missouri Law Review*, v. 86, 2021, p. 721.

imprecise chain of delegation.[25] This scenario reflected the sidelining of the parliament, which in practice transferred broad regulatory powers to prime ministers.[26]

In fact, the severity of the COVID-19 crisis has exposed the general weakness of several legislatures.[27] Particularly in Latin American and Eastern European countries, the pandemic reinforced bad examples of executive dominance, lack of parliamentary oversight, little democratic input, concentration of power by populist leaders, and a general disregard for proper constitutional order.[28] Adding to the confusion, several rules were introduced with little or no notice and sometimes with retroactive application. Uncertainty about the meaning of legal definitions used in the legislation also led to inconsistencies in its application. Ambiguous terms in the administrative decrees further exacerbated the regulatory chaos.[29]

25 The delegation was made by decree-laws (*decreti-legge*), legislative acts for times of urgency and necessity, which have the force of law. *See* Italian Decree-Law n. 6 of February 23, 2020, and Decree-Law n. 19 of March 25, 2020. The Decree-Law n. 19 of March 25, 2020, was converted with amendments by Law n. 35 of May 22, 2020, and subsequently supplemented and amended several times by other decree-laws. Those decree-laws determined that COVID-19 would be addressed through Decrees of the President of the Council of Ministers (DPCM), proposed by the minister of health, after consultation with the ministers of the interior, defense, economy, and other ministries concerned, as well as the presidents of the regions or the president of the Conference of Regions and Autonomous Provinces, depending on the territorial scope of the measures. *See also* article 77 of the Constitution of the Italian Republic:

> The Government may not, without an enabling act from the Houses, issue decrees having the force of ordinary law. When in extraordinary cases of necessity and urgency the Government adopts provisional measures having the force of law, it must on the same day present said measures for confirmation to the Houses which, even if dissolved, shall be summoned especially for this purpose and shall convene within five days. The decrees lose effect from their inception if they are not confirmed within sixty days from their publication. The Houses may however regulate by law legal relationships arising out of not confirmed decrees.

26 *See, e.g.*, Guzzetta, Giovanni. DPCM e Costituzione anche alla luce della sent. 198/2021 della Corte costituzionale. *Op. cit.*; Guzzetta, Giovanni. Le fonti dell'emergenza alla prova della pandemia. In: Marini, Francesco Saverio; Scaccia, Gino (Eds.). *Emergenza COVID-19 e ordinamento costituzionale*. Torino: G. Giappichelli editore, 2020, p. 73–82; Trabucco, Daniele. Il "virus" nel sistema delle fonti: decreti-legge e dpcm al tempo del Covid-19: tra principio di legalità formale e principio di legalità sostanziale. *Nomos*, n. 2, 2020, p. 1–21; Musella, Fortunato. I poteri di emergenza nella Repubblica dei Presidenti. *Diritti regionali*, n. 2, 2020, p. 107–139; Cavino, Massimo et al. Covid-19. Una prima lettura dei provvedimenti adottati dal Governo. *Federalismi.it*, n. 6, 2020, p. 1–9.

27 Cormacain, Ronan; Bar-Siman-Tov, Ittai. Legislatures in the time of Covid-19. *The Theory and Practice of Legislation*, v. 8, n. 1–2, 2020, p. 8; Griglio, Elena. Parliamentary oversight under the Covid-19 emergency: Striving against executive dominance. *The Theory and Practice of Legislation*, v. 8, n. 1–2, 2020, p. 49–70.

28 Inácio, Magna; Recch, Filipe; Valencia, Carolina Guerrero. The power of the administrative decisions of Latin American presidents. In: Llanos, Mariana; Marsteintredet, Leiv (Eds.). *Latin America in times of turbulence: Presidentialism under stress.* New York: Routledge, 2023, p. 75; Grogan, Joelle. States of emergency: Analysing global use of emergency powers in response to COVID-19. *Eur. JL Reform*, v. 22, 2020, p. 348.

29 Grogan, Joelle. COVID-19, the rule of law and democracy. Analysis of legal responses to a global health crisis. *Hague Journal on the Rule of Law*, v. 14, n. 2–3, 2022, p. 349–369.

This executive supremacy and unchecked regulatory activity are undesirable from a constitutional and democratic point of view, especially in an emergency.[30] Aware of this, democracies such as Germany, France, New Zealand, and Japan managed to involve their legislatures in the development of emergency measures, with the rapid passage of several laws specifically aimed at controlling the virus.[31] They recognized the importance of strengthening the system of checks and balances in times of crisis. Also, while some constitutional courts have preferred to adopt a deferential attitude toward government decisions, exercising almost no control over executive actions, others have expressed genuine opposition, invalidating decrees or accusing leaders of unconstitutional omissions.[32]

In this context, this book argues that a crisis scenario does not justify the dominance of the executive branch. Despite the need for speed and expertise in emergency management, parliamentary and judicial involvement is still important and necessary. Countries that have actively involved legislatures and courts in finding solutions have not lost efficiency or speed in dealing with the pandemic. In exceptional times, the legislature must play an active role in overseeing executive actions and in drafting new laws to respond to the crisis. It offers distinct advantages as an arena for political debate and serves as the ultimate *locus* of democratic legitimacy. Courts, in turn, must (i) monitor the procedural integrity of emergency declarations; (ii) conduct substantive review of restrictions on rights, balancing fundamental freedoms against public health concerns; and, in some cases, (iii) require the government to take active steps to address the crisis and its aftermath. Finally, subnational governments can tailor policies to local needs, conditions, and preferences.[33]

Certainly, cooperation produces more legitimate and reasoned responses than the national executive acting alone. This is especially important in situations where the optimal response is unclear. A crisis requires that the branches of government work together to formulate the response through mutual aid, contestation, and dialogue. Judicial review, legislative oversight, and subnational engagement can help identify blind spots and reduce the risk of errors in emergency responses.[34]

30 Gross, Oren; Aoláin, Fionnuala Ní. *Law in times of crisis: Emergency powers in theory and practice.* Cambridge: Cambridge University Press, 2006, p. 86–109.

31 Ginsburg, Tom; Versteeg, Mila. The bound executive: Emergency powers during the pandemic. *International Journal of Constitutional Law*, v. 19, n. 5, December 2021, p. 1498–1535.

32 Ginsburg, Tom; Versteeg, Mila. The bound executive: Emergency powers during the pandemic. *Op. cit.*

33 Ginsburg, Tom; Versteeg, Mila. The bound executive: Emergency powers during the pandemic. *Op. cit.*, p. 1.498–1.510.

34 Ginsburg, Tom; Versteeg, Mila. The bound executive: Emergency powers during the pandemic. *Public Law and Legal Theory Working Paper Series*, n. 747, 2020, p. 6. It should be noted that two versions of this article, one longer than the other, were published in the "*International Journal of Constitutional Law, v. 19, n. 5, December 2021*" and in the "*Public Law and Legal Theory Working Paper Series, n. 747, 2020*".

This book therefore posits that the frequent use of unilateral acts by the executive can lead to a process of serious democratic erosion. These acts have a strict scope that should not be expanded to serve as a political maneuvering tool for presidents or prime ministers who do not want to engage in dialogue with parliament. The unlimited expansion of unilateral action is incompatible with the principle of separation of powers and the basic elements of a constitutional democracy. The judicial and legislative branches, especially in times of crisis, must exercise firm control over executive acts. They should limit abuses and risks to democracy based on parameters that are attentive to democratic principles, institutional capacities, and the protection of fundamental rights.

The book is divided into seven chapters. The first chapter deals with the dominance of the executive and the imbalance between the branches of government. It points out the types of difficulties that the legislature and the judiciary usually encounter in controlling the executive. The second chapter then analyzes how presidents and prime ministers use decrees to circumvent Congress and unilaterally implement campaign promises that appeal to political constituencies. It seeks to answer the following questions: (i) why do presidents and prime ministers issue decrees? (ii) what are the democratic risks of the increasing use of these unilateral normative instruments? (iii) is the large number of decrees a sign of strength or weakness of the chief executive? (iv) does the number of decrees vary according to the personality of each leader or according to political and institutional factors? (v) when and under what circumstances do they issue decrees? (vi) what can be done to limit the abuse of unilateral powers?

Subsequently, Chapter 3 examines the justifications offered by authors such as Eric Posner and Adrian Vermeule for the dominance of the executive, particularly in times of crisis. It examines the reasons for unilateral executive action, such as the need for speed, flexibility, and expertise in certain sectors. Chapter 4 then outlines the main criticisms of Posner and Vermeule's theory of the "unbound executive", according to which the other branches should defer to the executive in emergencies. The chapter argues that this theory is inconsistent with the principles of legality and democratic deliberation. As happened in several countries during the pandemic, the decree power can be used to circumvent the constitution in a phenomenon that Mark Tushnet has termed "constitutional hardball",[35] in which normative instruments are used as political maneuvers to circumvent democratic rules.

In sequence, Chapter 5 analyzes the posture of the branches of government during the COVID-19 pandemic. While some countries failed to maintain an effective system of checks and balances, others were highly successful in maintaining robust legislative and judicial oversight. In Hungary, Turkey, and

35 Tushnet, Mark. Constitutional hardball. *The John Marshall Law Review*, v. 37, 2003, p. 523. *See also* Balkin, Jack M. Constitutional hardball and constitutional crises. *Quinnipiac Law Review*, v. 26, 2007, p. 579.

Poland, for example, the pandemic led to a growing autocratic executive and increased the verticalization and concentration of decision-making power in the hands of chief executives. In those countries, the coronavirus response was based on decrees without a clear legal basis and a lack of parliamentary and judicial oversight. On the other hand, democracies such as Germany, France, New Zealand, and Japan actively involved legislatures, courts, and subnational governments in the development of emergency measures.

Subsequently, Chapter 6 addresses the theories of constitutional and administrative law concerning restrictions on fundamental rights imposed by executive acts. According to the theory of "essentialness" or "materiality" (*Wesentlichkeitstheorie*), developed by the German Constitutional Court, essential questions of a particular political, social, or economic matter must be decided by an act of parliament.[36] From this perspective, laws that delegate normative powers to the executive must have a high normative density, specifying the content, purpose, and scope of executive regulations. Secondary legislation that does not have a clear, detailed, and precise legal basis should not be recognized as constitutional. Legislatures should set explicit limits, conditions, and checks on administrative power. This theory is important for assessing the validity of unilateral acts enacted during the COVID-19 pandemic, which produced core restrictions on fundamental rights.

Finally, the seventh chapter analyzes the legal response to the pandemic in Italy, Brazil, and Germany. This comparative perspective and the choice of these countries are due to a gradation between the levels of involvement of the legislative and judicial branches in the fight against the pandemic. In Italy, the participation of the other branches can be classified as a "weak-form review", since they exercised only a weak oversight over executive actions.[37] Indeed, Italian doctrine has criticized the inertia of parliament, which has limited itself to converting the decree-laws, which in turn entrusted the adoption of containment measures to the prime ministers, without parliamentary scrutiny.[38] The Italian Constitution provides for an instrument specifically designed for situations of need and urgency: the decree-law.[39] An extensive use of this instrument would have allowed the legislature to exercise more control.[40]

36 Staupe, Júrgen. *Parlamentsvorbehalt und Delegationsbefugnis - Zur "Wesentlichkeitstheorie" und zur Reichxveite legislativer Regelungskompetenz, insbesondere im Schulrecht.* Berlin: Duncker & Humblot, 1985, p. 24.

37 Claudiani, Simona. Brevi Note Sui DPCM: Tra Emergenza e Stabilizzazione, In: Morana, Donatella; Mabellini, Stefania (Eds.). *L'emergenza pandemica e l'impatto sul diritto pubblico: innovazione e prospettive future. Quaderni del Dottorato di Ricerca in Diritto Pubblico dell'Università degli Studi di Roma "Tor Vergata".* Milan: Wolters Kluwer, 2022, p. 69.

38 *See, e.g.*, Guzzetta, Giovanni. DPCM e Costituzione anche alla luce della sent. 198/2021 della Corte costituzionale. *Op. cit.*

39 Esposito, Carlo. Decreto Legge. In: *Enciclopedia del Diritto*, v. XI. Milano: Giuffrè Editore, 1962, p. 864–870.

40 Lucarelli, Alberto. Costituzione, fonti del diritto ed emergenza sanitaria. *Rivista AIC*, v. 2, 2020, *passim*.

In Brazil, the other branches of government exercised an intermediary level of control. On the one hand, there was a chaotic proliferation of decrees and regulations from local administrations implementing measures to deal with the crisis. But on the other hand, the National Congress passed numerous laws specifically related to COVID-19 and formed a Parliamentary Inquiry Commission (CPI) to investigate allegations of corruption and omissions on the part of the federal executive, headed by then-President Jair Bolsonaro.[41] In addition, the Supreme Court of Brazil has issued thousands of decisions regarding the pandemic and invalidated a series of executive acts that contradicted the guidelines of the World Health Organization (WHO). Furthermore, it has prohibited the dissemination of propaganda by the Bolsonaro government against social distancing measures. The Court also has ordered the government to develop a specific plan to protect Indigenous populations from the coronavirus.[42] Thus, considering that the judiciary and the legislature have not been silent, but their control has coexisted with the regulatory protagonism of local administrations, Brazil can be considered an example of a "mid-term review" of executive actions.

In Germany, despite the intensity of federal and local government intervention, other political actors were constantly active and performed a "strong-form review". Federal and local legislators passed several anti-COVID laws, which were continually updated and rediscussed by parliamentarians. At the same time, the German Infectious Diseases Protection Act (Infektionsschutzgesetz, IfSG),[43] as amended in November 2020, set clear and limited parameters for executive regulations, which constrained the administration. In the same vein, the German judiciary actively shaped the contours of what was permitted and prohibited during this period, ruling on a number of lawsuits that debated restrictions on fundamental rights.[44]

41 Brazil. Federal Senate. *CPI da Pandemia: principais pontos do relatório*. Available at: https://www12.senado.leg.br/noticias/materias/2021/10/20/cpi-da-pandemia-principais-pontos-do-relatorio.

42 Pinheiro, Victor Marcel; Ilarraz, Marcelo; Mestriner, Melissa Terni. The impacts of the COVID-19 crisis on the Brazilian legal system – a report on the functioning of the branches of the government and on the legal scrutiny of their activities. *The Theory and Practice of Legislation*, v. 8, n. 1–2, 2020, p. 201–202; Llanos, Mariana; Marsteintredet, Leiv. *Latin America in times of turbulence: Presidentialism under stress. Op. cit.*, p. 75–105.

43 Germany. *Gesetz zur Verhütung und Bekämpfung von Infektionskrankheiten beim Menschen (Act on the Prevention and Control of Infectious Diseases in Humans)*. Available at: https://www.gesetze-im-internet.de/ifsg/index.html.

44 Kaiser, Anna-Bettina; Hensel, Roman. Federal Republic of Germany: Legal response to Covid-19. In: *The Oxford compendium of national legal responses to Covid-19*. April 2021. Available at: https://oxcon.ouplaw.com/view/https://doi.org/10.1093/law-occ19/law-occ19-e2; Kaiser, Anna-Bettina. The state of exception under German law and the current pandemic: Comparative models and constitutional rights. *e-Pública*, v. 7, n. 3, 2020, p. 4–15. *See also* German Federal Constitutional Court (Bundesverfassungsgericht). *Constitutional complaints (BvR) – 2020 to 2022*. Available at: https://www.bundesverfassungsgericht.de/

These three countries were chosen for other reasons as well. All three share an authoritarian past in the 20th century and a generally strong and powerful executive.[45] Although Germany and Italy have parliamentary systems of government, their prime ministers are prominent figures on the political scene, often leading political reforms, and controversies. Their importance is not diminished or forgotten in the face of parliaments. In Italy, prime ministers such as Silvio Berlusconi, Romano Prodi, Bettino Craxi, or Giulio Andreotti centralized Italian political life and did not act as mere spokesmen for the parliament. In Germany, too, especially during the pandemic, the figure of Angela Merkel centralized great political prestige.[46] In Brazil, given the presidential system, there is a natural tendency for power to be concentrated in the executive, especially in the figure of the president of the republic.[47] In this scenario, all three countries have a history of a strong, active, and sometimes autocratic executive.

Furthermore, Chapter 7 offers a concise examination of the political systems of Brazil, Germany, and Italy. Providing this context is crucial for understanding the use of decrees, ensuring that the unilateral power of the executive is analyzed within the specific political and constitutional frameworks of each nation, rather than in isolation. By analyzing constitutional provisions and the allocation of power between national and regional authorities, the chapter reveals how these structures influence the functioning of their respective executives. This approach considers the unique constitutional factors that shape the executive's authority and decision-making processes in each country.

Finally, it is essential to define the object of this book. Unilateral executive acts are those that take effect without the prior involvement or control of the legislative branch. In general, there are two types of these unilateral acts. The first is decrees with the force of law, which are considered primary legislation and are aimed at creating or amending laws. This is the case, for example, of ***decreti-legge*** (decree-laws) in Italy[48] and ***medidas provisórias*** (provisional measures)

SiteGlobals/Forms/Suche/EN/Entscheidungensuche_Formular.html?nn=5403310&facettedYear=2021&language_=en.

45 Mammone, Andrea; Parini, Ercole Giap; Veltri, Giuseppe A. (Eds.). *The Routledge handbook of contemporary Italy: History, politics, society*. New York: Routledge, 2015; Childers, Thomas. *The third Reich: A history of Nazi Germany. New York: Simon and Schuster*, 2017; Kleßmann, Christoph; Sabrow, Martin. Contemporary history in Germany after 1989. *Contemporary European History*, v. 6, n. 2, 1997, p. 219–243; Santos, Desirree dos Reis. *Ditadura militar e democracia no Brasil: história, imagem e testemunho*. Rio de Janeiro: Ponteio, 2013.

46 Mammone, Andrea; Parini, Ercole Giap; Veltri, Giuseppe A. (Eds.). *The Routledge handbook of contemporary Italy: History, politics, society*. *Op. cit.*; Kleßmann, Christoph; Sabrow, Martin. Contemporary history in Germany after 1989. *Op. cit.*, p. 219–243.

47 Abranches, Sérgio. *Presidencialismo de coalizão: raízes e evolução do modelo político brasileiro*. São Paulo: Editora Companhia das Letras, 2018.

48 *See* article 77 of the Constitution of the Italian Republic:

> The Government may not, without an enabling act from the Houses, issue decrees having the force of ordinary law. When in extraordinary cases of necessity and urgency the Government

in Brazil.[49] These decrees with the force of law, issued by the government in cases of necessity and urgency, produce legal effects for a limited period of time (usually 30 to 60 days), and within this period, they must be converted into law by the parliaments.

The second type of unilateral acts – and the focus of this book – are the decrees, ordinances, and regulations that represent secondary legislation. These regulatory acts serve mainly to guarantee the applicability of laws, but they can also establish conditions for the organization and functioning of the executive bureaucracy. Although the book occasionally discusses the decrees with the force of law, the main focus is on this secondary regulation, which does not require scrutiny by the legislature.[50]

Another important point is that, despite the profound differences between presidential and parliamentary systems, various considerations and arguments about unilateral executive action can be applied to both. Crisis scenarios, for example, make decrees by both presidents and prime ministers flourish. Italy, as has been previously observed, is a country with a parliamentary system that has primarily addressed the challenges posed by the COVID-19 pandemic through the decrees of the prime minister (DPCM). For the aforementioned reasons, the book will clearly indicate when there are reasons to approximate or differentiate unilateral action in both systems.[51-52]

Additionally, the considerations presented in this book are primarily directed at the head of the executive branch and government ministers. The question of the independent regulatory agencies, which possess specialized expertise in

---

adopts provisional measures having the force of law, it must on the same day present said measures for confirmation to the Houses which, even if dissolved, shall be summoned especially for this purpose and shall convene within five days. The decrees lose effect from their inception if they are not confirmed within sixty days from their publication. The Houses may however regulate by law legal relationships arising out of not confirmed decrees.

49 In Brazil, *medidas provisórias* have the force of law. They can be understood as both a legally binding temporary executive order and an anticipated legislative proposal. During the first 120 days after the issuance of a *medida provisória*, it is considered a unilateral presidential directive, having the force of law. At the end of this period, the act must be voted on by Congress, so that it permanently becomes law. Otherwise, the *medida provisória* is terminated and no longer has legal validity.

50 In this sense, whenever a topic refers to "decrees, regulations or ordinances" it is referring to secondary legislation.

51 *See* Siaroff, Alan. Comparative presidencies: The inadequacy of the presidential, semi-presidential and parliamentary distinction. *European Journal of Political Research,* v. 42, n. 3, 2003, p. 287–312.

52 Despite the profound differences between the terms "parliament", "congress", "legislature", and "legislative branch", these will be used interchangeably to refer to these institutions whose primary function is to create laws in democratic systems. In the same sense, the term "chief executive", "head of the executive", or "executive leader" will be used to refer to presidents and prime ministers. Although we recognize the difference between them in presidential and parliamentary systems and in different countries, the choice of these different terms is intended to facilitate the flow of the text and to avoid excessive repetition.

specific matters, will not be addressed in detail. The focus is on the decrees and regulations issued by the president or premier and their ministers, who are eminently political and nontechnical authorities. Even if ministers such as the minister of health or the minister of economy can have great expertise in their specific field, it is undeniable that their nominations can be made for political reasons, rather than for scientific ones.[53] This is different from independent regulatory agencies, which, despite some criticism of the lack of political insulation in some of them, have strategic institutional mechanisms to make eminently technical and scientific decisions.[54]

In essence, this book posits that legislative, judicial, and subnational oversight of executive emergency actions is vital to safeguard democracy and the rule of law. The courts can invalidate abusive measures and enforce constitutional rights and institutional safeguards. Opposition parties can demand transparency and successfully conduct oversight. The free press can challenge the decisions of the government. Active local government and civil society can mobilize to hold national executives accountable. In practice, emergencies should not be used as an excuse to create an administrative Leviathan. Such circumstances do not justify a radical transfer of normative power from the legislature to the executive. In the future, the management of crises must be the responsibility of collegial, pluralistic bodies, rather than the sole domain of the chief executive.

Bibliography

Abranches, Sérgio. *Presidencialismo de coalizão: raízes e evolução do modelo político brasileiro.* São Paulo: Editora Companhia das Letras, 2018.

Ackerman, Bruce. The emergency constitution. *Yale Law Journal*, v. 113, 2003, p. 1.029.

Ackerman, Bruce. Good-bye, montesquieu. In: Rose-Ackerman, Susan; Lindseth, Peter L. (Eds.). *Comparative administrative law*. Cheltenham: Edward Elgar Publishing, 2010, p. 128–133.

Ackerman, Bruce. The new separation of powers. In: *The rule of law and the separation of powers.* New York: Routledge, 2017, p. 395–490.

Andeweg, Rudy B. Ministers as double agents? The delegation process between cabinet and ministers. *European Journal of Political Research*, v. 37, 2000, p. 377–395.

53 Andeweg, Rudy B. Ministers as double agents? The delegation process between cabinet and ministers. *European Journal of Political Research*, v. 37, 2000, p. 377–395; Klein, Elad; Umit, Resul. The electoral connection of ministerial selection in the UK. *The Journal of Legislative Studies*, v. 22, n. 2, 2016, p. 276–294; Dvořák, Petr; Pink, Michal. Nomination of ministers according to the areas of electoral support for political parties in elections to the chamber of deputies of the parliament of the Czech Republic. *Politics in Central Europe*, v. 18, n. 3, 2022, p. 433–460; Krook, Mona Lena; O'Brien, Diana Z. All the president's men? The appointment of female cabinet ministers worldwide. *The Journal of Politics*, v. 74, n. 3, 2012, p. 840–855.

54 *See, e.g.*, Gilardi, Fabrizio. *Delegation in the regulatory state: Independent regulatory agencies in western Europe*. Cheltenham: Edward Elgar Publishing, 2009.

Balkin, Jack M. Constitutional hardball and constitutional crises. *Quinnipiac Law Review*, v. 26, 2007, p. 579.
Blondel, Jean. *The presidential republic*. London: Palgrave Macmillan London, 2015, p. 23–41.
Calise, Mauro. Personalization of politics. In: Badie, Bertrand; Berg-Schlosser, Dirk; Morlino, Leonardo (Eds.). *International encyclopedia of political science*. London: Sage, 2011, p. 1.858–1.861.
Cavino, Massimo et al. Covid-19. Una prima lettura dei provvedimenti adottati dal Governo. *Federalismi.it*, n. 6, 2020, p. 1–9.
Childers, Thomas. *The third Reich: A history of Nazi Germany*. New York: Simon and Schuster, 2017.
Claudiani, Simona. Brevi Note Sui DPCM: Tra Emergenza e Stabilizzazione. In: Morana, Donatella; Mabellini, Stefania (Eds.). *L'emergenza pandemica e l'impatto sul diritto pubblico: innovazione e prospettive future. Quaderni del Dottorato di Ricerca in Diritto Pubblico dell'Università degli Studi di Roma "Tor Vergata"*. Milan: Wolters Kluwer, 2022, p. 69.
Cormacain, Ronan; Bar-Siman-Tov, Ittai. Legislatures in the time of Covid–19. *The Theory and Practice of Legislation*, v. 8, n. 1–2, 2020, p. 8.
Deere, Kelly J. Governing by executive order during the COVID-19 pandemic: Preliminary observations concerning the proper balance between executive orders and more formal rule making. *Missouri Law Review*, v. 86, 2021, p. 721.
Dvořák, Petr; Pink, Michal. Nomination of ministers according to the areas of electoral support for political parties in elections to the chamber of deputies of the parliament of the Czech Republic. *Politics in Central Europe*, v. 18, n. 3, 2022, p. 433–460.
Elgie, Robert; Passarelli, Gianluca. *The presidentialization of political executives. The Oxford handbook of political executives*. Oxford: Oxford University Press, 2020, p. 359–381.
Gilardi, Fabrizio. *Delegation in the regulatory state: Independent regulatory agencies in Western Europe*. Cheltenham: Edward Elgar Publishing, 2009.
Ginsburg, Tom; Versteeg, Mila. The bound executive: Emergency powers during the pandemic. *International Journal of Constitutional Law*, v. 19, n. 5, December 2021, p. 1498–1535.
Griglio, Elena. Parliamentary oversight under the Covid-19 emergency: Striving against executive dominance. *The Theory and Practice of Legislation*, v. 8, n. 1–2, 2020, p. 49–70.
Grogan, Joelle. Analysing global use of emergency powers in response to COVID-19. *European Journal of Law Reform*, v. 4, 2020, p. 338.
Grogan, Joelle. States of emergency: Analysing global use of emergency powers in response to COVID-19. *Eur. JL Reform*, v. 22, 2020, p. 348.
Grogan, Joelle. COVID-19, the rule of law and democracy. Analysis of legal responses to a global health crisis. *Hague Journal on the Rule of Law*, v. 14, n. 2–3, 2022, p. 349–369.
Gross, Oren; Aoláin, Fionnuala Ní. *Law in times of crisis: Emergency powers in theory and practice*. Cambridge: Cambridge University Press, 2006, p. 86–109.
Guzzetta, Giovanni. Le fonti dell'emergenza alla prova della pandemia. In: Marini, Francesco Saverio; Scaccia, Gino (Eds.). *Emergenza COVID-19 e ordinamento costituzionale*. Torino: G. Giappichelli editore, 2020, p. 73–82.
Howell, William G. Unilateral powers: A brief overview. *Presidential Stud. Q.*, v. 35, 2005, p. 417.
Inácio, Magna; Llanos, Mariana. The institutional presidency in Latin America: A comparative analysis. *Presidential Studies Quarterly*, v. 46, n. 3, 2016, p. 531–549.
Inácio, Magna; Recch, Filipe; Valencia, Carolina Guerrero. The power of the administrative decisions of Latin American presidents. In: Llanos, Mariana; Marsteintredet,

Leiv (Eds.). *Latin America in times of turbulence: Presidentialism under stress.* New York: Routledge, 2023, p. 75.
Kaiser, Anna-Bettina. The state of exception under German law and the current pandemic: Comparative models and constitutional rights. *e-Pública*, v. 7, n. 3, 2020, p. 4–15.
Kaiser, Anna-Bettina; Hensel, Roman. Federal Republic of Germany: Legal response to Covid-19. In: *The Oxford compendium of national legal responses to Covid-19.* April 2021. Available at: https://oxcon.ouplaw.com/view/https://doi.org/10.1093/law-occ19/law-occ19-e2.
Klein, Elad; Umit, Resul. The electoral connection of ministerial selection in the UK. *The Journal of Legislative Studies*, v. 22, n. 2, 2016, p. 276–294.
Kleßmann, Christoph; Sabrow, Martin. Contemporary history in Germany after 1989. *Contemporary European History*, v. 6, n. 2, 1997, p. 219–243.
Krook, Mona Lena; O'brien, Diana Z. All the president's men? The appointment of female cabinet ministers worldwide. *The Journal of Politics*, v. 74, n. 3, 2012, p. 840–855.
Kubicek, Paul. Delegative democracy in Russia and Ukraine. *Communist and Post-Communist Studies*, v. 27, n. 4, 1994, *passim*.
Lucarelli, Alberto. Costituzione, fonti del diritto ed emergenza sanitaria. *Rivista AIC*, v. 2, 2020, *passim*.
Mammone, Andrea; Parini, Ercole Giap; Veltri, Giuseppe A. (Eds.). *The Routledge handbook of contemporary Italy: History, politics, society.* New York: Routledge, 2015.
Musella, Fortunato. I poteri di emergenza nella Repubblica dei Presidenti. *Diritti regionali*, n. 2, 2020, p. 107–139.
Pinheiro, Victor Marcel; Ilarraz, Marcelo; Mestriner, Melissa Terni. The impacts of the COVID-19 crisis on the Brazilian legal system–a report on the functioning of the branches of the government and on the legal scrutiny of their activities. *The Theory and Practice of Legislation*, v. 8, n. 1–2, 2020, p. 201–202.
Poguntke, Thomas; Webb, Paul. The presidentialization of politics in democratic societies: A framework for analysis. In: Poguntke, T.; Webb, P. (Eds.). *The presidentialization of politics: A comparative study of modern democracies*, v. 1. Oxford University Press, 2005, p. 1–25.
Posner, Eric A.; Vermeule, Adrian. *The executive unbound: After the Madisonian republic.* Oxford: Oxford University Press, 2011, *passim*.
Rubio, Delia Ferreira; Goretti, Matteo. Cuando el presidente gobierna solo. Menem y los decretos de necesidad y urgencia hasta la reforma constitucional (julio 1989-agosto 1994). *Desarrollo Económico*, v. 36, n. 141, 1996, p. 443–474.
Rullo, Luigi. The COVID-19 pandemic crisis and the personalization of the government in Italy. *International Journal of Public Leadership*, v. 17, n. 2, 2021, p. 196–207.
Santos, Desirree dos Reis. *Ditadura militar e democracia no Brasil: história, imagem e testemunho.* Rio de Janeiro: Ponteio, 2013.
Siaroff, Alan. Comparative presidencies: The inadequacy of the presidential, semi-presidential and parliamentary distinction. *European Journal of Political Research*, v. 42, n. 3, 2003, p. 287–312.
Staupe, Júrgen. *Parlamentsvorbehalt und Delegationsbefugnis – Zur "Wesentlichkeitstheoríe" und zur Reichxveite legislativer Regelungskompetenz, insbesondere im Schulrecht.* Berlin: Duncker & Humblot, 1985, p. 24.
Trabucco, Daniele. Il "virus" nel sistema delle fonti: decreti-legge e dpcm al tempo del Covid-19: tra principio di legalità formale e principio di legalità sostanziale. *Nomos*, n. 2, 2020, p. 1–21.
Tushnet, Mark. Constitutional hardball. *The John Marshall Law Review*, v. 37, 2003, p. 523.

1 The executive dominance and the marginalization of parliaments

Governing by decree

Ordinarily, decrees and regulations are considered tools for day-to-day administrative matters of little political value, with discreet and residual effects.[1] But presidents and prime ministers have used these legal instruments to establish all kinds of public policies without parliamentary approval. Decrees can have important symbolic and political value, revealing the priorities of the government's agenda and providing an alternative for the chief executive to escape the legislative process. While representatives in parliament can only propose bills, presidents and prime ministers can go first and create legally binding public policies with the stroke of a pen. And they can do so without ever having to wait for political coalitions, the cooperation of committee chairs, or the support of party leaders.[2]

Studies of the executive powers devote much of their attention to the influence of presidents and prime ministers on the ordinary legislative process, based on their powers to initiate and veto legislation. However, their political agenda goes beyond this. Chief executives may seek to implement their political priorities through secondary regulations, such as decrees that implement laws, which can pose risks to democracy.[3] Indeed, an increasing number of populist, outsider, and anti-establishment leaders have raised concerns about the use of unilateral executive action to deal with political disagreements and crisis scenarios.[4] There are fears that an isolated executive, weakly controlled by the other branches of government, will lead to a profound democratic

1 Carey, John M.; Shugart, Matthew Soberg. Poder de decreto: Chamando os tanques ou usando a caneta? *Revista brasileira de ciências sociais*, v. 13, n. 37, 1998, p. 149–184.

2 Howell, William G. *Power without persuasion: The politics of direct presidential action*. Princeton University Press, 2003, p. 14.

3 Mayer, Kenneth R. *With the stroke of a pen: Executive orders and presidential power*. Princeton University Press, 2002, p. 97–102; Rotinghaus, Brandon; Warber, Adam L. Unilateral orders as constituency outreach: Executive orders, proclamations, and the public presidency. *Presidential Studies Quarterly*, v. 45, n. 2, 2015, p. 289–309.

4 Mudde, Cas; Kaltwasser, Cristóbal Rovira (Eds.). *Populism in Europe and the Americas: Threat or corrective for democracy?* Cambridge: Cambridge University Press, 2012.

DOI: 10.4324/9781003610816-2

backlash. In particular, the COVID-19 pandemic has revived fears of executive aggrandizement and unilateralism in the context of national emergencies.[5]

In this context, the following topics will analyze the historical process of executive dominance in light of the theory of the administrative state,[6] as well as the specific reasons for the deficiencies in legislative and judicial oversight.

1.1 The (im)balance between the branches of government: the imperial executive

Several democracies face a chronic imbalance between the three branches, which allows the chief executives to expand their legislative capacities and to dominate other political actors. The Brazilian political system, for example, has been conceptualized as a "constitutionally organized personal government" in which presidents consider themselves to be "the government itself, and not just the head of the government".[7] In a recent example, former Brazilian President Jair Bolsonaro said "I am the Constitution" to journalists who questioned his participation in a pro-military intervention protest calling for the closure of the National Congress and the Supreme Court.[8] In this institutional arrangement, the legislative and judicial branches do not usually act as effective counterbalances to the executive, limiting themselves to an attitude of deference to the president's decisions and directives. As will be seen, it is only when the media and public opinion turn against the chief executive that the other branches of government begin to monitor his actions more effectively.

According to Eric Posner and Adrian Vermeule, in most Western democracies, the government is centered on the figure of the executive leader, and legislative and judicial oversight of his actions is only "tenuous and punctual".[9] Legislatures and courts play a reactive and marginal role, modifying or

5 Griglio, Elena. Parliamentary oversight under the Covid-19 emergency: Striving against executive dominance. *The Theory and Practice of Legislation,* v. 8, n. 1–2, 2020, p. 50.

6 The administrative state theory originated in the German doctrine of the 1900s. *See* Schmitt, Carl. *Legality and legitimacy (1932).* Trans. by J. Seitzer. Durham: Duke University Press, 2004 and Forsthoff, Ernst. *Begriff und Wesen des sozialen Rechtsstaates*, v. 12. Berlin: Walter de Gruyter, 1954. Despite the importance of Carl Schmitt's theory, his work will not be studied directly in this book. This choice is largely due to the fact that his work has already been extensively explored and because we seek a contemporary and democratic view of the administrative state. Thus, we have chosen to examine the administrative state under the democratic reinterpretation proposed by Eric Posner and Adrian Vermeule in the book *The executive unbound: After the Madisonian republic*, published by the Oxford University Press in 2011.

7 Torres, João Camilo de Oliveira. *O presidencialismo no Brasil.* Rio de Janeiro: Ed. O Cruzeiro, 1962, p. 222.

8 Folha de São Paulo (Brazilian Newspaper). *Eu sou a Constituição, diz Bolsonaro ao defender democracia e liberdade um dia após ato pró-golpe militar.* April 20, 2020. Available at: https://www1.folha.uol.com.br/poder/2020/04/democracia-e-liberdade-acima-de-tudo-diz-bolsonaro-apos-participar-de-ato-pro-golpe.shtml.

9 Posner, Eric A.; Vermeule, Adrian. *The executive unbound: After the Madisonian republic.* Oxford: Oxford University Press, 2011, p. 4.

constraining executive initiatives, but rarely taking the political lead. Given the expansion of power and the size of the contemporary administrative state, Posner and Vermeule defend the "declaration of failure" of the traditional model of the separation of powers, which, if it is to survive, must be subjected to extensive rereading and updating. Due to the complexity of modern governance, the legislature and the judiciary are constantly lagging behind the pace of events in the administrative state, with major deficits in terms of speed, flexibility, and expertise.

In fact, the president and prime minister often act unilaterally, promoting far-reaching political and economic reforms with only the "power of the pen".[10] In Brazil, this preponderance, combined with the historical tendency toward personalism, makes presidents the epicenter of normative production, delimiting the government's broad control over the legislative agenda and allowing it to issue a large number of decrees and *medidas provisórias* (provisional measures).[11] Especially when the president enjoys ample political capital and media support, the other branches of government are unable to supervise and monitor his actions effectively, especially on symbolic issues or those with great popular approval.[12]

In several countries, this unilateral authority, combined with the power of patronage, which consists of the prerogative to nominate ministers and other public officials, has centralized the decision-making process in the hands of the executive and poses great democratic risks.[13] There's a tremendous imbalance in executive–legislative relations, which has proved problematic for the consolidation of real democracy.[14] For a long time, it was believed that the greatest threat to a country's democracy was an authoritarian military leader and his "extraordinary acts". Today, however, that threat can be a democratically elected civilian president acting in the exercise of his constitutional authority.

10 Carey, John M.; Shugart, Matthew Soberg. Poder de decreto: Chamando os tanques ou usando a caneta? *Revista Brasileira de Ciências Sociais*, v. 13, n. 37, 1998, p. 149–184; Power, Timothy. The pen is mightier than the Congress. Presidential decree power in Brazil. In: Carey, John M.; Shugart, Matthew Soberg (Eds.). *Executive decree authority*. Cambridge: Cambridge University Press, 1998, p. 216–217.

11 Ferreira Filho, Manoel Gonçalves. *Curso de direito constitucional*. São Paulo: Saraiva Educação, 1971, p. 145–146.

12 Posner, Eric A.; Vermeule, Adrian. *The executive unbound: After the Madisonian republic. Op. cit.*, p. 25–26.

13 Figueiredo, Argelina Cheibub. Agendas, instituições políticas e desempenho do governo na democracia brasileira. In: Reis, Elisa P.; Zilberman, Regina (Eds.). *Retratos do Brasil*. Porto Alegre: EDIPUCRS, 2004, p. 80; Figueiredo, Argelina Cheibub; Limongi, Fernando. *Executivo e Legislativo na nova ordem constitucional*. Rio de Janeiro: FGV, 1999, p. 41.

14 Power, Timothy. The pen is mightier than the Congress. Presidential decree power in Brazil. In: Carey, John M.; Shugart, Matthew Soberg (Eds.). *Executive decree authority, Op. cit.*, p. 224–225.

Many constituent assemblies ended up exchanging the "dictatorship of guns" for the "dictatorship of the pen".[15]

In Brazil, for example, the lack of attentive and effective control of the president by the other branches of government is proved by the very low number of presidential decrees suspended by the National Congress or annulled by the Supreme Court. The Brazilian Federal Constitution allows the Congress to control the regulations of the executive branch.[16] Since 1988, however, only two decrees have been suspended.[17] Likewise, of the hundreds of lawsuits filed in the Federal Supreme Court against the more than 4,000 presidential decrees issued between 1990 and 2020, only 20 have passed the admissibility stage, and of those, only 11 have had their requests for injunctions granted or their claims upheld on the merits.[18] There is, in fact, a blind spot when it comes to controlling the actions of presidents, who enjoy a great deal of discretion to legislate on their own.

15 Power, Timothy. The pen is mightier than the Congress. Presidential decree power in Brazil. In: Carey, John M.; Shugart, Matthew Soberg (Eds.). *Executive decree authority, Op. cit.*

16 Brazilian Federal Constitution of 1988. "Art. 49. It is the exclusive competence of the National Congress: (. . .) V – To suspend normative acts of the Executive Branch that exceed the regulatory power or the limits of legislative delegation". (In original: "Art. 49. É da competência exclusiva do Congresso Nacional: (. . .) V – sustar os atos normativos do Poder Executivo que exorbitem do poder regulamentar ou dos limites de delegação legislativa".).

17 Since the enactment of the Federal Constitution of 1988, only seven Legislative Decrees have been issued on the basis of Article 49, Section V of the Constitution. Of these seven Legislative Decrees, only two suspended the effects of Presidential Decrees: (i) through Legislative Decree n. 3/1992, Congress suspended Decree n. 430 of January 20, 1992, issued by former president Fernando Collor de Mello, and (ii) through Legislative Decree n. 3/1989, Congress suspended the effects of Decree n. 97.455/1989, issued by former president José Sarney. The other legislative decrees sought to suspend other illegal acts, such as executive orders and resolutions: (iii) Legislative Decree n. 293/2015: suspends the effects of Interministerial Order n. 192 of 05.10.2015, of the Ministry of Agriculture, Livestock and Supply and the Environment; (iv) Legislative Decree n. 273/2014: suspends Resolution – RDC n. 52, of October 6, 2011, of the National Health Surveillance Agency – ANVISA; (v) Legislative Decree no. 207/2002: suspends the effects of Note Conjur-Minfra n. 24/92, of the Minister of State for Infrastructure; (vi) Legislative Decree n. 177/2017: suspends art. 1 and the only paragraph of art. 2 of the Ministry of Health Regulation n. 1.253/2013; (vii) Legislative Decree n. 170/2018: suspends the MDIC-MMA Interministerial Decree n. 78/2019. Cf. Mendes, Gilmar Ferreira; Branco, Paulo Gonet. *Curso de Direito Constitucional*, 15. ed. São Paulo: Saraiva Educação, 2020, p. 1.799.

18 Brazil. Federal Supreme Court (STF). Ação Direta de Inconstitucionalidade (ADI) n. 4.661 MC, Tribunal Pleno, Min. Marco Aurélio, DJe 23.03.2012; ADI n. 2.795 MC, Tribunal Pleno, Rel. Min. Maurício Corrêa, DJe 20.06.2003; ADI n. 1.599 MC, Tribunal Pleno, Rel. Min. Maurício Corrêa, DJe 18.05.2001; ADI n. 1.480 MC, Tribunal Pleno, Rel. Min. Celso de Mello, DJe 18.05.2001; ADI n. 1.435 MC, Tribunal Pleno, Rel. Min. Francisco Rezek, DJe 06.08.1999; ADI n. 1.178 MC, Tribunal Pleno, Rel. Min. Marco Aurélio, DJe 18.05.2001; ADI n. 1.155 MC, Tribunal Pleno, Rel. Min. Marco Aurélio, DJe 18.05.2001; ADI n. 673 MC, Tribunal Pleno, Min. Paulo Brossard, DJe 11.10.2001; ADI n. 313, Tribunal Pleno, Rel. Min. Paulo Brossard, DJe 30.04.1992; ADI n. 533 MC, Tribunal Pleno, Rel. Min. Carlos Velloso, DJe 27.09.1991 e ADI n. 6.121 MC, Tribunal Pleno, Min. Marco Aurélio, DJe 28.11.2019.

In this scenario, the legal doctrine led by Posner and Vermeule believes that the limits of executive power no longer lie in the law or in a specific constitutional design, but in the dynamics of politics and public opinion – the only factors capable of blocking abuses of power.[19] For them, even if the legislature and the courts are not effective checks and balances, the chief executive is constrained by elections and the daily scrutiny of civil society, as he needs popularity and credibility to gain support for his decisions.[20] This is because, in the long run, presidents and prime ministers are concerned with their political legacies and their places in history, so they engage in a constant trade-off between their political will and maintaining their popularity. In the words of Posner and Vermeule, "No matter how extensive a president's powers are, he must always build political support and a base of confidence for his actions".[21]

Thus, public opinion and media pressure would be the primary sources of checks on the use of unilateral powers and would serve to stimulate the other branches of government to exercise effective oversight as well. The less popular support and media support the president enjoys, the greater the chance that the judiciary or legislature will invalidate his actions.[22-23]

1.2 Deficiencies in legislative oversight of the executive branch

Historically, this centrality of the executive is largely due to the obstacles that the legislature faces in exercising oversight. Even in countries with a presidential system, such as Brazil and the United States of America, there has been a general tendency for legislative bodies to align themselves with the chief executive.[24] The phenomenon of "coalition presidentialism" combines proportionality, multipartyism, and "imperial presidentialism" so that the executive is organized on the basis of broad coalitions of parties. As Brazilian political scientist Fernando Limongi observes, in order to influence public policy, it is necessary to be aligned with the president. In his words, "The parliamentarians

19 Posner, Eric A.; Vermeule, Adrian. *The executive unbound: After the Madisonian republic. Op. cit.*, p. 5.

20 Posner, Eric A.; Vermeule, Adrian. *The executive unbound: After the Madisonian republic. Op. cit.*, p. 61.

21 Posner, Eric A.; Vermeule, Adrian. *The executive unbound: After the Madisonian republic. Op. cit.*

22 Kaufman, Aaron R.; Rogowski, Jon C. *The unilateral presidency, 1933–2017.* March 8, 2018, p. 9. Available at: http://www.aaronrkaufman.com/wp-content/uploads/2018/03/Kaufman-Rogowski.pdf.

23 Howell, William G. *Power without persuasion: The politics of direct presidential action. Op. cit.*, p. 169.

24 Moe, Terry M; Howell, William G. The presidential power of unilateral action. *The Journal of Law, Economics, and Organization*, v. 15, n. 1, 1999, p. 132–179; Posner, Eric A.; Vermeule, Adrian. *The executive unbound: After the Madisonian republic. Op. cit.*, p. 5; Limongi, Fernando. A democracia no Brasil: presidencialismo, coalizão partidária e processo decisório. *Novos estudos CEBRAP*, n. 76, 2006, p. 17–41.

therefore have basically two alternatives: to be part of the presidential coalition in the current legislature, or to close ranks with the opposition, hoping to reach the presidency in the next legislature".[25]

Given the fragmentation of the party system, the chief executive often tries to ensure governability through a system of negotiations and concessions to parliamentarians.[26] In presidential systems, with the exception of political crises that can lead to impeachment, the legislature does not represent a massive and constant opposition to presidents, who generally seek alliances and dialogue with Congress. The design of legislative chambers, deliberative institutions *par excellence*, creates a political fragmentation that often prevents joint action against the president. Although the legal literature treats the legislature as a unitary actor with a large capacity for overlapping with other branches of government, in reality, it is constituted by a collective decision-making body permeated by veto points.[27]

Indeed, there are several stages at which proposed legislation can be stalled or altered. These multiplicity of veto points within the legislative process makes it challenging for parliaments to assert themselves effectively. The complexity of committee reviews, floor debates, and bicameral negotiations makes it difficult for legislatures to act quickly and cohesively, especially in opposition to the executive. Presidents and prime ministers, who have agenda-setting power and the ability to act unilaterally in certain areas, can then exploit legislative gridlock to advance their policies without significant opposition.[28]

These structural obstacles are closely related to political fragmentation, collective action problems, the personal motivations of legislators, and the influence of the executive over the legislative process. Parliaments are collective bodies composed of members with diverse interests and agendas. This diversity can lead to internal divisions and hinder cohesive action against executive overreach. Legislatures are, by design, composed of members with diverse constituencies and policy priorities. It lacks the unified ambition that characterizes the executive branch.[29]

This political fragmentation is particularly prevalent in proportional representation and multiparty systems. In such political environments, voter

25 Limongi, Fernando. A democracia no Brasil: presidencialismo, coalizão partidária e processo decisório. *Op. cit.*, p. 41.

26 Abranches, Sérgio Henrique de. *Presidencialismo de Coalizão: o dilema institucional brasileiro. Op. cit.*; Figueiredo, Argelina; Limongi, Fernando. Bases institucionais do presidencialismo de coalizão. *Lua Nova*, n. 44, 1998, p. 81–106.

27 Moe, Terry M.; Howell, William G. The presidential power of unilateral action. *The Journal of Law, Economics, and Organization*, v. 15, n. 1, 1999, p. 132–179.

28 Moe, Terry M.; Howell, William G. The presidential power of unilateral action. *The Journal of Law, Economics, and Organization*, v. 15, n. 1, 1999, p. 132–179.

29 Shugart, Matthew S. *Presidents and assemblies: Constitutional design and electoral dynamics.* Cambridge: Cambridge University Press, 1992, *passim*; Tsebelis, George. *Veto players: How political institutions work.* New York: Russell Sage Foundation and Princeton University Press, 2002, *passim*.

preferences lead to a proliferation of political parties with diverse agendas and ideologies, none of which typically commands an outright majority. This fragmentation necessitates the formation of coalition governments to achieve a functional majority capable of governing effectively. In presidential systems, such as Brazil and the United States, this diversity makes it difficult to form a unified legislative front capable of confronting the executive.

The necessity for parties to collaborate to form a government can then result in the dilution of distinct policy positions and an increased propensity to defer to executive leadership to maintain coalition stability. When legislative bodies are gridlocked due to political fragmentation or partisan polarization, it becomes easier for executives to resort to unilateral measures to advance their policy objectives. The chief executive often capitalizes on this fragmentation to ensure governability through negotiations and concessions to individual parliamentarians or party blocs. As Matthew Shugart and John Carey note, presidents may leverage their positions to build coalitions, often through patronage and policy concessions, to secure legislative support.[30] This dynamic can undermine the legislature's ability to function as an independent and cohesive body.

Also, many parliamentarians are more concerned with their own reelections than with a possible institutional defense of the legislature against the executive, especially in scenarios where the executive enjoys broad popular support. Although members of parliament will condemn any abuse of power, they will only occasionally seek to "protect their own institution and curb the constant delegation of power to the executive".[31] In the precise words of Terry M. Moe, professor of political science at Stanford University:

> [T]he presidency tends to seek more power. The legislator does not tend to seek more power. On issues that affect the institutional balance between the three branches, presidents seek reforms that promote their institutional power, while parliamentarians typically do not. Members of Congress are unlikely to oppose any expansion of presidents' power unless the issue directly affects the interests of their electorate (. . .). Members of Congress are generally unwilling to do "whatever it takes" to increase Parliament's institutional power.[32]

The personal motivations of legislators can significantly influence the power dynamics between parliaments and the executive. Legislators often prioritize their electoral prospects and constituent services over institutional

30 Shugart, Matthew S. *Presidents and assemblies: Constitutional design and electoral dynamics.* Cambridge: Cambridge University Press, 1992, *passim.*

31 Howell, William G. *Power without persuasion: The politics of direct presidential action. Op. cit.*, p. 111.

32 Moe, Terry M. The presidency and the bureaucracy: The presidential advantage. *The Presidency and the Political System*, v. 5, 1998, p. 443–474.

considerations. This focus can lead to a reluctance to challenge the executive, especially when such opposition might jeopardize their political standing or access to resources controlled by the executive. As a result, legislators may acquiesce in executive initiatives, even when those initiatives encroach on legislative prerogatives.

The executive also has significant influence over the budget and appointments, which can be used to secure legislative support.[33] This dynamic creates a patronage system in which legislators support the executive in exchange for benefits that enhance their reelection prospects. Legislators may then avoid challenging the executive to avoid political fallout or to maintain favorable relations with the administration. In the legislative context, individual members may be reluctant to invest resources in opposing the executive if they believe others will not join them or if the benefits of such opposition are diffuse. The lack of a unified ambition, as opposed to the centralized authority and clear objectives of the executive, puts the legislature at a disadvantage in asserting its institutional power.

When the executive enjoys broad popular support, it can be politically costly for individual legislators to oppose it. They may fear alienating voters or losing access to executive-controlled resources that benefit their districts. This dynamic discourages legislators from challenging the executive, even when institutional checks are warranted. In Brazil, for example, although the constitution gives Congress the power to suspend illegal executive regulations, legislators rarely use this tool. According to article 49, item V, of the Brazilian Federal Constitution, "It is the exclusive competence of the National Congress: (. . .) to suspend the normative acts of the Executive Power that exceed the regulatory power or the limits of legislative delegation". This provision represents an innovation introduced by the 1988 Constitution, which was not present in previous republican constitutions.[34] However, this tool has seen limited success: between 1988 and 2020, only two presidential decrees were suspended through legislative decrees enacted by Congress.[35]

It can therefore be said that, except in scenarios of severe political crisis or when public opinion is strongly against the president, a culture of deference to the executive prevails, which has resulted in weak control over the unilateral acts. Addressing this imbalance requires a multifaceted approach.

33 Limongi, Fernando. A democracia no Brasil: presidencialismo, coalizão partidária e processo decisório. *Op. cit.*, p. 41.

34 Cunha, Anna Cândida Ferraz da. Comentários ao art. 49, V, da Constituição Federal de 1988. In: Canotilho, J. J. Gomes; Mendes, Gilmar Ferreira; Sarlet, Ingo Wolfgang; Streck, Lenio Luiz; Leoncy, Leo Ferreira (Org.). *Comentários à Constituição do Brasil*. São Paulo: Saraiva Jur, 2018. E-book. p. 1956.

35 Brazil. Decreto Legislativo nº 293/2015; Decreto Legislativo nº 273/2014; Decreto Legislativo nº 207/2002; Decreto Legislativo nº 177/2017 e Decreto Legislativo nº 170/2018. *See* Mendes, Gilmar Ferreira; Branco, Paulo Gonet. *Curso de Direito Constitucional*, 15. ed. São Paulo: Saraiva Educação, 2020. E-book. cap. 10, p. 1799, nota 233.

Strengthening legislative institutions involves enhancing their capacity for collective action, improving oversight mechanisms, and recalibrating the incentives that drive individual legislators' behavior. Institutional reforms may include revising electoral systems to reduce fragmentation, promoting internal cohesion within parliaments, and reinforcing the legal frameworks that delineate the separation of powers. Moreover, fostering a political culture that values institutional integrity over individual political gains is crucial. Legislators must recognize the long-term consequences of yielding authority to the executive and prioritize the preservation of democratic norms and constitutional checks.

In conclusion, the enfeeblement of parliaments is a complex phenomenon rooted in structural factors such as political fragmentation, coalition dynamics, and the executive's capacity for unilateral action. The interplay of these elements results in a gradual erosion of legislative power and an expansion of executive authority. Recognizing and addressing these structural challenges is essential to revitalizing parliamentary institutions and ensuring the resilience of democratic governance.

1.3 Deficiencies in judicial oversight of the executive branch

The judiciary is also deferential to the executive.[36] While there are occasional shocks between the two, the long-term tendency of the courts is toward alignment.[37] In cases that discuss the limits of executive power, judges tend to adopt a complacent attitude, validating in the name of the "democratic principle" normative acts that clearly exceed legal or constitutional limits.[38]

In Brazil, the courts have historically ensured the expansion of the president's powers, even when he manifests clear authoritarian and usurping

36 Ferejohn, John A.; Kramer, Larry D. Independent judges, dependent judiciary: Institutionalizing judicial restraint. *New York University Law Review*, v. 77, 2002, p. 377; Posner, Eric A.; Vermeule, Adrian. *The executive unbound: After the Madisonian republic. Op. cit.*, p. 36–37; Eichler, Jessika; Sonkar, Sumit. Challenging absolute executive powers in times of corona: Re-examining constitutional courts and the collective right to public contestation as instruments of institutional control. *Review of Economics and Political Science*, v. 6, n. 1, 2021, p. 3–23.

37 Posner, Eric A.; Vermeule, Adrian. *The executive unbound: After the Madisonian republic. Op. cit.*, p. 36–37; Howell, William G. *Power without persuasion: The politics of direct presidential action. Op. cit.*, p. xviii (preface); Mayer, Kenneth R. *With the stroke of a pen: Executive orders and presidential power*. Princeton University Press, 2002, p. 11; Cooper, Phillip J. By order of the president: Administration by executive order and proclamation. *Administration & Society*, v. 18, n. 2, 1986, p. 233–262; Carvalho, Ernani Rodrigues de. *Sua Majestade, o Presidente da República: estudo de caso do controle de constitucionalidade dos atos do Executivo (1994–1998)*. Universidade Federal de Pernambuco, 2000, p. 92; Pacheco, Cristina Carvalho. *O Supremo Tribunal Federal e a reforma do Estado: uma análise das Ações Diretas de Inconstitucionalidade julgadas no primeiro governo de Fernando Henrique Cardoso (1995–1998)*. Curitiba: Appris Editora, 2019, p. 42.

38 Howell, William G. *Power without persuasion: The politics of direct presidential action. Op. cit.*, p. 139–147.

tendencies.[39] Except in times of crisis, the Federal Supreme Court has been deferential to presidential policies, and the attitude has often been one of cooperation.[40] In fact, judicial review in Brazil "serves the political interests (authoritarian or democratic) of the central power and has a strategic function for the Brazilian executive, which has historically been characterized as strong, centralizing and authoritarian".[41] Thus, there is a historical role of subordination of the judiciary to the executive and a lower willingness of the Supreme Court to invalidate presidential acts, such as *medidas provisórias* (emergency measures) and decrees, compared to other legislative acts.[42]

The judicial deference to presidents and prime ministers is not explained solely by the individual ideology of judges. Rather, it is the result of specific political contexts and institutional needs. In a realistic view of the separation of powers, judges almost always have "good reasons to be deferential" to the chief executive.[43] And when they do not, it is because other relevant political forces have expressed opposition to executive action. In general, the judiciary cooperates because (i) the effectiveness of its rulings depends on the cooperation of the chief executive or the public administration; (ii) it fears reprisals and seeks to preserve its reputation and institutional strength; and (iii) the members of the constitutional courts are often appointed by executive leaders.[44]

Indeed, the judiciary has no "key safe" or "power of the sword", so it depends on other powers to survive and ensure compliance with its decisions.[45] In this sense, courts try not to issue orders that will be clearly ignored by presidents or prime ministers. Alexander Hamilton, in the 18th century, already warned that courts "ultimately depend on the assistance of the executive branch for the effectiveness of their judgments".[46]

Moreover, many of the decisions of the judiciary stem from a deep concern for its institutional position within the system of separation of powers. In this

39 Carvalho, Ernani Rodrigues de. *Sua Majestade, o Presidente da República: estudo de caso do controle de constitucionalidade dos atos do Executivo (1994–1998).* Dissertação (Mestrado em Ciência Política). Recife, Universidade Federal de Pernambuco, 2000, p. 92; Pacheco, Cristina Carvalho. *O Supremo Tribunal Federal e a reforma do Estado: uma análise das Ações Diretas de Inconstitucionalidade julgadas no primeiro governo de Fernando Henrique Cardoso (1995–1998).* Curitiba: Appris Editora, 2019, p. 42.

40 Ribeiro, Pedro José de Almeida. *A Construção do Judiciário, Capital Institucional e Quota de Decisões Contramajoritárias do STF. Op. cit.*, p. 95.

41 Arantes, Rogério Bastos. *Judiciário e política no Brasil.* São Paulo: Idesp, 1997.

42 Carvalho, Ernani Rodrigues de. *Sua Majestade, o Presidente da República: estudo de caso do controle de constitucionalidade dos atos do Executivo (1994–1998). Op. cit.*, p. 92.

43 Howell, William G. *Power without persuasion: The politics of direct presidential action. Op. cit.*, p. 174.

44 Howell, *Power without persuasion*, p. 138–170.

45 Garoupa, Nuno; Ginsburg, Tom. *Judicial reputation: A comparative theory.* Chicago: University of Chicago Press, 2015.

46 Hamilton, Alexander. The federalist n. 78. In: Madison, James; Hamilton, Alexander; Jay, John. *The federalist.* Campinas: Russell Editores, 2013.

perspective, the courts decide cases in favor of the executive in order to guarantee their own strength and institutional interests, since a large part of the court's reputation and prestige derives from its ability to subordinate other political actors to its orders.[47] So, there would be a strategic approach with the executive precisely to compensate for some limitations. In the words of Terry Moe and William Howell, the courts "cannot simply act on principles and without institutional concerns, as this type of strategy is counterproductive":[48]

> [A]lthough the judiciary is an independent branch of the state, its power and prestige are deeply dependent on the executive. Court decisions, even if legally well founded (. . .), are meaningless pieces of paper unless they are put into practice – and they can only be put into practice if the executive is willing to implement them. If the executive refuses to cooperate – or if it acts too slowly, ineffectively, or distorts judicial intent – the Court's pronouncements remain empty, and the integrity and standing of the judiciary as a political institution is seriously compromised (. . .). Academics recognize that courts cannot simply act on principle and without institutional concerns, as such a strategy proves self-defeating (. . .). Judges have incentives to be pragmatic and to exercise a kind of self-control appropriate to the fragile position in which they find themselves.[49]

In fact, assuming that the judiciary depends on its institutional capital, very negative reactions from the chief executive's co-religionists can jeopardize the stability of the system and inaugurate scenarios of profound political crisis. Whenever the judiciary has aligned itself with the executive, it has developed and expanded as an institution, while the broad and prolonged conflict tends to drain its resources and political capital. Also, when the judiciary comes into conflict with public opinion or the executive, the risk of a backlash is high: history is replete with cases of the abolition of courts, significant changes in the number of members, suppression of powers, impeachment of judges, and restrictions on the budget and salaries of its members.[50] Given that the judiciary

47 Hamilton, Alexander. The federalist n. 78. In: Madison, James; Hamilton, Alexander; Jay, John. *Op. cit.*, p. 138.

48 Moe, Terry M.; Howell, William G. The presidential power of unilateral action. *The Journal of Law, Economics, and Organization*, v. 15, n. 1, 1999, p. 132–179.

49 Moe, Terry M.; Howell, William G. The presidential power of unilateral action. *Op. cit.*

50 *See* Llanos, Mariana; Weber, Cordula Tibi. Court–executive relations during the COVID-19 pandemic. In: Llanos, Mariana; Marsteintredet, Leiv (Eds.). *Latin America in times of turbulence*: Presidentialism Under Stress. New York: Routledge, 2023, p. 128:

> The most severe type of executive reaction, formal interference, includes all types of intervention aimed at packing or curbing the court (Kosař and Šipulová, 2022): impeachments, the alteration of judicial selection and removal processes, changing jurisdiction, modifying court structure or procedures, slashing the budget, altering court size. Such measures

does not have "standing armies" to ensure compliance with its orders, it is always necessary to count on the cooperation of the executive and to try to build a good image in the face of occasional majorities.[51]

During COVID-19, for example, the Hungarian government, under the leadership of Prime Minister Viktor Orbán, implemented significant restrictions on access to justice. These measures were enacted allegedly in response to the urgent need to limit the spread of the virus. Only those cases deemed "extremely urgent" or "critical" were allowed to proceed. The ordinary courts were completely closed, and the possibility of reviewing the proportionality of executive emergency measures was excluded. This complete exclusion of these emergency unilateral acts from the scope of judicial review was a matter of deep concern among human rights advocates, especially in a country where the courts lack independence and where there is little room for political or popular objection through elections or protests.[52]

Finally, the way in which members of the courts are appointed also explains deference to the executive branch. Presidents appoint judges whose ideologies and legal positions align with their own in order to advance their agendas and exercise their own brand of leadership.[53] In fact, research has shown that US Supreme Court justices are less likely to overturn executive orders issued by the presidents who appointed them.[54]

1.4 The judiciary, the executive, and the public opinion

It is important to stress that courts are only likely to invalidate decrees when public opinion is against the chief executive. According to Moe and Howell, "When the President's unilateral actions are clearly unpopular, the Court can gain prestige by declaring them illegal or unconstitutional".[55] Based on empirical data, the authors demonstrated that public attention to a court case can act unfavorably to the chief executive. For example, when *The New York Times* writes at least one article about a court case involving a presidential executive order before the trial, the chances of the decision being favorable to the

change the composition of a given court, resulting in a majority of judges loyal to the government, or significantly reduce its overall power. While facing such interference, courts have very limited scope for action in defending their independence and power. These circumstances will have a strong negative short- to medium- term impact (and potential long-term one too) on the court's status.

51 O'Connor, Sandra Day. Public trust as a dimension of equal justice: Some suggestions to increase public trust. *University of Chicago Law Review*, 1999, p. 10–13.

52 Grogan, Joelle. Analysing global use of emergency powers in response to COVID-19. *European Journal of Law Reform*, v. 4, 2020, p. 350.

53 Moe, Terry M.; Howell, William G. The presidential power of unilateral action. *The Journal of Law, Economics, and Organization*, v. 15, n. 1, 1999, p. 132–179.

54 Howell, William G. *Power without persuasion: The politics of direct presidential action. Op. cit.*, p. 151.

55 Moe, Terry M.; Howell, William G. The presidential power of unilateral action. *Op. cit.*, p. 149.

president decrease from 85% to 61%.[56] In other words, when public opinion is attentive to a trial, the tendency of the courts is to follow the popular will, even if this means antagonizing the position of the executive.

In this scenario, it is worth making a brief digression on the influence of public opinion on judicial decisions. It is well established in the literature that the reaction of the public and the media influences the evolution of jurisprudence, motivating judges to reproduce theses with positive repercussions in the media and to align their positions with the understanding of the majorities.[57] In many democracies such as Brazil and the United States, there is a growing tendency for judges, especially in constitutional courts, to take public opinion into account and to bring their decisions closer to the dominant view in society.[58] The judiciary is not exempt from the conflicts of interest and external influences that affect the legislative and judicial decision-making processes.[59-60] Public opinion tends to influence not only the outcome of the judgment but also important aspects such as the length of time the case takes or the granting of a preliminary injunction.

In the United States, research shows that counter-majoritarian decisions are mere exceptions in the Supreme Court: most of the time, the results of its judgments align with opinion polls on the respective issues.[61] According to Thomas Marshall, the US Supreme Court has behaved as closely to public

56 Howell, William G. *Power without persuasion: The politics of direct presidential action. Op. cit.*, p. 162.

57 Friedman, Barry. *The will of the people: How public opinion has influenced the Supreme Court and shaped the meaning of the Constitution*. New York: Farrar, Straus and Giroux, 2009; Friedman, Barry. The politics of judicial review. *Tex. L. Rev.*, v. 84, 2005, p. 257; Barrett Lain, Corinna. Upside-down judicial review. *Georgetown Law Journal*, v. 101, 2012, p. 113; Caldeira, Gregory A. Neither the purse nor the sword: Dynamics of public confidence in the Supreme Court. *American Political Science Review*, v. 80, n. 4, 1986, p. 1209–1226; Tushnet, Mark. Skepticism about judicial review: A United States perspective. In: *Limits of constitutionality control*. Rio de Janeiro: Lumen Juris, 2009, p. 226; Epstein, Lee; Martin, Andrew D. Does public opinion influence the Supreme Court-possibly yes (but we're not sure why). *University of Pennsylvania Journal of Constitutional Law*, v. 13, 2010, p. 263; Marshall, Thomas R. *Public opinion and the Supreme Court*. Boston: Unwin Hyman, 1989.

58 *See, e.g.*, Friedman, Barry. *The will of the people: How public opinion has influenced the Supreme Court and shaped the meaning of the Constitution*. New York: Farrar, Straus and Giroux, 2009; Friedman, Barry. The politics of judicial review. *Tex. L. Rev.*, v. 84, 2005, p. 257; Barrett Lain, Corinna. Upside-down judicial review. *Georgetown Law Journal*, v. 101, 2012; Caldeira, Gregory A. Neither the purse nor the sword: Dynamics of public confidence in the Supreme Court. *American Political Science Review*, v. 80, n. 4, 1986, p. 1209–1226; Mello, Patrícia Perrone Campos. *Nos bastidores do Supremo Tribunal Federal*. Rio de Janeiro: Editora Forense, 2015.

59 Mello, Patrícia Perrone Campos. *Nos bastidores do Supremo Tribunal Federal*. Rio de Janeiro: Editora Forense, 2015; Elhauge, Einer R. Does interest group theory justify more intrusive judicial review? *Yale Law Journal*, v. 101, 1991, p. 31–110.

60 Novelino, Marcelo. O Supremo Tribunal Federal brasileiro e a opinião pública. In: Novelino, Marcelo; Leite, George Salomão; Rocha, Lilian Rose Lemos (Eds.). *Liberdade e Fraternidade: a Contribuição de Ayres Britto Para o Direito*. Salvador: JusPodivm, 2018, p. 169.

61 Barrett Lain, Corinna. Upside-down judicial review. *Georgetown Law Journal*, v. 101, 2012, p. 158.

opinion as the other branches of government.[62] Even the decisions considered to be counter-majoritarian originated in growing mobilizations by organized sectors of society which, little by little, managed to change the winds of public opinion in their favor. As Michael Klarman rightly points out, "The courts protect only those minorities who are viewed favorably by the majority":

> [S]ince the social and political context plays a very important role in judges' decisions on constitutional issues, the romantic image of the courts as the great saviors of the weak and oppressed is probably unrealistic. (. . .) *courts only protect minorities that are viewed favorably by the majority. Ironically, at times of greatest oppression, when minority groups most need judicial protection, they are unlikely to receive it.* Judges wouldn't have dreamed of protecting the rights of women or homosexuals under the equal protection clause before the feminist movement and the gay rights movement. Similarly, racial segregation began to seem unconstitutional to judges only when Afro-Americans became a vital part of the New Deal, achieving middle-class status, professional success, winning military honors and a Nobel Peace Prize.[63]

Of course, judges are also part of public opinion and are subject to the same events and forces that affect other members of society.[64] They do not live in isolation, nor are they beings without social roots. They are subject to the same influences and come into contact with the same social flows that cause changes in the conviction of the majority.[65] Like everyone else, judges want to preserve their images and win the recognition and esteem of the members of their communities. Thus, gaining popularity and recognition by public opinion can be an important object of desire.[66] In the words of Lawrence Baum, "The approval of certain audiences is what guides judicial action".[67]

The preceding analysis reveals that the courts are not an optimal checkpoint for executive action. While they may challenge the president or premier in specific cases, particularly those that garner public attention, the general tendency is to prioritize the interests of the chief executive. As will be demonstrated in

62 Marshall, Thomas R. *Public opinion and the Supreme Court*. Boston: Unwin Hyman, 1989.

63 Klarman, Michael J. *Brown v. board of education and the civil rights movement*. Oxford: Oxford University Press, 2007, p. 218 (emphasis added).

64 Epstein, Lee; Martin, Andrew D. Does public opinion influence the Supreme Court – possibly yes (but we're not sure why). *University of Pennsylvania Journal of Constitutional Law*, v. 13, 2010, p. 263.

65 Novelino, Marcelo. O Supremo Tribunal Federal brasileiro e a opinião pública. *Op. cit.*, p. 183.

66 Baum, Lawrence. *Judges and their audiences: A perspective on judicial behavior*. Princeton: Princeton University Press, 2009, p. 66.

67 Baum, Lawrence. *Judges and their audiences: A perspective on judicial behavior*. *Op. cit.*

the subsequent chapters, this lack of control has facilitated the flourishing of unilateral acts, particularly decrees.

Bibliography

Abranches, Sérgio Henrique de. *Presidencialismo de Coalizão: o dilema institucional brasileiro. Op. cit.*; Figueiredo, Argelina; Limongi, Fernando. Bases institucionais do presidencialismo de coalizão. *Lua Nova*, n. 44, 1998, p. 81–106.

Arantes, Rogério Bastos. *Judiciário e política no Brasil.* São Paulo: Idesp, 1997.

Barrett Lain, Corinna. Upside-down judicial review. *Georgetown Law Journal*, v. 101, 2012, p. 158.

Baum, Lawrence. *Judges and their audiences: A perspective on judicial behavior.* Princeton: Princeton University Press, 2009, p. 66.

Caldeira, Gregory A. Neither the purse nor the sword: Dynamics of public confidence in the Supreme Court. *American Political Science Review*, v. 80, n. 4, 1986, p. 1209–1226.

Carey, John M.; Shugart, Matthew Soberg. Poder de decreto: Chamando os tanques ou usando a caneta? *Revista Brasileira de Ciências Sociais*, v. 13, n. 37, 1998, p. 149–184.

Carvalho, Ernani Rodrigues de. *Sua Majestade, o Presidente da República: estudo de caso do controle de constitucionalidade dos atos do Executivo (1994–1998).* Dissertação (Mestrado em Ciência Política). Recife, Universidade Federal de Pernambuco, 2000, p. 92.

Eichler, Jessika; Sonkar, Sumit. Challenging absolute executive powers in times of corona: Re-examining constitutional courts and the collective right to public contestation as instruments of institutional control. *Review of Economics and Political Science*, v. 6, n. 1, 2021, p. 3–23.

Epstein, Lee; Martin, Andrew D. Does public opinion influence the Supreme Court-possibly yes (but we're not sure why). *University of Pennsylvania Journal of Constitutional Law*, v. 13, 2010, p. 263.

Ferreira Filho, Manoel Gonçalves. *Curso de direito constitucional.* São Paulo: Saraiva Educação, 1971, p. 145–146.

Figueiredo, Argelina Cheibub. Agendas, instituições políticas e desempenho do governo na democracia brasileira. In: Reis, Elisa P.; Zilberman, Regina (Eds.). *Retratos do Brasil.* Porto Alegre: Edipucrs, 2004, p. 80.

Figueiredo, Argelina Cheibub; Limongi, Fernando. *Executivo e Legislativo na nova ordem constitucional.* Rio de Janeiro: FGV, 1999, p. 41.

Friedman, Barry. The politics of judicial review. *Tex. L. Rev.*, v. 84, 2005, p. 257; Barrett Lain, Corinna. Upside-down judicial review. *Georgetown Law Journal*, v. 101, 2012, p. 113.

Friedman, Barry. *The will of the people: How public opinion has influenced the Supreme Court and shaped the meaning of the constitution.* New York: Farrar, Straus and Giroux, 2009.

Garoupa, Nuno; Ginsburg, Tom. *Judicial reputation: A comparative theory.* Chicago: University of Chicago Press, 2015.

Griglio, Elena. Parliamentary oversight under the Covid-19 emergency: Striving against executive dominance. *The Theory and Practice of Legislation*, v. 8, n. 1–2, 2020, p. 50.

Grogan, Joelle. Analysing global use of emergency powers in response to COVID-19. *European Journal of Law Reform*, v. 4, 2020, p. 350.

Hamilton, Alexander. The federalist n. 78. In: Madison, James; Hamilton, Alexander; Jay, John. *The federalist.* Campinas: Russell Editores, 2013.

Howell, William G. *Power without persuasion: The politics of direct presidential action.* Princeton University Press, 2003, p. 14.
Kaufman, Aaron R.; Rogowski, Jon C. *The unilateral presidency, 1933–2017.* March 8, 2018, p. 9. Available at: http://www.aaronrkaufman.com/wp-content/uploads/2018/03/Kaufman-Rogowski.pdf.
Klarman, Michael J. *Brown v. board of education and the civil rights movement.* Oxford: Oxford University Press, 2007, p. 218.
Limongi, Fernando. A democracia no Brasil: presidencialismo, coalizão partidária e processo decisório. *Novos estudos CEBRAP*, n. 76, 2006, p. 17–41.
Marshall, Thomas R. *Public opinion and the Supreme Court.* Boston: Unwin Hyman, 1989.
Mayer, Kenneth R. *With the stroke of a pen: Executive orders and presidential power.* Princeton University Press, 2002, p. 97–102.
Mello, Patrícia Perrone Campos. *Nos bastidores do Supremo Tribunal Federal.* Rio de Janeiro: Editora Forense, 2015.
Mendes, Gilmar Ferreira; Branco, Paulo Gonet. *Curso de Direito Constitucional*, 15. ed. São Paulo: Saraiva Educação, 2020. E-book. cap. 10, p. 1799, nota 233.
Mendes, Gilmar Ferreira; Sarlet, Ingo Wolfgang; Streck, Lenio Luiz; Leoncy, Leo Ferreira (Org.). *Comentários à Constituição do Brasil.* São Paulo: Saraiva Jur, 2018. E-book. p. 1956.
Moe, Terry M. The presidency and the bureaucracy: The presidential advantage. *The Presidency and the Political System*, v. 5, 1998, p. 443–474.
Moe, Terry M.; Howell, William G. The presidential power of unilateral action. *The Journal of Law, Economics, and Organization*, v. 15, n. 1, 1999, p. 132–179.
Mudde, Cas; Kaltwasser, Cristóbal Rovira (Eds.). *Populism in Europe and the Americas: Threat or corrective for democracy?* Cambridge: Cambridge University Press, 2012.
Novelino, Marcelo. O Supremo Tribunal Federal brasileiro e a opinião pública. In: Novelino, Marcelo; Leite, George Salomão; Rocha, Lilian Rose Lemos (Eds.). *Liberdade e Fraternidade: A Contribuição de Ayres Britto Para o Direito.* Salvador: JusPodivm, 2018, p. 169.
O'Connor, Sandra Day. Public trust as a dimension of equal justice: Some suggestions to increase public trust. *University of Chicago Law Review*, 1999, p. 10–13.
Pacheco, Cristina Carvalho. *O Supremo Tribunal Federal e a reforma do Estado: uma análise das Ações Diretas de Inconstitucionalidade julgadas no primeiro governo de Fernando Henrique Cardoso (1995–1998).* Curitiba: Appris Editora, 2019, p. 42.
Posner, Eric A.; Vermeule, Adrian. *The executive unbound: After the Madisonian republic.* Oxford: Oxford University Press, 2011, p. 4.
Rotinghaus, Brandon; Warber, Adam L. Unilateral orders as constituency outreach: Executive orders, proclamations, and the public presidency. *Presidential Studies Quarterly*, v. 45, n. 2, 2015, p. 289–309.
Shugart, Matthew S. *Presidents and assemblies: Constitutional design and electoral dynamics.* Cambridge: Cambridge University Press, 1992.
Torres, João Camilo de Oliveira. *O presidencialismo no Brasil.* Rio de Janeiro: Ed. O Cruzeiro, 1962, p. 222.
Tsebelis, George. *Veto players: How political institutions work.* New York: Russell Sage Foundation and Princeton University Press, 2002.
Tushnet, Mark. Skepticism about judicial review: A United States perspective. In: *Limits of constitutionality control.* Rio de Janeiro: Lumen Juris, 2009, p. 226.

2 When do presidents and prime ministers rule by decree?

Despite the importance that most democratic constitutions give to the legislature, the unilateral power of the executive is still "substantial, persistent and, in many cases, destructive".[1] In Brazil, for example, it is no exaggeration to say that the vast majority of policy changes since the return to democracy in 1985 have come from the unilateral hands of the president. The Bolsa Família program, a social welfare policy, was instituted by President Luiz Inácio Lula da Silva through the *Medida Provisória* (Provisional Measure) n. 132 of October 20, 2003.[2] Similarly, a decree issued by former president Jair Bolsonaro, significantly changed the country's firearms ownership policy.[3] The fact that presidents can unilaterally initiate reforms of this magnitude in different sectors is a worrying sign of the broad powers they enjoy.

In the administrative state, the public authorities are expected to take countless measures in the areas of health, education, public transportation, and social security, which generates high expectations of executive action. Overwhelmed by these expectations and wishing to consolidate their political power and historical legacy, presidents and prime ministers use unilateral action to escape legislative constraints and veto points, instituting new social policies and economic reforms more quickly. As William Howell says, they do *more* precisely because the public expects *more of* them.[4]

Addressing the growing decree power of presidents and prime ministers in several contemporary democracies, Guillermo O'Donnell coined the term "delegated democracy" to characterize regimes in which "the winner of the executive election is empowered to govern as he sees fit, constrained only by

1 Mayer, Kenneth R. Executive orders and presidential power. *The Journal of Politics*, v. 61, n. 2, 1999, p. 445–466. *See also* Moe, Terry M.; Howell, William G. The presidential power of unilateral action. *The Journal of Law, Economics, and Organization*, v. 15, n. 1, 1999, p. 132–179.

2 Brazil. Official website of federal legislation. Available at: https://www4.planalto.gov.br/legislacao/portal-legis/legislacao-1/medidas-provisorias.

3 Brazil. Official website of federal legislation. Available at: https://www4.planalto.gov.br/legislacaoportal-legis/legislacao-1/decretos1/decretos-1.

4 Howell, William G. *Power without persuasion: The politics of direct presidential action. Op. cit.*, p. 180.

DOI: 10.4324/9781003610816-3

the conjunctures of existing political relations and by a constitutionally limited term of office".[5] Thus, chief executives no longer need to call in the tanks to surround legislatures or the judiciary: they can exercise their unilateral powers in much less dramatic circumstances, when the legislature is functioning and within the limits formally established by the Constitution or the law.[6]

In this context, despite legal and constitutional limitations, decrees have become important instruments for consolidating executive power and promoting political reform. Even policies enacted by decree within the public administration spill over into the private sector: a small reform in the executive bureaucracy can have major consequences outside it. For example, administrative changes in a ministry of agriculture have an enormous impact on the private sector, especially the rural population and agribusiness. In this regard, former Brazilian President Jair Bolsonaro issued a decree abolishing several departments of the National Institute for Agrarian Reform (INCRA).[7] Although this act was purely administrative, it had far-reaching effects on agrarian reform policies, the lives of rural workers, social and labor relations in the countryside, and the Brazilian economy itself.

Also, it is important to mention that the frequency and contours of these normative acts cannot be explained solely by the personality of those in government, but rather by political and institutional forces.[8] The "imperial executive" is in fact the result of a specific governmental and institutional structure, in which the political strengths and weaknesses of certain centers of power stand out. This chapter will thus analyze the sources, motives, and political strategies behind decrees. It will examine the ability of the president and prime minister to make public policy without the explicit consent of parliament and how this unilateral action is constrained in a system of separation of powers.

The chapter also attempts to answer the following questions: (i) why do presidents and prime ministers issue decrees? (ii) what are the democratic risks of the increasing use of unilateral normative instruments by the executive? (ii) is the large number of decrees a sign of strength or weakness of the chief executive? (iii) does the number of decrees vary according to the personality of each president/prime minister or according to political and institutional factors? (iv) when and under what circumstances do they issue these decrees? (vi) what can be done to limit abuse?

The literature on the subject indicates that the frequency of issuing decrees varies according to the party composition of parliament, that is, whether the

5 O'Donnell, Guillermo. Delegative democracy? *Journal of Democracy*, v. 51, p. 55–69, 1994, p. 59.

6 Carey, John M.; Shugart, Matthew Soberg. Poder de decreto: Chamando os tanques ou usando a caneta? *Revista Brasileira de Ciências Sociais*, v. 13, n. 37, 1998, p. 149–184.

7 Brazil. Official website of federal legislation. Available at: https://www4.planalto.gov.br/legislacaoportal-legis/legislacao-1/decretos1/decretos-1.

8 Moe, Terry M.; Howell, William G. The presidential power of unilateral action. *The Journal of Law, Economics, and Organization*, *Op. cit.*, p. 134.

head of the executive has a legislative majority or not. It also varies depending on the popularity of the president or prime minister; the length of his term; the proximity of the election period; and the existence of an economic, political, or social crisis. Unilateral action in this context would be the result of the chief executive's interaction with the legislature, the courts, the media, the public, and the business sector.[9]

Finally, it should be noted that the literature on these topics largely analyzes presidential systems. Despite the profound differences, some of the considerations made here can also be applied to parliamentary systems. For each topic, the possibility (or not) of transferring the arguments between systems will be highlighted.

2.1 The party composition of the Congress[10]

In presidential systems, it is believed that presidents resort to decrees when they don't have a solid base in Congress or when their political ideology is very different from the majority of deputies and senators.[11] They would act unilaterally to bypass a hostile Congress and manage to govern. Brazilian political scientists have said, for example, that the high number of decrees issued by former president Bolsonaro was mainly due to the absence of a consolidated base with a majority in Congress and a lack of dialogue with the legislature.[12] Bolsonaro opted for confrontation rather than building articulated policies with parliamentarians and, precisely for this reason, he had "governed by decree".[13]

However, contrary to what might be assumed at first glance, empirical evidence indicates that in the majority of cases, the greater the presidential influence over Congress, the greater the number of decrees that are signed. According to Professor Magna Maria Inácio, in Latin America, it is not presidents with small coalitions and weak bases who govern through these acts. For her, "presidents with majority support in Congress use more decrees because they also pass more laws and implement them quickly. In addition, those who form coalitions use these decrees to manage their allies within the

9 Howell, William G. *Power without persuasion: The politics of direct presidential action. Op. cit.*, p. 10–12; Carey, John M.; Shugart, Matthew Soberg. Poder de decreto: Chamando os tanques ou usando a caneta? *Op. cit.*, p. 151.

10 Because of the profound differences between the relationship between presidents and prime ministers and the composition of the legislatures, this specific topic will deal only with presidential systems.

11 *See* Deering, Christopher J.; Maltzman, Forrest. The politics of executive orders: Legislative constraints on presidential power. *Political Research Quarterly*, v. 52, n. 4, 1999, p. 767–783.

12 G1 (Brazilian Newspaper). *Com média de 1,3 por dia, governo Bolsonaro só fez menos decretos que Collor nos 6 primeiros meses.* June 29, 2019. Available at: https://gauchazh.clicrbs.com.br/politica/noticia/2019/05/bolsonaro-edita-em-media-um-decreto-por-dia-cjvvkpuru05xg01mapiet70k2.html.

13 Carey, John M.; Shugart, Matthew Soberg. Poder de decreto: Chamando os tanques ou usando a caneta? *Op. cit.*, p. 166.

Executive".[14] Furthermore, according to Magna Inácio, ideological orientation does not influence the number of presidential decrees in Latin America. In her words, "These unilateral decisions depend on the powers the president has and the size of the majority that supports him. They are used by presidents with different ideological orientations".[15]

These conclusions, which seem to be "counterintuitive", have also been confirmed in the United States of America.[16] According to the data analyzed by George Krause and David Cohen, US presidents exercise their unilateral power more frequently when the government is unified, that is, when the same party governs the executive and legislative branches. Because of the congressional support they receive, presidents feel more encouraged to exercise their unilateral powers, using executive orders to complement or reinforce legislative successes in Congress. In the words of Krause and Cohen, "Presidents will issue more executive orders when their success rate in passing laws increases, so that this type of unilateral action reinforces the power that the president has in Congress".[17] On the other hand, when the government is divided, presidents would worry about the more intense scrutiny of Congress and thus would be afraid to issue these acts and then suffer the political burden of seeing them invalidated *a posteriori*.[18]

There is also a third position, which argues that the partisan composition of Congress does not actually have a significant impact on the adoption of unilateral acts.[19] In Brazil, for example, studies by Carlos Pereira, Timothy Power,

14 BBC NEWS BRAZIL. *From the USA to Brazil, how presidents try to govern without Congress.* June 17, 2019. Available at: https://www.bbc.com/portuguese/brasil-48505310; Inácio, Magna; Llanos, Mariana. The institutional presidency in Latin America: A comparative analysis. *Presidential Studies Quarterly*, v. 46, n. 3, 2016, p. 531–549.

15 BBC NEWS BRAZIL. *From the USA to Brazil, how presidents try to govern without Congress.* June 17, 2019. Available at: https://www.bbc.com/portuguese/brasil-48505310; Inácio, Magna; Llanos, Mariana. The institutional presidency in Latin America: A comparative analysis. *Op. cit.*, p. 531–549. In the United States, however, data shows that Democratic presidents tend to issue more executive orders than Republicans. Mayer, Kenneth. *With the stroke of a pen: Executive orders and presidential power. Op. cit.*, p. 102.

16 Krause, George A.; Cohen, David B. Presidential use of executive orders, 1953–1994. *American Politics Quarterly*, v. 25, n. 4, 1997, p. 458–481. In the same vein: Shull, Steven A. *Presidential-congressional relations: Policy and time approaches.* Michigan: University of Michigan Press, 2000.

17 Krause, George A.; Cohen, David B. Presidential use of executive orders, 1953–1994. *Op. cit.*, p. 470.

18 Bolton, Alexander; Thrower, Sharece. Legislative capacity and executive unilateralism. *American Journal of Political Science*, v. 60, n. 3, 2016, p. 649–663; Deering, Christopher J.; Maltzman, Forrest. The politics of executive orders: Legislative constraints on presidential power. *Political Research Quarterly*, v. 52, n. 4, 1999, p. 767–783.

19 Fine, Jeffrey A.; Warber, Adam L. Circumventing adversity: Executive orders and divided government. *Presidential Studies Quarterly*, v. 42, n. 2, 2012, p. 256–274; Pereira, Carlos; Power, Timothy J.; Rennó, Lucio R. Under what conditions do presidents resort to decree power? Theory and evidence from the Brazilian case. *The Journal of Politics*, v. 67, n. 1, 2005,

and Lucio Rennó[20] indicate that the use of *medidas provisórias* (provisional measures) is highly dependent on political and economic factors, but that there is no direct and inexorable relationship between unified or divided governments, especially considering the political system of coalition presidentialism in force in the country.

In view of the intense controversy, Kenneth Mayer, one of the leading researchers on the subject, went as far as to say that "it is still not fully understood how the dynamic between the president and Congress affects the issuing of unilateral acts".[21] It can therefore be seen that the relationship between the frequency of unilateral action and holding a majority in Congress remains uncertain. It is likely to depend on specific political arrangements, which are not always observable from the majority/minority dichotomy in the legislature.

2.2 Popularity ratings

Part of the literature states that presidents and prime ministers tend to act unilaterally when they experience low levels of popular support.[22] They adopt a compensatory strategy to make political decisions and reforms to boost their popularity.[23] Decrees would thus be used as a form of direct dialogue with the population – especially with their original support base.[24] They would also serve to give extra publicity to a given political position, as a way for the executive chief to show attention and solidarity to a given social problem and give direct *feedback* to the population. In short, to improve their image, they would try to "do things on their own, in their own way" to demonstrate that they still have political strength.[25]

Again, however, these data don't seem to apply in every scenario. In Brazil, for example, former president Dilma Rousseff was one of the least popular

p. 178–200; Mayer, Kenneth R. Executive orders and presidential power. *The Journal of Politics*, v. 61, n. 2, 1999, p. 445–466.

20 Pereira, Carlos; Power, Timothy J.; Rennó, Lucio R. Under what conditions do presidents resort to decree power? Theory and evidence from the Brazilian case. *Op. cit.*, p. 196.

21 Mayer, Kenneth. Executive orders. In: Bessette, J. M.; Tulis, J. K. (Org.). *The constitutional presidency*. Baltimore: John Hopkins, 2009, p. 168.

22 Mayer, Kenneth. With the stroke of a pen: Executive orders and presidential power. *Op. cit.*, p. 97 and 102. In the same vein, *see* Deering, Christopher J.; Maltzman, Forrest. The politics of executive orders: Legislative constraints on presidential power. *Political Research Quarterly*, v. 52, n. 4, 1999, p. 767–783 and Fine, Jeffrey A.; Warber, Adam L. Circumventing adversity: Executive orders and divided government. *Presidential Studies Quarterly*, v. 42, n. 2, 2012, p. 256–274.

23 Mayer, Kenneth R. Executive orders and presidential power. *The Journal of Politics*, v. 61, n. 2, 1999, p. 445–466.

24 Rotinghaus, Brandon; Warber, Adam L. Unilateral orders as constituency outreach: Executive orders, proclamations, and the public presidency. *Presidential Studies Quarterly*, v. 45, n. 2, 2015, p. 289–309.

25 Rotinghaus, Brandon; Warber, Adam L. Unilateral orders as constituency outreach: Executive orders, proclamations, and the public presidency. *Op. cit.*

presidents in recent history, yet she issued a considerably low number of decrees. Also, Brazilian presidents who enjoyed high levels of popularity, such as Lula and Fernando Henrique Cardoso, issued a high number of these unilateral acts, much higher than Dilma Rousseff's average. Furthermore, Jair Bolsonaro enjoyed positive popularity ratings during his first year in office, precisely when he issued a record number of these acts.[26] Thus, it is unclear whether there is a direct correlation between popularity and the enactment of decrees that could be applied in any political context.

2.3 Start or end of term[27]

Another interesting question relates to the frequency with which these acts are issued over the course of a mandate. It is assumed that presidents and prime ministers tend to issue more decrees in their first and last months in government. This is based on the observation that the number of decrees issued tends to increase in the period immediately following their election and then again in the period immediately preceding their departure from office.[28] In the initial phase of a mandate, chief executives typically enjoy considerable political influence, which they seek to maintain by promptly implementing campaign promises. During this period, they want to change the *status quo* in order to differentiate themselves from their predecessors, carrying out reforms and molding the executive to the new guidelines.

Especially in the first "100 days" of government, which receive a lot of media attention, executive leaders often point out the mistakes of the previous administration and issue a greater number of acts to adapt the bureaucracy to the "new times" and to leave their "trademark".[29] In effect, presidents and premiers generally resort to unilateral administrative measures as a way of revoking decisions made by previous administrations and aligning executive branch bodies with their own political agendas.[30-31] In this manner, they will criticize and disassociate themselves from previous administrations.

26 Brazil. Official website of federal legislation. Available at: https://www4.planalto.gov.br/legislacaoportal-legis/legislacao-1/decretos1/decretos-1.

27 Given that in some parliamentary systems the prime minister can continue in office for long periods, the focus of this chapter is on presidential systems in which there is a fixed term of office.

28 Rotinghaus, Brandon; Warber, Adam L. Unilateral orders as constituency outreach: Executive orders, proclamations, and the public presidency. *Op. cit.*, p. 294.

29 Ruhl, J. B.; Salzman, James. Presidential exit. *Duke Law Journal*, v. 67, 2017, p. 1.732.

30 BBC NEWS BRAZIL. *From the USA to Brazil, how presidents try to govern without Congress.* June 17, 2019. Available at: https://www.bbc.com/portuguese/brasil-48505310. Inácio, Magna; Llanos, Mariana. The institutional presidency in Latin America: A comparative analysis. *Op. cit.*, p. 531–549.

31 Inácio, Magna; Recch, Filipe; Valencia, Carolina Guerrero. The power of the administrative decisions of Latin American presidents. In: Llanos, Mariana; Marsteintredet, Leiv (Eds.).

On the other hand, it is also common to issue decrees at the very end of their terms, precisely to bind the next executive leaders and perpetuate a certain policy or reform.[32] This creates a political burden for the next president or premier to annul his predecessor's measures. American doctrine points out, for example, that in the last months of office, presidents often issue executive orders with highly symbolic and controversial content, relating to labor rights, the health system, and the environment.[33] These acts are also more often issued in reelection years to demonstrate that the chief executive is "in charge" and "doing his job",[34] and are generally aimed at supporters, reinforcing political positions and consolidating reforms.

2.4 Crisis scenarios[35]

The number of decrees tends to peak during times of crisis.[36] In Latin American countries, for example, the serious economic crises that often hit them are usually tackled through economic reform packages drawn up unilaterally by presidents.[37] In Argentina, former president Carlos Menem abused his normative power in the 1990s by using the economic crisis as an excuse to act in a discretionary and unconstitutional manner. Many of the emergency measures were not in response to a pressing need of society, but rather of the government, which used decrees to impose its own political agenda and bypass Congress.[38] In post-socialist European states, too, the economic and political

---

Latin America in times of turbulence*: Presidentialism under stress*. New York: Routledge, 2023, p. 83.

32 Mayer, Kenneth. *With the stroke of a pen: Executive orders and presidential power*. *Op. cit.*, p. 96.

33 Mayer, Kenneth R. Executive orders and presidential power. *The Journal of Politics*, *Op. cit.*, p. 450–452.

34 Rotinghaus, Brandon; Warber, Adam L. Unilateral orders as constituency outreach: Executive orders, proclamations, and the public presidency. *Presidential Studies Quarterly*, v. 45, n. 2, 2015, p. 289–309. In the same vein, Mayer, Kenneth. *With the stroke of a pen: Executive orders and presidential power*. *Op. cit.*, p. 97.

35 The considerations in this topic apply to both parliamentary and presidential systems.

36 There are three categories of emergencies: (i) those caused by intentional human action (such as a large-scale terrorist attack), (ii) those that are the product of human action but not human design (such as an economic crisis or Chernobyl), and (iii) those caused by nature. The boundaries between these categories are blurred – for example, the damage caused by "natural" disasters can be the joint product of nature and prior human action. *See* Posner, Eric, Vermeule, Adrian. Emergencies, tradeoffs, and deference. In: Dyzenhaus, David (Ed.). *Civil rights and security*. Ed. Routledge, 2017, p. 50.

37 Carey, John M.; Shugart, Matthew Soberg. Poder de decreto: Chamando os tanques ou usando a caneta? *Revista Brasileira de Ciências Sociais*, v. 13, n. 37, 1998, p. 149–184.

38 Rubio, Delia Ferreira; Goretti, Matteo. Cuando el presidente gobierna solo. Menem y los decretos de necesidad y urgencia hasta la reforma constitucional (julio 1989–agosto 1994). *Desarrollo Económico*, v. 36, n. 141, 1996, p. 443–474.

reforms of the early 1990s were carried out by acts of the chief executives, with minimal participation from parliaments.[39]

In Brazil, the role of the executive in economic crisis scenarios was well summarized in an interview given by former president Fernando Collor de Mello, who sought to curb the country's high inflation with economic plans conveyed by *medidas provisórias* (provisional measures) and secondary legislation. With these instruments, he initiated many privatization processes of public companies. When asked about the importance of using these measures, the former president replied:

> [H]ow could we have frozen all liquid assets [without the use of provisional measures]? How could we carry out all these measures by saying: "Listen, we need to freeze all assets for a year, (. . .) in order to reduce the amount of money in circulation and thus get rid of inflation"? *These were strategies that would have been impossible to adopt without the use of "medidas provisórias" [provisional measures].* (. . .) every heterodox economic plan here in Brazil has used a "medida provisória", without which it would never have passed. That doesn't mean that I defend them. I'm against them. *But it is the only instrument of governability and administration available to us today.* That's it. There's no other way.[40]

Another example of a crisis dealt with by decrees in several countries is the COVID-19 pandemic. As already mentioned, there was a proliferation of unilateral acts coming from all executive levels of government to impose restrictions on public transport and urban mobility, order the closure of commercial establishments, limit freedom of assembly, and so on. It can be said that these decisions were taken through unilateral acts precisely because of their speed and flexibility, since the crisis scenario theoretically did not allow waiting for legislative majorities to be formed and for the normal legislative process to run its course.[41]

A detailed analysis of the behavior of the chief executives during the pandemic is presented in Chapter 5 of this book. For now, it's enough to point out that periods of crisis usually lead to a flourishing of executive decrees, both those that constitute primary legislation – such as the Brazilian *medidas*

39 Kubicek, Paul. Delegative democracy in Russia and Ukraine. *Communist and Post-Communist Studies*, v. 27, n. 4, 1994.

40 Power, Timothy. The pen is mightier than the Congress. Presidential decree power in Brazil. In: Carey, John M.; Shugart, Matthew Soberg (Org.). *Executive decree authority*. Cambridge: Cambridge University Press, 1998, p. 216–217 (emphasis added).

41 *See* for all Petrov, Jan. The COVID-19 emergency in the age of executive aggrandizement: What role for legislative and judicial checks? *The Theory and Practice of Legislation*, v. 8, n. 1–2, 2020, p. 71–92 and Deere, Kelly J. Governing by executive order during the COVID-19 pandemic: Preliminary observations concerning The proper balance between executive orders and more formal rule making. *Missouri Law Review*, v. 86, 2021, p. 721.

provisórias or the Italian *decreti-legge* – and those that represent secondary legislation.

2.5 Institutional and political limits to unilateral power

Presidents and prime ministers know the importance and impact of unilateral action on their political present and future. They know that the media and the public will support or condemn their acts, and that there may be backlash or retaliation from legislatures or the courts. They make political calculations in advance and try to anticipate the reaction of the other branches of government to assess whether a particular action should be taken unilaterally or in cooperation with Congress. The decision to act alone is not trivial and carries political costs, so executive branch leaders "think politically" before issuing decrees.[42]

In fact, chief executives often face real obstacles: a large and entrenched bureaucracy, an independent and often recalcitrant parliament, a self-interested media, an increasingly vigilant public, and a judiciary that sometimes shows its face.[43] In this context, the abuse of unilateral power can be combated on several fronts, both formal and informal. Formal control mechanisms include the possibility for parliaments to suspend executive decrees and for the judiciary to control them through lawsuits. Informal mechanisms include the media and public opinion, which play an important role against the abuse of decree power and represent a real source of "checks" on the head of the government.

For example, an important kind of oversight is the publication of newspaper reports that warn and alert the public to the frequent use of unilateral instruments. In Brazil, it was common to see headlines proclaiming: "Bolsonaro sets record for decrees in first 150 days"[44] and "With an average of 1.3 per day, Bolsonaro's government only made fewer decrees than Collor's in the first six months".[45] Such reports are important to alert the public to an abusive executive habit and to the democratic risks of excessive use of decrees.[46] Perhaps more than the courts and legislatures, it's this kind of informal and political

42 Bailey, Jeremy D.; Rottinghaus, Brandon. Reexamining the use of unilateral orders: Source of authority and the power to act alone. *American Politics Research*, v. 42, n. 3, 2014, p. 472–502.

43 Posner, Eric A.; Vermeule, Adrian. *The executive unbound: After the Madisonian republic. Op. cit.*, p. 14.

44 Correio Braziliense (Brazilian Newspaper). *Bolsonaro bate recorde de decretos nos primeiros 150 dias desde Collor.* April 6, 2019. Available at: https://www.correiobraziliense.com.br/app/noticia/politica/2019/06/04/interna_politica,760088/bolsonaro-edita-recorde-de-decretos-desde-collor.shtml.

45 G1 (Brazilian Newspaper). *Com média de 1,3 por dia, governo Bolsonaro só fez menos decretos que Collor nos 6 primeiros meses.* June 29, 2019. Available at: https://g1.globo.com/politica/noticia/2019/06/29/com-media-de-13-decreto-por-dia-governo-bolsonaro-so-editou-menos-que-collor-em-seis-meses.ghtml.

46 Christenson, Dino P.; Kriner, Douglas L. Political constraints on unilateral executive action. *Case Western Reserve Law Review*, v. 65, 2014, p. 931.

constraint that explains why presidents and prime ministers in many countries don't act alone so aggressively on a day-to-day basis.[47]

But the media must be only one of several tools for checking the president and prime minister. A democracy cannot rely solely on its press to stay within constitutional limits. Especially with the rise of information technology and social networks, many leaders ignore or minimize the warnings of the traditional media and seek support on digital platforms such as *Twitter* and *Facebook*. Thus, it is not enough that the press publishes reports criticizing the use of decrees: what is needed is a legislature and a judiciary with the courage to act in a counter-majoritarian manner and to impose limits on the chief executive, especially when he uses his popularity to govern alone. As William Howell observes, "[W]hen Congress is weak and the judiciary is lenient, presidential unilateral power flourishes; when Congress is strong and united and the judiciary decides to limit presidential power, presidents have limited unilateral power".[48]

Bibliography

Bailey, Jeremy D.; Rottinghaus, Brandon. Reexamining the use of unilateral orders: Source of authority and the power to act alone. *American Politics Research*, v. 42, n. 3, 2014, p. 472–502.

Bolton, Alexander; Thrower, Sharece. Legislative capacity and executive unilateralism. *American Journal of Political Science*, v. 60, n. 3, 2016, p. 649–663; Deering, Christopher J.; Maltzman, Forrest. The politics of executive orders: Legislative constraints on presidential power. *Political Research Quarterly*, v. 52, n. 4, 1999, p. 767–783.

Carey, John M.; Shugart, Matthew Soberg. Poder de decreto: Chamando os tanques ou usando a caneta? *Revista Brasileira de Ciências Sociais*, v. 13, n. 37, 1998, p. 149–184.

Christenson, Dino P.; Kriner, Douglas L. Political constraints on unilateral executive action. *Case Western Reserve Law Review*, v. 65, 2014, p. 931.

Deere, Kelly J. Governing by executive order during the COVID-19 pandemic: Preliminary observations concerning the proper balance between executive orders and more formal rule making. *Missouri Law Review*, v. 86, 2021, p. 721.

Deering, Christopher J.; Maltzman, Forrest. The politics of executive orders: Legislative constraints on presidential power. *Political Research Quarterly*, v. 52, n. 4, 1999, p. 767–783.

Fine, Jeffrey A.; Warber, Adam L. Circumventing adversity: Executive orders and divided government. *Presidential Studies Quarterly*, v. 42, n. 2, 2012, p. 256–274.

Inácio, Magna; Recch, Filipe; Valencia, Carolina Guerrero. The power of the administrative decisions of Latin American presidents. In: Llanos, Mariana; Marsteintredet, Leiv (Eds.). *Latin America in times of turbulence: Presidentialism under stress*. New York: Routledge, 2023, p. 83.

Krause, George A.; Cohen, David B. Presidential use of executive orders, 1953–1994. *American Politics Quarterly*, v. 25, n. 4, 1997, p. 458–481.

47 Posner, Eric A.; Vermeule, Adrian. *The executive unbound: After the Madisonian republic. Op. cit.*, p. 14.

48 Howell, William G. *Power without persuasion: The politics of direct presidential action. Op. cit.*, p. 176.

Kubicek, Paul. Delegative democracy in Russia and Ukraine. *Communist and Post-Communist Studies*, v. 27, n. 4, 1994.
Mayer, Kenneth R. Executive orders and presidential power. *The Journal of Politics*, v. 61, n. 2, 1999, p. 445–466.
Mayer, Kenneth R. *With the stroke of a pen: Executive orders and presidential power. Op. cit.*, p. 97 and 102.
Mayer, Kenneth R. Executive orders. In: Bessette, J. M.; Tulis, J. K. (Org.). *The constitutional presidency*. Baltimore: John Hopkins, 2009, p. 168.
Moe, Terry M.; Howell, William G. The presidential power of unilateral action. *The Journal of Law, Economics, and Organization*, v. 15, n. 1, 1999, p. 132–179.
O'Donnell, Guillermo. Delegative democracy? *Journal of Democracy*, v. 51, 1994, p. 55–69.
Pereira, Carlos; Power, Timothy J.; Rennó, Lucio R. Under what conditions do presidents resort to decree power? Theory and evidence from the Brazilian case. *The Journal of Politics*, v. 67, n. 1, 2005, p. 178–200.
Petrov, Jan. The COVID-19 emergency in the age of executive aggrandizement: What role for legislative and judicial checks? *The Theory and Practice of Legislation*, v. 8, n. 1–2, 2020, p. 71–92.
Posner, Eric; Vermeule, Adrian. Emergencies, tradeoffs, and deference. In: Dyzenhaus, David (Ed.). *Civil rights and security*. Ed. Routledge, 2017, p. 50.
Power, Timothy. The pen is mightier than the Congress. Presidential decree power in Brazil. In: Carey, John M.; Shugart, Matthew Soberg (Org.). *Executive decree authority*. Cambridge: Cambridge University Press, 1998, p. 216–217.
Rotinghaus, Brandon; Warber, Adam L. Unilateral orders as constituency outreach: Executive orders, proclamations, and the public presidency. *Presidential Studies Quarterly*, v. 45, n. 2, 2015, p. 289–309.
Rubio, Delia Ferreira; Goretti, Matteo. Cuando el presidente gobierna solo. Menem y los decretos de necesidad y urgencia hasta la reforma constitucional (julio 1989-agosto 1994). *Desarrollo Económico*, v. 36, n. 141, 1996, p. 443–474.
Ruhl, J. B.; Salzman, James. Presidential exit. *Duke Law Journal*, v. 67, 2017, p. 1.732.
Shull, Steven A. *Presidential-congressional relations: Policy and time approaches*. Michigan: University of Michigan Press, 2000.

3 Justifying unilateral executive action

Executive dominance has been the subject of numerous criticisms and justifications. Some see the frequent use of unilateral acts as a danger to a democratic constitutional order.[1] Others argue that the escalation of decree power is necessary in the contemporary economic and social scenario, which requires quick and technical responses from the government.[2] In general, critics claim that the abusive use of decrees violates (i) the principle of separation of powers, because it is a way of bypassing Congress and the ordinary legislative process, and (ii) the democratic principle, because the process of drafting decrees does not involve prior public deliberation and can only be subject to *a posteriori* control.

In turn, the high volume of decrees would be justified by the need (i) for speed, expertise, and flexibility in developing certain policies; (ii) for direct dialogue between the chief executive and his support base; (iii) for filling in regulatory gaps; and, finally, (iv) because Congress sometimes prefers presidents and prime ministers to unilaterally elaborate policies, since, thus, the political risks move from the legislative to the executive. In this perspective, John Carey and Matthew Shugart argue that the frequent exercise of executive decree authority does not necessarily constitute a form of usurpation of congressional power. In their view, more often than is generally recognized, the executive decree power could be tolerated – or even preferred – by legislatures because it shifts the political burdens and risks of enacting a particular policy from the legislative branch to the executive.[3]

1 Branum, Tara L. President or king - the use and abuse of executive orders in modern-day America. *Journal of Legislation*, v. 28, 2002, p. 1–86.
2 Posner, Eric A.; Vermeule, Adrian. *The executive unbound: After the Madisonian republic. Op. cit.*, p. 19.
3 Carey, John M.; Shugart, Matthew Soberg. Calling out the tanks or filling out the forms? In: Carey, John M.; Shugart, Matthew Soberg (Eds.). *Executive decree authority*. Cambridge: Cambridge University Press, 1998, p. 1–29.

DOI: 10.4324/9781003610816-4

3.1 Celerity

One factor that makes regulations and decrees attractive to presidents and prime ministers is speed. Legislative processes are often slow and may not be effective in solving urgent problems. Especially in times of crisis, these executive actions are often preferred to the normal legislative process.[4] According to Steven Calabresi, this expansion of a president's and prime minister's freedom to act alone reflects democratic interests, as the exercise of concentrated power seems more efficient for tackling complex problems that require urgent solutions.[5] The heads of the executive branch would have institutional advantages over Congress and could develop faster and more effective actions, especially in crisis contexts.

It can be said, for example, that major decisions taken during the COVID-19 pandemic came by unilateral acts because of their speed and flexibility. In the context of the crisis scenario, it would not be possible to wait for the formation of legislative majorities and the subsequent course of the ordinary legislative procedure. The length, formality, and complexity of parliamentary decision-making procedures, based on the participation of a significant number of parliamentarians, may seem incompatible with the urgency of a pandemic.

However, this need for speed should not be used as a license for administrators to abuse their decree authority. Especially in crisis scenarios, executive leaders need to establish a dialogue with the legislature so that both can find cooperative solutions without the regulatory burden falling entirely on the executive. Technological communication tools and faster legislative processes, such as Brazil's "extremely urgent" legislative regime (*urgência urgentíssima*),[6] allow legislators to participate in policymaking in times of crisis, producing more democratic and responsive solutions to the different political forces that exist in society.

3.2 Expertise

In some areas, the executive has more expertise than the legislature in formulating public policy. In matters involving a high degree of specialization, such

4 Carey, John M.; Shugart, Matthew Soberg. Calling out the tanks or filling out the forms? *Op. cit.*, p. 160.

5 Calabresi, Steven G. Some normative arguments for the unitary executive. *Arkansas Law Review, v.* 48, 1995, p. 23–104.

6 Internal regulations of the Chamber of Deputies of Brazil.

> Art. 155. Even if the session in which it is presented begins, a proposal that deals with a topic of relevant and urgent national interest can be automatically included in the agenda for discussion and immediate voting, at the request of the absolute majority of the composition. of the Chamber, or of the Managers representing this number, approved by the absolute majority of Deputies, without the constraint referred to in §2 of the previous article.

as international policy or armaments, the public administration usually has greater technical and informational aptitude.[7] In the words of Cass Sunstein, "Of the three branches of the national government, the executive branch possesses by far the most information, not only in foreign policy but also in the domestic domain":[8]

> If public managers are to solve the nation's problems, they have to access a large amount of information, most of it highly technical. Of the three branches of the national government, the Executive has by far the most information, not only in foreign policy but also in the domestic domain. Although this informational advantage could not have been easily anticipated by the generation of the Constituents, it continues to grow every year. In particular, the gap between the knowledge of the executive branch and that of Congress is widening.[9]

Similarly, Adrian Vermeule and Eric Posner argue that the executive is structurally superior to the legislative and judicial branches. According to them, "The scope of the executive's responsibility is vast so that legislative and judicial institutions lack the capacity to monitor any important fraction of what the executive does":

> In many of the most important fields, and those most difficult to monitor – those involving intelligence, foreign policy and national security, or highly complex questions of economic policy – legislators and courts are defeated, for resistant structural reasons that prevail no matter the contingent political constellation.[10]

It's understandable that some technical and complex decisions take place within the administration, among specialists, rather than among politicians in the legislature. In the field of international relations, for example, the president or prime minister has access to confidential information provided by diplomats, ambassadors, or members of intelligence agencies, which could not be disclosed or openly discussed in a plenary session of Congress. In the field of public security, police coordination can provide more effective responses in crisis scenarios, especially because of the information superiority and secrecy imposed on certain data collected.

7 Carey, John M.; Shugart, Matthew Soberg. Poder de decreto: Chamando os tanques ou usando a caneta? *Revista Brasileira de Ciências Sociais*, v. 13, n. 37, 1998, p. 149–184.

8 Sunstein, Cass R. The most knowledgeable branch. *University of Pennsylvania Law Review*, v. 164, 2015, p. 1.608.

9 Sunstein, Cass R. The most knowledgeable branch. *Op. cit.*

10 Posner, Eric A.; Vermeule, Adrian. *The executive unbound: After the Madisonian republic. Op. cit.*, p. 19.

Indeed, independent regulatory agencies can also have the best institutional conditions to make complex decisions that require the highest levels of information, *expertise*, technical knowledge, and operational aptitude. They are naturally better placed to deal with technical and scientific issues. Parliamentarians, in turn, tend to avoid complex issues with which they are unlikely to be familiar or which do not pay electoral dividends. This means that they end up delegating these decisions to the executive, thereby reducing coalition costs.[11]

Health care regulatory agencies, for example, are the ideal place to decide which drugs should or should not be marketed in a given country. In this regard, the Brazilian Supreme Court highlighted the importance of the expertise of these regulatory agencies in a case involving the approval of the marketing and distribution of the "synthetic phosphoethanolamine", known as the "cancer pill".[12] The Court ruled that the National Health Surveillance Agency (Anvisa), a special agency linked to the Ministry of Health, is the body that has the expertise and technical capacity to authorize, or not, the marketing of the drug.

In his opinion, Judge Roberto Barroso pointed out that there is a legitimate area of administrative action that must be respected by the legislature in the name of the principle of separation of powers. In his words, the regulatory agency (Anvisa) has the "best institutional conditions to make such decisions" and the "highest level of information, expertise, technical knowledge and operational aptitude in relation to the health registration procedure, which is characterized by great complexity".[13] Therefore, it would not be legitimate to transfer the decision to authorize the use of the substance from the executive to the legislative branch.

However, we defend that this argument of expertise cannot be used as a trump card to approve exorbitant regulations that clearly go beyond the exegetical limits of the laws. Although the executive has greater technical and informational capacity to regulate certain matters, it should not use this institutional superiority to alienate the legislatures from issues that should clearly be the subject of broad democratic deliberation. Indeed, it is important for the executive to share relevant technical information with the legislative bodies, rather than using it as a pretext for unilateral action. Armed with this relevant data, parliamentarians could engage in open and productive discussions, leading to greater publicity and increased popular participation.

Moreover, the complete rationality of government decisions will always be questionable. There is no absolute truth in policymaking. The relevant facts,

11 Epstein, David; O'Halloran, Sharyn. *Delegating powers: A transactional cost politics approach to policy making under separation of powers*. Cambridge: Cambridge University Press, 1999.

12 Brazilian Supreme Federal Court. Ação Direta de Inconstitucionalidade (ADI) n. 5.501 MC, Rel. Min. Marco Aurélio, decision published on February 14, 2017.

13 Brazilian Supreme Federal Court. Ação Direta de Inconstitucionalidade (ADI) n. 5.501 MC, Rel. Min. Marco Aurélio, decision published on February 14, 2017.

their assessment, the policy's goal, and the appropriate way to achieve it are the objects of political struggle. Executive rules must be legitimate beyond their technical soundness.[14] Even if certain decisions are primarily scientific or technical, they may also involve political and legal controversies. During the COVID-19 pandemic, decisions to completely close all businesses or places of worship also involved a political and constitutional controversy – to the point that the German Constitutional Court, for example, allowed some places of worship to remain open as long as distancing measures were respected.[15]

Also, especially when it comes to acts issued by presidents, prime ministers, or government ministers, the argument of expertise loses some of its strength. This is because they cannot be compared to a specialized regulatory agency, which in fact has greater technical and informational capacity to discipline certain issues. Government ministers are generally chosen by political nominations and are not institutionally trained to make technical decisions. As a matter of example, during a period of the COVID-19 crisis, the Brazilian Minister of Health, Eduardo Pazuello, was a military man with no medical qualifications.[16]

Finally, legislators can understand the elements of science-based policy, often advised by a team of experts. During the pandemic, many countries passed lengthy and complex legislation to combat the virus: parliamentarians were advised by experts who helped draft the legal texts. For these reasons, important decisions that affect the lives of citizens should not be taken by the solitary hands of a president, prime minister, or government minister without a clear legal basis. Some issues should be the subject of broad deliberation, with all political forces and divergent opinions opposing each other. In this manner, the parliament can discuss solutions under the watchful eye of the public and the media, in effective respect of the democratic principle.

3.3 Flexibility

Another reason for issuing decrees and secondary regulations is their flexibility. They are easily revoked: with the stroke of a pen, presidents and prime ministers can overturn hundreds of previous regulations in one fell swoop.[17]

14 Pünder, Hermann. Democratic legitimation of delegated legislation - a comparative view on the American, British, and German law. *International & Comparative Law Quarterly*, v. 58, n. 2, 2009, p. 353–378.

15 *See, e.g.*, Kaiser, Anna-Bettina; Hensel, Roman. Federal Republic of Germany: Legal response to Covid-19. In: *The Oxford compendium of national legal responses to Covid-19*. April 2021. Available at: https://oxcon. ouplaw. com/view/https://doi.org/10.1093/law-occ19/law-occ19-e2.

16 BBC. *Who is Eduardo Pazuello, the general taking over the ministry of health on an interim basis?* May 16, 2020. Available at: https://www.bbc.com/portuguese/brasil-52686114.

17 Fleishman, Joel L.; Aufses, Arthur H. Law and orders: The problem of presidential legislation. *Law and Contemporary Problems*, v. 40, n. 3, 1976, p. 1–45.

Repealing a law, on the other hand, requires the passage of another law, and thus the formation of new coalitions and a new parliamentary majority. Especially in crisis situations, when new problems and issues are constantly emerging, the flexibility of decrees, regulations, and ordinances proves useful in allowing authorities to quickly replace strategies with more effective ones.

The ease with which thousands of decrees can be repealed was demonstrated in the first year of former Brazilian president Jair Bolsonaro's administration, which quickly revoked 2,019 decrees issued since 1910.[18] The presidential justification was the need to simplify the legislation and to reduce the regulatory framework to what was strictly necessary. According to the then minister of the Civil House, Onyx Lorenzoni, the repeal fulfilled the government's commitment to "reduce bureaucracy, simplify and reduce the size of the Brazilian state, a promise made during the electoral campaign". In his words, it was necessary to remove from the legal system "hundreds of unnecessary decrees that today only serve to add volume to our already bloated state and create bureaucracies that only get in the way".[19]

It should be noted, however, that this repeal was not preceded by a public debate. Although presidents and prime ministers have the formal authority to take this type of measure, there are democratic risks that should not be overlooked, because among the set of repealed decrees there may be norms of marked political, social, or economic relevance. In point of fact, the constant repeal of regulations confuses citizens and disorients their perception of the legal system. The constant repealing and issuing of decrees without a clear, predictable, and isonomic criterion empties the very foundation of the regulatory power, which is to make positive law clearer, more objective, and more precise. A chaotic regulatory activity makes it challenging for legal professionals and citizens to understand the legal system's expectations.[20]

The danger of this posture was also illustrated with the issuing of a decree by former Brazilian president Jair Bolsonaro that extinguished councils for civil society participation within the federal public administration. The act was partially suspended by the Federal Supreme Court precisely because, among the numerous bodies generically extinguished, there were councils created by

18 Brazil. Official website of federal legislation. *Governo Federal revoga cerca de 5,5 decretos ao dia*. December 17, 2019. Available at: https://www.gov.br/secretariageral/pt-br/noticias/governo-federal-revoga-cerca-de-5–5-decretos-ao-dia.

19 PORTAL G1. *Decreto faz 'revogaço' de normas; objetivo é simplificar legislação, diz governo.* Available at: https://g1.globo.com/politica/noticia/2019/04/11/decreto-faz-revogaco-de-normas-objetivo-e-simplificar-legislacao-diz-governo.ghtml.

20 Brandão, Rodrigo; Capecchi Nunes, Daniel. *Poder regulamentar e 'jogo duro constitucional': o caso dos decretos de armas. Jota.* July 10, 2019. Available at: https://www.jota.info/opiniao-e-analise/artigos/poder-regulamentar-e-jogo-duro-constitucional-o-caso-dos-decretos-de-armas-10072019.

law, which, due to the principle of symmetry, could only be extinguished by another primary law. According to the Court,

> [I]n view of the principle of the separation of powers, it is contrary to the Federal Constitution to abolish, by an act unilaterally issued by the Chief Executive, collegial bodies which, after having been formally established by a law, allow the participation of the population in the implementation of public policies.[21]

Flexibility is therefore a double-edged sword. On the one hand, it makes it easier to regulate areas that are in constant change; on the other hand, it allows for the immediate modification or repeal of countless regulations without proper and prior public deliberation. Certainly, these "major repeals" should send a warning signal to the other branches of government, as they promote change without popular control, on a very undemocratic basis.

3.4 Escaping the formal legislative process

Presidents and prime ministers use decrees strategically to implement their political agendas and escape the formal legislative process.[22] Instead of waiting for a lengthy legislative process before approving or vetoing a law, they simply create a new policy and leave it to Congress and the courts to control it *a posteriori*. If the other branches of government decide to remain inactive, either by not suspending the decree or by ruling in favor of the chief executive in a court case, the act is perpetuated and continues to produce its effects freely.[23] The decrees would thus be tools to compensate for congressional opposition,[24] bypassing the other institutional actors and fulfilling political promises directly and immediately, pleasing voters and the electoral support base.[25]

In the words of William Howell, chief executives use unilateral tools to avoid "endless debates and negotiations", since "a decree can be as powerful as a law – and considerably easier to obtain".[26] For the author, "There are

21 Supreme Federal Court of Brazil. ADI n. 6.121 MC, Rel. Min. Marco Aurélio. Publication: November 28, 2019.
22 Rotinghaus, Brandon; Warber, Adam L. Unilateral orders as constituency outreach: Executive orders, proclamations, and the public presidency. *Presidential Studies Quarterly*, v. 45, n. 2, 2015, p. 289–309; Fleishman, Joel L.; Aufses, Arthur H. Law and orders: The problem of presidential legislation. *Law and Contemporary Problems*, v. 40, n. 3, 1976, p. 1–45.
23 Howell, William G. *Power without persuasion: The politics of direct presidential action. Op. cit.*, p. 14.
24 Fleishman, Joel L.; Aufses, Arthur H. Law and orders: The problem of presidential legislation. *Law and Contemporary Problems*, v. 40, n. 3, 1976, p. 1–45.
25 Mayer, Kenneth R. Executive orders and presidential power. *The Journal of Politics*, v. 61, n. 2, 1999, p. 445–466.
26 Howell, William G. *Power without persuasion: The politics of direct presidential action.* Princeton University Press, 2003.

clear advantages associated with going it alone. When presidents decide to produce policies unilaterally, they present Congress (and the courts) with a fait accompli". The other branches of government only need to approve or invalidate the normative act without participating in its creation *ab initio*.[27] In addition, it is common for the president or prime minister to use decrees when they have already tried the ordinary legislative process and been defeated, as a way of forcing a negotiation process with the legislature.[28]

3.5 Instruments of legislative interpretation

Decrees can be a useful way for executive leaders to express their views on the meaning of legislation and to give it the concrete form they deem appropriate.[29] These unilateral acts represent a constitutional tool for legal interpretation, since through them the chief executive can reveal and consolidate specific meanings for existing laws, among the various possible hermeneutical possibilities. Especially when the legal text is vague or ambiguous, regulations and decrees are often used to define the scope and reach of the rules.

For some scholars, the leader of the executive branch would have ample democratic legitimacy to choose one of these possible interpretative paths and regulate the law according to his policy preferences.[30] A more traditional literature, however, is critical of the executive's ability to shape the meaning of laws to its own liking. In this perspective, the executive cannot impose its own interpretation on the pretext of regulating a given law, because "where the law creates doubt, it is not for the executive to sweep it away".[31]

In this regard, this book defends that the president or prime minister should interpret the law in accordance with hermeneutic rules and the framework established by the delegating law. They can interpret the primary legislation literally, systematically, historically, or teleologically, but not against its normative content, objective, and spirit. An infra-legal rule cannot violate the spirit of the primary law it regulates. Regulatory power must be exercised in express accordance with the objectives that explicitly and implicitly guide the

27 Howell, William G. *Power without persuasion: The politics of direct presidential action. Op. cit.*, p. 22.

28 Krause, George A.; Cohen, David B. Presidential use of executive orders, 1953–1994. *American Politics Quarterly*, v. 25, n. 4, 1997, p. 458–481, and Bailey, Jeremy D.; Rottinghaus, Brandon. The development of unilateral power and the problem of the power to warn: Washington through McKinley. *Presidential Studies Quarterly*, v. 43, 2013, p. 186–204.

29 Bradley, Curtis A.; Posner, Eric A. Presidential signing statements and executive power. *Constitutional Commentary*, v. 23, 2006, p. 307–364.

30 Lawson, Gary; Moore, Christopher D. The executive power of constitutional interpretation. *Iowa Law Review*, v. 81, 1996, p. 1.261.

31 Gasparini, Diógenes. *Poder regulamentar*. São Paulo: Ed. José Bushatsky, 1978, p. 123. Analyzing this traditional view in Italy, *see* Delpino, Federico; Del Giudice, Luigi. *Manuale di diritto amministrativo*. Napoli: Edizioni Giuridiche Simone, 2019.

legal text. Decrees cannot have the effect of emptying the meaning of legality itself.[32]

As an example of regulations that go against the very purpose of the law, we can highlight the decrees issued by Jair Bolsonaro to facilitate the carrying and possession of firearms.[33] These acts certainly violated the spirit of the Brazilian Disarmament Statute (Federal Law n. 10.826/2003), which was enacted with the clear intention of limiting the population's access to firearms. The objective of Bolsonaro's decrees was clearly the opposite of that of the law: while the latter sought to restrict the possession of guns, the central objective of the decrees was to arm the population and reverse the public policy provided for in the law. These decrees are a clear example of abuse of regulatory power, since the change in the Brazilian firearms ownership regime should have been submitted to Congress through a bill, and not imposed through a unilateral act by the president.

3.6 Filling regulatory gaps

Decrees can also be used to fill normative gaps in matters that are not reserved for the primary legislation.[34] In Brazil, the so-called autonomous decrees can (i) implement reforms in the administrative bureaucracy that do not require an increase in public spending and (ii) deal with matters not yet specifically regulated by law, as long as they don't violate areas that require primary legislation.[35] These autonomous or independent decrees do not definitively replace the law: they only fill its absence in certain fields until the law provides it. Once the law is enacted, the decree is superseded.[36]

In fact, the gaps in the law and the unpredictability of certain facts require that the executive be granted regulatory power. By means of decrees, ordinances, or other regulations, the executive may provide for situations not foreseen by the legislature.[37]

In Brazil, the Federal Supreme Court has often recognized the validity of autonomous decrees. The Court upheld the constitutionality of a decree

32 Brandão, Rodrigo; Capecchi Nunes, Daniel. *Poder regulamentar e 'jogo duro constitucional': o caso dos decretos de armas. Jota.* July 10, 2019. Available at: https://www.jota.info/opiniao-e-analise/artigos/poder-regulamentar-e-jogo-duro-constitucional-o-caso-dos-decretos-de-armas-10072019.

33 Brazil. Presidential Decree n. 9.981, issued on August 20, 2019. *See also* The Guardian. *Brazil's Bolsonaro signs decree loosening gun ownership rules.* Available at: https://www.theguardian.com/world/2019/jan/15/brazil-bolsonaro-signs-decree-easing-gun-restrictions.

34 Duncan Jr., John C. A critical consideration of executive orders: Glimmerings of autopoiesis in the executive role. *Vermont Law Review*, v. 35, 2010, p. 345.

35 Meirelles, Hely Lopes. *Brazilian administrative law*, 13. ed. São Paulo: Revista dos Tribunais, 1987, p. 138.

36 Meirelles, Hely Lopes. *Brazilian administrative law*, 13. ed. *Op. cit.*

37 Meirelles, Hely Lopes. *Brazilian administrative law*, 13. ed. *Op. cit.*, p. 124.

issued by President Luiz Inácio Lula da Silva to regulate the process of identifying, recognizing, demarcating, delimiting, and titling the lands of *quilombolas*, which are rural black communities founded by the descendants of African slaves. The decree directly regulates an article of the Brazilian Constitution that guarantees the right of the remnants of quilombo communities to ownership of the lands they occupy. In the ruling, the Court explicitly stated that a decree can directly regulate the constitutional text without the intermediary of a law.[38]

3.7 The symbolic role of decrees

In addition to the justifications already mentioned, presidents and prime ministers also act unilaterally to provide quick and immediate benefits to their constituencies or support bases. Decrees have an important symbolic and rhetorical function and are used to appease old supporters, attract new ones, and reward electors for their votes.[39] They are a valuable tool to seek public support and fulfill campaign promises, creating social mobilizations in their favor and accumulating greater political capital.[40] In order to cultivate support, decrees are used for ceremonial or even exhortative purposes to favor or appeal to an electoral base made up of specific groups, such as ethnic or social minorities, environmentalists, trade unionists, or industrialists.[41] With them, chief executives can satisfy their support base more quickly, avoid legislative obstacles, and get all the credit for implementing a particular policy.

In Brazil, highly symbolic decrees aimed at a specific support base have been common in every presidential term since re-democratization. One example was a decree issued by former president Fernando Henrique Cardoso to "grant compensation to the family of a person who disappeared or died as a result of participation, or accusation of participation, in political activities during the military dictatorship".[42] In this way, the former president showed his repudiation of the political crimes committed during the military dictatorship, defining a clear political position in solidarity with the victims of the regime.

38 Brazilian Federal Supreme Court. ADI n. 3.239, Rel. Min. Cezar Peluso, Rel. p/ Acórdão: Min. Rosa Weber, Full Court, published in 01.02.2019.

39 Rotinghaus, Brandon; Warber, Adam L. Unilateral orders as constituency outreach: Executive orders, proclamations, and the public presidency. *Presidential Studies Quarterly*, v. 45, n. 2, 2015, p. 289–309.

40 Rotinghaus, Brandon; Warber, Adam L. Unilateral orders as constituency outreach: Executive orders, proclamations, and the public presidency. *Op. cit.*, p. 295–296.

41 Rotinghaus, Brandon; Warber, Adam L. Unilateral orders as constituency outreach: Executive orders, proclamations, and the public presidency. *Op. cit.*, p. 291.

42 Brazil. *Federal Decree n. 1898, of May 9, 1996: Grants compensation to the family of a person who disappeared due to participation or accusation of participation in political activity.* Available at: http://www4.planalto.gov.br/legislacao/portal-legis/legislacao-1/decretos1/1996-decretos.

In another example, the already mentioned decree issued by Brazilian President Lula to regulate the ownership of "quilombola land" also had a highly political and symbolic content. The president's electoral promises were characterized by equal access to land and the protection of vulnerable minorities. The decree served to concretize a policy that was unlikely to be approved by Congress, which has historically been conservative on agrarian issues. Faced with possible opposition to the measure in the legislature, Lula chose to implement it unilaterally, directly regulating the constitutional text without the intermediation of the legislature.

In effect, the symbolic or political use of these acts is a common strategy in democratic governments and should not be condemned *a priori*. It is important for presidents and prime ministers to have normative tools to define positions, make political promises, and speak directly to their supporters. To achieve these goals, however, they must not ignore constitutional limits and bypass institutions by issuing exorbitant decrees that violate democratic principles. They can and must fulfill their promises and please their electorate, but always with the appropriate normative instrument and within the limits of the Constitution and the laws.

3.8 Decrees shift the political burden from the legislature to the executive

Finally, decrees can also be used to shift the political burden from the legislature to the executive. In this regard, John Carey and Matthew Shugart[43] take a position contrary to the *mainstream* literature on unilateral executive power. They argue that this prerogative does not necessarily constitute a form of usurpation of legislative authority. For them, it is possible that parliamentarians *prefer* certain political decisions to be made unilaterally by the executive rather than through ordinary legislative process.[44] Decrees, then, do not necessarily represent the marginalization of Congress's institutional and political interests, but simply another way to design reforms with greater political efficiency. In the words of Carey and Shugart:

> We agree that the executive's use of decrees has often led to the usurpation of legislative powers, especially in presidential systems. This, however, is far from a universal truth, and the usurpation argument has often been exaggerated (. . .). We suggest that, more commonly than is currently accepted, the executive decree is tolerated and even preferred by

43 Carey, John M.; Shugart, Matthew Soberg. Poder de decreto: Chamando os tanques ou usando a caneta? *Revista Brasileira de Ciências Sociais*, v. 13, n. 37, 1998, p. 149–184.

44 Carey, John M.; Shugart, Matthew Soberg. Poder de decreto: Chamando os tanques ou usando a caneta? *Op. cit.*, p. 150.

> parliamentary majorities. (. . .) The use of decrees by the executive is not always the same thing as "calling in the tanks".[45]

Indeed, these acts allow Congress to escape responsibility for approving policies that may be unpopular, leaving the political burden entirely on the president or premier.[46] Legislators must deal with lobbying from various interest groups and sometimes choose the "sin of inaction" over casting a vote on controversial legislation. In several cases, it is better for Congress to "delegate powers to the president and then sit back, criticizing or applauding, depending on the popularity or unpopularity of the presidential action".[47] The legislature may prefer to make the chief executive solely responsible – or "guilty" – for certain policies. In the same vein, Fleishman and Aufses[48] point out that when the political goals of parliament are similar to those of the president or prime minister, unilateral actions may informally be the result of congressional delegation and serve as a means for the executive to anticipate the preferences of the legislature. Thus, rather than circumventing the will of Congress, decrees may actually serve as a means of implementing that will.[49]

Bibliography

Bailey, Jeremy D.; Rottinghaus, Brandon. The development of unilateral power and the problem of the power to warn: Washington through McKinley. *Presidential Studies Quarterly*, v. 43, 2013, p. 186–204.

Bradley, Curtis A.; Posner, Eric A. Presidential signing statements and executive power. *Constitutional Commentary*, v. 23, 2006, p. 307–364.

Brandão, Rodrigo; Capecchi Nunes, Daniel. *Poder regulamentar e 'jogo duro constitucional': o caso dos decretos de armas. Jota.* 10 July 2019. Available at: https://www.jota.info/opiniao-e-analise/artigos/poder-regulamentar-e-jogo-duro-constitucional-o caso-dos-decretos-de-armas-10072019

Branum, Tara L. President or king – the use and abuse of executive orders in modern-day America. *Journal of Legislation*, v. 28, 2002, p. 1–86.

Calabresi, Steven G. Some normative arguments for the unitary executive. *Arkansas Law Review*, v. 48, 1995, p. 23–104.

45 Carey, John M.; Shugart, Matthew Soberg. Poder de decreto: Chamando os tanques ou usando a caneta? *Op. cit.*, p. 150 and p. 181.

46 Pereira, Carlos; Power, Timothy J.; Rennó, Lucio R. Agenda power, executive decree authority, and the mixed results of reform in the Brazilian congress. *Legislative Studies Quarterly*, v. 33, n. 1, 2008, p. 5–33.

47 Fleishman, Joel L.; Aufses, Arthur H. Law and orders: The problem of presidential legislation. *Law and Contemporary Problems*, v. 40, n. 3, 1976, p. 1–45.

48 Fleishman, Joel L.; Aufses, Arthur H. Law and orders: The problem of presidential legislation. *Op. cit.*, p. 33.

49 Carey, John M.; Shugart, Matthew Soberg. Poder de decreto: Chamando os tanques ou usando a caneta? *Op. cit.*, p. 151.

Carey, John M.; Shugart, Matthew Soberg. Calling out the tanks or filling out the forms? In: Carey, John M.; Shugart, Matthew Soberg (Eds.). *Executive decree authority*. Cambridge: Cambridge University Press, 1998a, p. 1–29.

Carey, John M.; Shugart, Matthew Soberg. Poder de decreto: Chamando os tanques ou usando a caneta? *Revista Brasileira de Ciências Sociais*, v. 13, n. 37, 1998b, p. 149–184.

Delpino, Federico; Del Giudice, Luigi. *Manuale di diritto amministrativo*. Napoli: Edizioni Giuridiche Simone, 2019.

Duncan, J. R.; John, C. A critical consideration of executive orders: Glimmerings of autopoiesis in the executive role. *Vermont Law Review*, v. 35, 2010, p. 345.

Epstein, David; O'Halloran, Sharyn. *Delegating powers: A transactional cost politics approach to policy making under separation of powers*. Cambridge: Cambridge University Press, 1999.

Fleishman, Joel L.; Aufses, Arthur H. Law and orders: The problem of presidential legislation. *Law and Contemporary Problems*, v. 40, n. 3, 1976, p. 1–45.

Gasparini, Diógenes. *Poder regulamentar*. São Paulo: Ed. José Bushatsky, 1978, p. 123.

Kaiser, Anna-Bettina; Hensel, Roman. Federal Republic of Germany: Legal response to Covid-19. In: *The Oxford compendium of national legal responses to Covid-19*. April 2021. Available at: https://oxcon.ouplaw.com/view/https://doi.org/10.1093/law-occ19/law-occ19-e2.

Krause, George A.; Cohen, David B. Presidential use of executive orders, 1953–1994. *American Politics Quarterly*, v. 25, n. 4, 1997, p. 458–481.

Lawson, Gary; Moore, Christopher D. The executive power of constitutional interpretation. *Iowa Law Review*, v. 81, 1996, p. 1.261.

Mayer, Kenneth R. Executive orders and presidential power. *The Journal of Politics*, v. 61, n. 2, 1999, p. 445–466.

Meirelles, Hely Lopes. *Brazilian administrative law*, 13. ed. São Paulo: Revista dos Tribunais, 1987, p. 138.

Pereira, Carlos; Power, Timothy J.; Rennó, Lucio R. Agenda power, executive decree authority, and the mixed results of reform in the Brazilian congress. *Legislative Studies Quarterly*, v. 33, n. 1, 2008, p. 5–33.

Pünder, Hermann. Democratic legitimation of delegated legislation – A comparative view on the American, British, and German law. *International & Comparative Law Quarterly*, v. 58, n. 2, 2009, p. 353–378.

Rotinghaus, Brandon; Warber, Adam L. Unilateral orders as constituency outreach: Executive orders, proclamations, and the public presidency. *Presidential Studies Quarterly*, v. 45, n. 2, 2015, p. 289–309.

Sunstein, Cass R. The most knowledgeable branch. *University of Pennsylvania Law Review*, v. 164, 2015, p. 1.608.

4 Unilateral executive action in times of crisis

The justifications for unilateral executive action discussed in the previous chapter are amplified in times of crisis, which require even more rapid and flexible government action. In moments of great urgency and necessity, questions arise about the role of the legislative, judicial, and local branches of government in challenging the actions of the national executive. In these scenarios, should the other branches defer to the executive's decisions? Or should they increase their scrutiny and oversight? This chapter analyzes the attitudes of presidents, prime ministers, and government ministers in emergencies, particularly during the COVID-19 pandemic, and examines the ways in which other institutional actors can control executive unilateral action.

4.1 Should the other branches of government be deferential to the executive in emergencies?

A part of the legal literature holds that the executive should be "unbounded" in times of crisis.[1] According to Eric Posner and Adrian Vermeule, only this branch has the information, resources, decision-making capacity, speed, and flexibility to respond to emergencies. From this point of view, the system of checks and balances should, in practice, disappear during a crisis. The judiciary and legislature should transfer much of their power to the executive and adopt a posture of deference.[2] Given the scenario of uncertainty and the anxiety of the citizens, there should be a massive delegation of normative power: all laws

1 Posner, Eric, Vermeule, Adrian. *The executive unbound: After the Madisonian republic. Op. cit.*; Posner, Eric, Vermeule, Adrian. *Terror in the balance: Security, liberty, and the courts.* Oxford: Oxford University Press, 2007; Posner, Eric, Vermeule, Adrian. Emergencies, tradeoffs, and deference. In: Dyzenhaus, David (Ed.). *Civil rights and security.* New York: Ed. Routledge, 2017; Posner, Eric; Vermeule, Adrian. Accommodating emergencies. *Stanford Law Review,* 2003, p. 605–644 and Rossi, Jim. State executive lawmaking in crisis. *Duke Law Journal,* v. 56, 2006.

2 Posner, Eric; Vermeule, Adrian. Emergencies, tradeoffs, and deference. In: Dyzenhaus, David (Ed.). *Civil rights and security.* New York: Ed. Routledge, 2017, p. 24.

DOI: 10.4324/9781003610816-5

created to deal with the emergency should contain open and vague delegating norms, giving the government a blank check to decide how to act.[3] Legislators should then "hand the reins to the executive" and hope for the best.[4]

According to this literature, the judiciary should also be deferential during crises. There would be "no general reason to think that judges can do a better job than the government and (. . .) no reason to expect that the courts can systematically improve the government's emergency policies".[5] Judges should recognize a presumption of legitimacy for the executive's discretionary actions and not uphold claims against it. In this regard, Robert Cooter identifies the following institutional deficiencies of the judiciary in controlling macro-structural public policies:

> Unlike the executive who creates an agenda, judges take cases as they arise. Unlike legislators who sit in an assembly where political factions bargain, judges mostly decide disputes. Unlike elected officials, judges cannot speak freely with voters, retain staff to survey public opinion and aggregate data, or seek a mandate from voters. The independence of judges circumscribes their competence in making public policy. For example, judges cannot manage macroeconomic policy.[6]

Finally, regarding the relationship between national and local government, Posner and Vermeule suggest that in times of emergency, power should flow from the subnational to the national level. This is because emergencies require a quick and decisive response from a single actor, which should be the national executive.[7]

However, contrary to this view, other authors such as Tom Ginsburg and Mila Versteeg believe that, during crises, the systems of checks and balances should be even stronger and more active.[8] In such times, there would be greater risks to democracy, as leaders could opportunistically use emergency powers to increase their power. History is full of examples of disasters,

3 Posner, Eric A.; Vermeule, Adrian. *The executive unbound: After the Madisonian republic. Op. cit.*, p. 606–620.

4 Posner, Eric A.; Vermeule, Adrian. *The executive unbound: After the Madisonian republic. Op. cit.*, p. 27.

5 Posner, Eric; Vermeule, Adrian. Emergencies, tradeoffs, and deference. *Op. cit.*, p. 39.

6 Cooter, Robert D. *The strategic constitution.* Princeton: Princeton University Press, 2000, p. 311.

7 Posner, Eric; Vermeule, Adrian. *Terror in the balance: Security, liberty, and the courts. Op. cit.*, p. 16.

8 Ginsburg, Tom; Versteeg, Mila. The bound executive: Emergency powers during the pandemic. *International Journal of Constitutional Law*, v. 19, n. 5, December 2021. In the same sense, *see* Chemerinsky, Erwin. Controlling inherent presidential power: Providing a framework for judicial review. *S. Cal. L. Rev.*, v. 56, 1982, p. 863; Prakash, Saikrishna B.; Ramsey, Michael D. The Goldilocks executive. *University of Texas Law Review*, v. 90, 2011; Huq, Aziz Z. Binding the executive (by law or by politics). *U. Chi. L. Rev.*, v. 79, 2012, p. 777.

wars, and other public crises that have challenged and reshaped the constitutional system in favor of autocratic regimes. Benito Mussolini's first act as prime minister of Italy in 1925 was to demand emergency powers, which he then used against his political enemies. The burning of the Reichstag in Germany provided the impetus for Adolf Hitler to concentrate power and begin implementing a dictatorship.[9] Moreover, during the COVID-19 pandemic, autocrats invoked emergency powers to dissolve parliament, suspend the constitution, and rule without restraint. In countries such as Hungary, ruled by Viktor Orbán, and Turkey, ruled by Tayyip Erdoğan, the health crisis has been manipulated to consolidate dictatorial regimes and persecute political opponents and minorities.[10]

Especially in times of crisis, presidents and prime ministers tend to seek the image of "saviors of the nation" as a means to ensure their reelections and to leave legacies for posterity. When citizens are afraid, they tend to look to leaders' powers to protect them, and when exercising discretionary powers, these leaders look to popular demands to justify and legitimize unilateral actions. Emergencies are particularly conducive to exploring this dynamic.[11]

This attitude, as proven by history, can lead to abuses and reduce the rationality of anti-crisis measures. Chief executives can sometimes take unnecessary or disproportionate risks to get to the emergency more quickly. Excessive concern for their own public image would lead them to act less rationally and efficiently, trying at all costs to avoid being held responsible for the negative consequences of the emergency events. They would seek a positive image with the public, the media, and the financial sector, which could ultimately lead to distortions in the necessary measures.

In this context, this book argues that the excessive and abusive use of unilateral executive action poses a threat to constitutionalism and to the principle of the separation of powers.[12] Although decrees are necessary in certain circumstances, they can be a form of usurpation of legislative power and abuse of authority.[13] It's not uncommon for presidents or prime ministers to opportunistically use their unilateral normative authority to expand their

9 Paxton, Robert O. *The anatomy of fascism*. New York: Vintage Books, 2005, p. 107. *See also* Ginsburg, Tom; Versteeg, Mila. The bound executive: Emergency powers during the pandemic. *Op. cit.*, p. 1.507.

10 Ginsburg, Tom; Versteeg, Mila. *Op. cit.*, p. 1.507.

11 Crocker, Thomas. P. Presidential power and constitutional responsibility. *Boston College Law Review*, n. 52, 2011, p. 1564.

12 *See* Branum, Tara L. President or king – the use and abuse of executive orders in modern-day America. *Journal of Legislation*, v. 28, 2002, p. 1–86; Dodds, Graham G. *Take up your pen: Unilateral presidential directives in American politics*. Philadelphia: University of Pennsylvania Press, 2013; Carey, John M.; Shugart, Matthew Soberg. Poder de decreto: Chamando os tanques ou usando a caneta? *Revista brasileira de ciências sociais*, v. 13, n. 37, 1998, p. 149–184.

13 Carey, John M.; Shugart, Matthew Soberg. Poder de decreto: Chamando os tanques ou usando a caneta? *Op. cit.*, p. 149.

prerogatives and impose public policies against the will of the legislature. In Brazil, for example, presidents have often used *medidas provisórias* (provisional measures)[14] to control Congress's agenda, and exorbitant secondary decrees to circumvent the ordinary legislative process.[15] Unilateral acts can be evidence that legislatures are marginalized, and democratic institutions are ineffective.[16]

In other words, the excessive and abusive use of decrees not only subverts the constitutional system of separation of powers but can also give the chief executive direct control over the legislative branch. The best way to protect democracy from arbitrary and tyrannical rule is to demand that administrators remain faithful to the democratic legislative process outlined in the Constitution. It is necessary to value formal law and to seek the "dignity of legislation", as Jeremy Waldron posits.[17]

Indeed, the misuse of the decree authority weakens the mechanisms of vertical and horizontal accountability, underestimates the importance of the legislative process in a democratic regime, and ultimately undermines the confidence of citizens and other political actors in government decisions that come to be seen as autocratic and anti-democratic.[18] In this escape from Congress, the president, or premier ends up sacrificing popular consent and responsiveness,[19] unbalancing the forces between the executive and the legislative.[20] The problem with the abuse of regulatory power, as Tara Branum rightly says, is that "policies are being imposed outside of the democratic process. No good can come out of such a situation".[21]

Moreover, it must be remembered that the top of the executive branch tends to be highly centralized, controlled by people from the same political party or even by people with no party affiliation, who act in complete deference or subordination to the will of the president or prime minister. There are

14 In Brazil, *medidas provisórias* have the force of law. They can be understood as both a legally binding temporary executive order and an anticipated legislative proposal. During the first 120 days after the issuance of a *medida provisória*, it is considered a unilateral presidential directive, having the force of law. At the end of this period, the act must be voted on by Congress, so that it permanently becomes law. Otherwise, the *medida provisória* is terminated and no longer has legal validity.

15 Bradley, Curtis A.; Posner, Eric A. Presidential signing statements and executive power. *Constitutional Commentary*, v. 23, 2006, p. 307–364.

16 Branum, Tara L. President or king – the use and abuse of executive orders in modern-day America. *Journal of Legislation*, v. 28, 2002, p. 1–86.

17 Waldron, Jeremy. *The dignity of legislation*. Cambridge: Cambridge University Press, 1999.

18 Negretto, Gabriel L. ¿Gobierna solo el Presidente? Poderes de decreto y diseño institucional en Brasil y Argentina. *Desarrollo Económico*, 2002, p. 377–404.

19 Fleishman, Joel L.; Aufses, Arthur H. Law and orders: The problem of presidential legislation. *Law and Contemporary Problems*, v. 40, n. 3, 1976, p. 1–45.

20 Diver, Colin S. Presidential powers. *American University Law Review*, v. 36, 1986, p. 530.

21 Branum, Tara L. President or king – the use and abuse of executive orders in modern-day America. *Journal of Legislation*, v. 28, 2002, p. 1–86.

usually no members of opposition parties or people with views clearly opposed to those of the chief executive at the top administrative level. In this context, decrees are not the result of deliberations or compromises between clashing political forces but the result of discussions and debates among people who generally think the same. Decrees of high political content, therefore, end up entering the legal scenario and producing all its effects without the healthy and necessary discussion and prior control of other political actors.

It should also be noted that the process of drafting decrees is completely different from the process of drafting laws. From the proposal of a law to its final sanction, there may be numerous social and media manifestations regarding its content, which makes parliamentarians seek a compromise result and pay attention to all political forces involved. Decrees, on the other hand, depend only on the stroke of a pen: they are presented to the public as a *fait accompli*, and it is up to the legislature, the judiciary, and other political actors to carry out *a posteriori* control, trying to minimize or stop their effects.

In sum, the decrees represent a major challenge to democratic theory. Allowing presidents and prime ministers to innovate the legal order and to legislate alone, creating rights and duties, violates the principle of separation of powers and the framework that democratic constitutions create for the executive branch. Concentrating the drafting of normative acts of broad political relevance in the hands of a single person carries a high democratic risk, especially in new democracies. Decrees should not be used as an excuse to circumvent political and partisan difficulties in Congress. They should be used only in limited situations and for specific purposes.

4.2 Authoritarian infra-legalism, abusive constitutionalism, and "constitutional hardball"

There is a close relationship between the frequent use of decrees and the phenomena of "abusive constitutionalism", a term coined by David Landau to identify measures that, although formally legal and constitutional, end up damaging the very democratic order of a country. In his words, "abusive constitutionalism" consists of "using mechanisms of constitutional change to make a state significantly less democratic than it was before".[22] Landau uses recent examples from Hungary, Colombia, and Venezuela to illustrate this threat. In these countries, the tools of constitutional change have been used to undermine democracy with relative facility. For him, abusive constitutional practices can produce constitutions that are formally democratic but, in practice, authoritarian in the way institutions operate.

22 Landau, David. Abusive constitutionalism. *U.C. Davis Law Review*, v. 47, 2013, p. 191–192.

Although Landau deals with cases involving a constitutional amendment itself, his reflections are important to illustrate the risks of abusive use of any normative tool, including decrees. In his words,

> While traditional methods of democratic overthrow such as the military coup have been on the decline for decades, the use of constitutional tools to create authoritarian and semi-authoritarian regimes is increasingly prevalent. Powerful incumbent presidents and parties can engineer constitutional change so as to make themselves very difficult to dislodge and so as to defuse institutions such as courts that are intended to check their exercises as power. (. . .) In contrast to past practice, where authoritarian regimes were generally formed through military coup or other unconstitutional practices, would-be autocrats now have significant incentives to appear to be playing by the constitutional rules.[23]

Mark Tushnet, for his part, uses the term "constitutional hardball" to describe political practices – legislative or executive – that are within the bounds of constitutional doctrine and practice but are used to cheat the Constitution and to weaken political opponents. A normative act can be characterized as "constitutional hardball" when it violates or oversteps a constitutional competence or norm for partisan purposes.[24] According to Steven Levitsky, it means

> using institutions as a political weapon against political opponents. Using the letter of the law in a way that diminishes the spirit of the law. It is the fruit of polarization, when both sides begin to fear and despise the other, they begin to use any means necessary to prevent the other from winning.[25]

In Tushnet's words:

> A shorthand sketch of constitutional hardball is this: it consists of political claims and practices – legislative and executive initiatives – that are without much question within the bounds of existing constitutional doctrine and practice but that are nonetheless in some tension with existing pre-constitutional understandings. It is hardball because its practitioners see themselves as playing for keeps in a special kind of way; they believe the stakes of the political controversy their actions provoke are

23 Landau, David. Abusive constitutionalism. *Op. cit.*, p. 191–195.
24 Tushnet, Mark. Constitutional hardball. *J. Marshall L. Rev.*, v. 37, 2004, p. 523; Fishkin, Joseph; Pozen, David E. Asymmetric constitutional hardball. *Columbia Law Review*, v. 118, n. 3, 2018, p. 915–982.
25 BBC NEWS. *Steven Levitsky: Why this Harvard professor believes Brazilian democracy is at risk.* October 19, 2018. Available at: https://www.bbc.com/portuguese/brasil-45829323.

quite high, and that their defeat and their opponents' victory would be a serious, perhaps permanent setback to the political positions they hold.[26]

Finally, the "authoritarian infra-legalism" refers to the phenomenon in which an authoritarian political agenda is created through the issuance of administrative decrees, ordinances, and regulations. All with the aim to erode or neutralize various rights and values established by the Constitution and supported by para-institutional pressures on public agents.[27] In this scenario, chief executives issue decrees that, under the pretext of regulating laws, contradict them and mischaracterize public policies. The judicialization of these decrees and secondary acts can be made more difficult by the executive's strategy of frequently revoking its acts and then issuing similar ones. With each new act, the attempt to prosecute may be frustrated, and a new lawsuit must be filed in court.[28]

Thus, it can be seen that apparently legal and constitutional instruments can be used to undermine democracy. The current concern of constitutionalists should be with presidents and prime ministers who use formally legal instruments to gain more power. Through the constant issuance of administrative decrees – seemingly innocuous instruments – an entire state bureaucracy can become subservient to the directives of a potentially authoritarian leader. As noted earlier, decrees are important tools and should be the subject of extensive study and scrutiny.

In this context, we argue that legislative and judicial oversight is not "undue interference" in executive actions – on the contrary, it is an important part of a constitutional democratic system. Decrees cannot – and should not – exceed or contradict legal provisions. Only the checks and balances of the courts, the legislature, local governments, the media, and civil society can prevent the spread and normalization of authoritarian "pen strokes".

4.3 Decrees and the democratic principle

Laws have more normative force than decrees precisely because they are drafted jointly by the legislative and executive branches. In the ordinary legislative process, parliamentarians discuss and approve the bill, which is then sanctioned by the president or prime minister and becomes law. The decree of the head of the executive branch, on the other hand, is a secondary act and has less normative force because it does not go through parliamentary discussion

26 Tushnet, Mark. Constitutional hardball. *J. Marshall L. Rev.*, v. 37, 2004, p. 523.

27 Vieira, Oscar Vilhena; Glezer, Rubens; Barbosa, Ana Laura Pereira. Supremocracia e Infralegalismo Autoritário: o comportamento do Supremo Tribunal Federal durante o governo Bolsonaro. *Novos estudos CEBRAP*, v. 41, 2023, p. 592.

28 Vieira, Oscar Vilhena; Glezer, Rubens; Barbosa, Ana Laura Pereira. Supremocracia e Infralegalismo Autoritário: o comportamento do Supremo Tribunal Federal durante o governo Bolsonaro. *Op. cit.*

and approval but is simply drafted and signed by the chief executive. In other words, it has a narrower scope precisely because it does not go through a largely democratic, transparent, and deliberative process.

A democracy is not synonymous with the dominance of the will of the majority. It presupposes that all people, especially members of minority groups, have a voice and can influence political decisions. Therefore, despite the extremely broad democratic legitimacy that elections confer on the chief executive, there must be a permanent participatory process, a continuous formation of collective will, and engagement in public debate. According to Robert Post, the essence of democracy is precisely "the opportunity to participate in the formation of the 'will of the community' through a 'continuous confrontation' between the majority and the minority".[29]

In addition to periodic participation in elections, democratic systems require that rights and duties be created by norms that result from deliberation and compromise between majorities and minorities. As Hans Kelsen rightly observed, in a democracy, the content of the legal order is not determined exclusively by the interests of the majority but is the result of a compromise between antagonistic political groups. In his words, "free discussion between majority and minority is essential to democracy because it creates an atmosphere favorable to compromise",[30] which is the very essence of democracy. Compromise is the "resolution of a conflict by a rule that is neither entirely in the interest of one party nor entirely against the interest of the other".[31] He continues:

> Since in a democracy the content of the legal order is not determined exclusively by the interests of the majority, but is the result of a compromise between the two groups, the voluntary submission of all individuals to the legal system is more easily achieved than in any other political organization. And it is precisely because of this tendency to compromise that democracy approaches the ideal of complete self-determination.[32]

So, the decrees do not have a primary normative force because they are completely in line with the interests of the government of the day, without any possibility of influence by the opposition parties. These acts are determined solely by the interests of the majority and are not the result of a compromise between them and political minorities. The very broad democratic legitimacy of the chief executive should not justify the adoption of exorbitant or unconstitutional unilateral acts, since a democratic regime, in addition to elections

29 Post, Robert. *Constitutional domains: Democracy, community, management.* Cambridge: Harvard University Press, 1995.

30 Kelsen, Hans. *Teoria geral do direito e do estado.* São Paulo: Martins Fontes, 2005, p. 412.

31 Kelsen, Hans. *Teoria geral do direito e do estado. Op. cit.*

32 Kelsen, Hans. *Teoria geral do direito e do estado. Op. cit.*

and "self-government", also involves participation in public debate, the protection of political minorities, and the guarantee of fundamental rights.

4.4 Executive underreach in a crisis

Chief executives need to be closely watched in times of crisis, not only when they do too much, exceeding legal limits, but also when they are inactive and negligent – when they do too little. In such cases, there is an intentional failure by the executive branch to address a significant public problem that it is legally and functionally equipped to address. During the COVID-19 pandemic, for example, the omission of leaders like Donald Trump and Jair Bolsonaro, who minimized or denied the threat of the virus, was correlated with high infection and mortality rates.[33] Trump refused to provide national medical supplies to state governments;[34] threatened to withdraw the United States from the World Health Organization (WHO);[35] refused to wear a face mask in public;[36] encouraged protest against governors who have imposed virus restrictions;[37] and in June 2020 began holding indoor rallies, largely without masks, to drum up support for his reelection.[38]

Bolsonaro, in his turn, also minimized the danger posed by the pandemic, calling coronavirus a "little flu",[39] promoting the effectiveness of unproven treatments like "chloroquine"[40] and hiding Brazil's coronavirus death toll and case totals.[41] Also, when questioned about the death toll, Bolsonaro brushed

33 Pozen, Davi; Scheppele, Kim L. Executive underreach, in pandemics and otherwise. *American Journal of International Law*, v. 114, 2020, p. 608–617.

34 Bloomberg. *Trump told governors to buy own virus supplies, then outbid them.* March 19, 2020. Available at: https://www.bloomberg.com/news/articles/2020-03-19/trump-told-governors-to-buy-own-virus-supplies-then-outbid-them.

35 The Washington Post. *Trump administration sends letter withdrawing U.S. from World Health Organization over coronavirus response.* July 7, 2020. Available at: https://www.washingtonpost.com/world/trump-united-states-withdrawal-world-health-organization-coronavirus/2020/07/07/ae0a25e4-b550–11ea-9a1d-d3db1cbe07ce_story.html.

36 CNN. *Trump says he won't wear a mask in front of cameras.* May 21, 2020. Available at: https://edition.cnn.com/2020/05/21/politics/donald-trump-michigan-masks/index.html.

37 The New York Times. *Trump encourages protest against governors who have imposed virus restrictions.* April 17, 2020. Available at: https://www.nytimes.com/2020/04/17/us/politics/trump-coronavirus-governors.html.

38 NBC News. *Inside Trump's Tulsa rally, no distancing despite empty seats, few masks and plenty of doubt about coronavirus.* June 20, 2020. Available at: https://www.nbcnews.com/politics/2020-election/inside-trump-s-tulsa-rally-no-distancing-few-masks-plenty-n1231654.

39 CNN. *Bolsonaro calls coronavirus a 'little flu.' Inside Brazil's hospitals, doctors know the horrifying reality.* May 25, 2020. Available at: https://edition.cnn.com/2020/05/23/americas/brazil-coronavirus-hospitals-intl/index.html.

40 Reuters. *Bolsonaro says Brazil to issue new chloroquine protocol on Wednesday.* May 19, 2020. Available at: https://www.reuters.com/article/us-health-coronavirus-brazil-bolsonaro/bolsonaro-says-brazil-to-issue-new-chloroquine-protocol-on-wednesday-idUSKBN22V39L/.

41 The Guardian. *Global report: Bolsonaro hides Brazil's coronavirus death toll and case totals.* June 7, 2020. Available at: https://www.theguardian.com/world/2020/jun/07/bolsonaro-strips-death-toll-and-case-totals-from-brazils-coronavirus-updates.

it off saying, "I'm not a grave-digger".[42] He then encouraged protests against local lockdowns,[43] defied the social distancing guidelines issued by his own health ministry,[44] and condemned state governors for "shutting down the economy".[45]

In this perspective, the constitutional system is also violated when the executive does not properly allocate resources in a crisis and underestimates its risks, undermining citizens' rights to health, safety, and security. In crises, negligence diminishes the capacity of the state, exacerbates inequality, and encourages dangerous or inefficient forms of self-help on the part of private actors. There is no reason to systematically worry more about executive overreaching than underreaching.[46]

In several countries, the constitutional courts have even tried to force the executive to take proactive measures against the virus through structural injunctions. However, due to the difficulties in making these processes effective, and the unwillingness of the executive to obey orders, these decisions often did not stop humanitarian tragedies from occurring during the pandemic.[47]

These negative effects of nonexistent, weak, or chaotic governance, characterized by decisions that lack scientific logic, can be mitigated by a strong system of checks and balances. When the executive is disorganized, uncoordinated, inconsistent, and unpredictable, the other institutional actors must make coordinated efforts to ensure the protection of rights and manage the crisis. Intensive, continuous, and effective oversight by the legislature, the judiciary, and local authorities during crises can prevent these unconstitutional omissions. An attitude of deference to the executive can lead to real tragedies if the president or prime minister of a country is not committed to overcoming the crisis. The other branches of government should not give the executive *carte blanche* – one must always consider the possibility that those in power will not act in a constitutional manner. Thus, weakening the

42 BBC. *Coronavirus: How pandemic turned political in Brazil.* June 12, 2020. Available at: https://www.bbc.com/news/world-latin-america-53021248.

43 CNN. *Brazil president Jair Bolsonaro defends joining anti-lockdown protest.* Available at: https://edition.cnn.com/2020/04/20/americas/bolsonaro-defends-coronavirus-protest-intl/index.html.

44 EuroNews. *Brazil's Jair Bolsonaro fined 75 euros for not wearing a face mask at a biker rally.* June 13, 2021. Available at: https://www.euronews.com/2021/06/13/brazil-s-jair-bolsonaro-fined-75-euros-for-not-wearing-a-face-mask-at-a-biker-rally.

45 BBC. *Brazil's Bolsonaro calls governors 'tyrants' over lockdowns.* March 22, 2021. Available at: https://www.bbc.com/news/world-latin-america-56479614.

46 Pozen, Davi; Scheppele, Kim L. Executive underreach, in pandemics and otherwise. *American Journal of International Law*, v. 114, 2020, p. 608–617.

47 Brazil. Supreme Federal Court. ADPF 709 MC-Ref. Rel. Roberto Barroso, published in October 7, 2020. *See also* Supreme Federal Court. *Barroso determina que governo federal adote medidas para conter avanço da Covid-19 entre indígenas.* Available at: https://portal.stf.jus.br/noticias/verNoticiaDetalhe.asp?idConteudo=447103&ori=1.

system of checks and balances can lead to abuse of power or unconstitutional inaction.

4.5 The different types of crises and levels of control

Finally, it is important to mention that crises are diverse and don't always require the same type of response. Indeed, there are several types of crises: the political crisis of Weimar Republicanism, the economic crisis of Argentina, the crisis of Roosevelt's welfare state, the subprime financial crisis, the COVID-19 pandemic, and so on. Some say that crises are cyclical, others say that they are a response to a collective addiction to greater abundance.[48] In all these cases, and for whatever reason, crises can spread unchecked and take on systemic proportions. What they have in common is the scarcity of resources and the solidarity of costs.

Posner and Vermeule developed their "executive unbound" theory thinking about the national security emergency that occurred in the United States after the terrorist attacks of September 11, 2001.[49] Thus, in addition to generating democratic risks, their insights are also inappropriate for other types of emergencies, such as natural disasters or health emergencies. In particular, in crises such as a pandemic – where information is dispersed, the crisis is ongoing, and it is local governments that have the most information about the details of the spread of the disease in each region – the central executive is structurally more limited than in national security crises.[50]

In a pandemic, there is also no need for secrecy in formulating the response. The various political actors can freely debate and deliberate to arrive at the best solutions. Therefore, subnational entities or the legislature may have some institutional advantages in dictating part of the crisis response.[51] In its turn, a national security crisis requires a unified response, including a centralized force to respond to attacks.

During a sanitary crisis, each location, each region, requires different efforts and measures. In Brazil, while some small towns had few cases of COVID-19, other towns with the same number of inhabitants experienced a collapse of the health services system.[52] That's why this type of emergency requires a great

48 Teubner, Gunther. A constitutional moment? The logics of 'Hit the Bottom'. In: Teubner, Gunther; Kjaer, Poul (Eds.). *After the catastrophe: Economy, law and politics in times of crisis.* Oxford: Hart Oxford, 2010.

49 Posner, Eric A.; Vermeule, Adrian. *The executive unbound: After the Madisonian republic. Op. cit.*, p. 606–620.

50 Ginsburg, Tom; Versteeg, Mila. *The bound executive: Emergency powers during the pandemic. Op. cit.*, p. 1.502–1.506.

51 Ginsburg, Tom; Versteeg, Mila. *The bound executive: Emergency powers during the pandemic. Op. cit.*

52 Pinheiro, Victor Marcel; Ilarraz, Marcelo; Mestriner, Melissa Terni. The impacts of the COVID-19 crisis on the Brazilian legal system – a report on the functioning of the branches

deal of proactivity on the part of local governments – not just a grandiose central executive that often doesn't have the necessary information to deal with local peculiarities. Especially in a federalist system, states can refuse to implement emergency regulations that they deem too harsh, or they can impose stricter measures than the national government if they consider the national response inadequate.

In addition, events in national security crises are often rapid and unpredictable. In these cases, the executive branch at the national level has access to exclusive information from central intelligence agencies, such as the CIA in the United States. This concentration of information, both at the center of government and in one of its branches, makes it very difficult for other branches or subnational actors to challenge the executive's decisions. Similarly, economic crises at the national level require a unified and highly technical response from central banks and finance ministries. Other government actors are unlikely to have the necessary expertise to take appropriate action.[53]

In the COVID-19 pandemic, on the other hand, information must be aggregated from thousands of health service providers. Also, the quality of government information may not be any better than that of the private sector. Universities, foundations, pharmaceutical companies, and other actors have specialized knowledge that sometimes exceeds that of the government agencies themselves, and they interact with each other in a complex information ecosystem. As a result, local authorities and private actors can have information that is superior to that held by the central executive.[54]

But despite these differences, we argue that the system of checks and balances should not be forgotten or abandoned during any type of crisis. Even in national security or economic crises, the control of other entities remains extremely important, especially for the preservation of human rights and fundamental freedoms. In the United States, for example, the attacks of September 11, 2001, led to the creation of the Guantánamo prison, a place where human rights violations often take place. This type of occurrence cannot be justified in a constitutional democracy and should be contained by the other branches of government.[55] A crisis must not lead to the erosion of the constitutional order.

---

of the government and on the legal scrutiny of their activities. *The Theory and Practice of Legislation*, v. 8, n. 1–2, 2020, p. 201–202.

53 Pinheiro, Victor Marcel; Ilarraz, Marcelo; Mestriner, Melissa Terni. The impacts of the COVID-19 crisis on the Brazilian legal system – a report on the functioning of the branches of the government and on the legal scrutiny of their activities. *Op. cit.*

54 Pinheiro, Victor Marcel; Ilarraz, Marcelo; Mestriner, Melissa Terni. The impacts of the COVID-19 crisis on the Brazilian legal system – a report on the functioning of the branches of the government and on the legal scrutiny of their activities. *Op. cit.*

55 Margulies, Joseph. *Guantanamo and the abuse of presidential power*. New York: Simon and Schuster, 2007.

Bibliography

Bradley, Curtis A.; Posner, Eric A. Presidential signing statements and executive power. *Constitutional Commentary*, v. 23, 2006, p. 307–364.

Branum, Tara L. President or king – the use and abuse of executive orders in modern-day America. *Journal of Legislation*, v. 28, 2002, p. 1–86.

Chemerinsky, Erwin. Controlling inherent presidential power: Providing a framework for judicial review. *S. Cal. L. Rev.*, v. 56, 1982, p. 863.

Cooter, Robert D. *The strategic constitution*. Princeton: Princeton University Press, 2000, p. 311.

Crocker, Thomas P. Presidential power and constitutional responsibility. *Boston College Law Review*, n. 52, 2011, p. 1564.

Diver, Colin S. Presidential powers. *American University Law Review*, v. 36, 1986, p. 530.

Fishkin, Joseph; Pozen, David E. Asymmetric constitutional hardball. *Columbia Law Review*, v. 118, n. 3, 2018, p. 915–982.

Fleishman, Joel L.; Aufses, Arthur H. Law and orders: The problem of presidential legislation. *Law and Contemporary Problems*, v. 40, n. 3, 1976, p. 1–45.

Ginsburg, Tom; Versteeg, Mila. The bound executive: Emergency powers during the pandemic. *International Journal of Constitutional Law*, v. 19, n. 5, December 2021.

Huq, Aziz Z. Binding the executive (by law or by politics). *U. Chi. L. Rev.*, v. 79, 2012, p. 777.

Kelsen, Hans. *Teoria geral do direito e do estado*. São Paulo: Martins Fontes, 2005, p. 412.

Landau, David. Abusive constitutionalism. *U.C. Davis Law Review*, v. 47, 2013, p. 191–192.

Margulies, Joseph. *Guantanamo and the abuse of presidential power*. New York: Simon and Schuster, 2007.

Negretto, Gabriel L. ¿Gobierna solo el Presidente? Poderes de decreto y diseño institucional en Brasil y Argentina. *Desarrollo Económico*, 2002, p. 377–404.

Paxton, Robert O. *The anatomy of fascism*. New York: Vintage books, 2005, p. 107. See also Ginsburg, Tom; Versteeg, Mila. The bound executive: Emergency powers during the pandemic. *Op. cit.*, p. 1.507.

Pinheiro, Victor Marcel; Ilarraz, Marcelo; Mestriner, Melissa Terni. The impacts of the COVID-19 crisis on the Brazilian legal system–a report on the functioning of the branches of the government and on the legal scrutiny of their activities. *The Theory and Practice of Legislation*, v. 8, n. 1–2, 2020, p. 201–202.

Posner, Eric; Vermeule, Adrian. Accommodating emergencies. *Stanford Law Review*, 2003, p. 605–644 and Rossi, Jim. State executive lawmaking in crisis. *Duke Law Journal*, v. 56, 2006.

Posner, Eric; Vermeule, Adrian. *Terror in the balance: Security, liberty, and the courts*. Oxford: Oxford University Press, 2007.

Posner, Eric; Vermeule, Adrian. Emergencies, tradeoffs, and deference. In: Dyzenhaus, David (Ed.). *Civil rights and security*. New York: Ed. Routledge, 2017.

Post, Robert. *Constitutional domains: Democracy, community, management*. Cambridge: Harvard University Press, 1995.

Pozen, Davi; Scheppele, Kim L. Executive underreach, in pandemics and otherwise. *American Journal of International Law*, v. 114, 2020, p. 608–617.

Prakash, Saikrishna B.; Ramsey, Michael D. The Goldilocks executive. *University of Texas Law Review*, v. 90, 2011.

Teubner, Gunther. A constitutional moment? The logics of 'hit the bottom'. In: Teubner, Gunther; Kjaer, Poul (Eds.). *After the catastrophe: Economy, law and politics in times of crisis*. Oxford: Hart Oxford, 2010.

Tushnet, Mark. Constitutional hardball. *J. Marshall L. Rev.*, v. 37, 2004, p. 523.
Vieira, Oscar Vilhena; Glezer, Rubens; Barbosa, Ana Laura Pereira. Supremocracia e Infralegalismo Autoritário: o comportamento do Supremo Tribunal Federal durante o governo Bolsonaro. *Novos estudos CEBRAP*, v. 41, 2023, p. 592.
Waldron, Jeremy. *The dignity of legislation*. Cambridge: Cambridge University Press, 1999.

5 Checks and balances during the COVID-19 pandemic

The legal response to the COVID-19 pandemic in several countries such as Hungary, Turkey, and Poland has been based on decrees and regulations without a clear legal basis, executive dominance, or a lack of parliamentary and judicial oversight.[1] In a crisis, this is not how things should be. This chapter will analyze these extreme anti-models of crisis management, demonstrating the dangers of abusive infra-legalism.

5.1 Executive dominance, democratic backlash, and autocratic populism

During the COVID-19 crisis, there was a trend in some countries toward a democratic decline through the increasing autocratization of governments. Based on emergency powers, populist and authoritarian leaders have caused an intense democratic backlash and growing illiberalism.[2] Democratic decline operated mainly through attacks on civil rights, depriving minorities of their rights, or through the illegitimate control of public institutions.[3] As Alexander Cooley and Daniel Nexon have noted, "illiberal governments worldwide are using the pandemic as cover for restricting media freedom and cracking down

1 Cormacain, Ronan; Bar-Siman-Tov, Ittai. Legislatures in the time of Covid-19. *The Theory and Practice of Legislation*, v. 8, n. 1–2, 2020, p. 8; Grogan, Joelle. Extraordinary or extra-legal responses? COVID-19 and the rule of law in Europe. *Democracy Reporting International*, 2021, p. 9; Grogan, Joelle. COVID-19, the rule of law and democracy. Analysis of legal responses to a global health crisis. *Hague Journal on the Rule of Law*, v. 14, n. 2–3, 2022, p. 349–369; Ginsburg, Tom; Versteeg, Mila. *The bound executive: Emergency powers during the pandemic. Op. cit.*, p. 1.527–1.530.

2 Eichler, Jessika; Sonkar, Sumit. Challenging absolute executive powers in times of corona: Re-examining constitutional courts and the collective right to public contestation as instruments of institutional control. *Review of Economics and Political Science*, v. 6, n. 1, 2021, p. 3–23; Roth, Kenneth. How authoritarians are exploiting the Covid-19 crisis to grab power. *Human Rights Watch*, v. 3, 2020, p. 15.

3 Roth, Kenneth. How authoritarians are exploiting the Covid-19 crisis to grab power. *Op. cit.*, p. 16.

DOI: 10.4324/9781003610816-6

on political opposition and civil society".[4] The pandemic was then exploited by leaders to use their emergency powers in unjustified ways to achieve political goals and adopt measures unrelated to the public health crisis.[5]

In Hungary, for example, parliament passed a law allowing Prime Minister Victor Orbán to rule by decree. The legislature gave him indefinite, extraordinary, sweeping, and unlimited powers to tackle the pandemic. Parliament could eventually invalidate the delegation, but only with a two-thirds majority. Among other features, the law introduced jail terms of up to five years for intentionally spreading misinformation, which led to dozens of arrests of government critics. Other institutional restrictions were also introduced, such as the temporary suspension of the functioning of the courts, which prevented judicial review of executive actions. In this scenario, Hungarian citizens lost a significant part of their civic rights and gained very little protection against COVID-19.[6]

In Turkey, the pandemic has allowed President Recep Tayyip Erdoğan to deepen his autocratic rule by silencing critics and quickly passing restrictive new laws to limit dissent. In 2020, the president used the emergency as an excuse to ban demonstrations by opposition parties and government critics. The government passed new laws to deepen censorship of social media platforms and to limit the authority of bar associations that speak out about Turkey's rule of law crisis. In late 2020, it approved legislation allowing arbitrary restrictions on civil society organizations and threatening the right to freedom of association. In the words of Hugh Williamson, director of the Human Rights Watch's for Europe and Central Asia, "The Covid-19 pandemic has become an excuse for the Erdogan government to double down on autocratic rule and crack down on criticism and opposition, to the detriment of uniting the country during a public health crisis".[7]

In authoritarian regimes such as China, Cuba, Saudi Arabia, and Cambodia, the response to the pandemic has also been based entirely on executive decrees and regulations, and their formal legal basis has never been officially clarified. In these countries, the pandemic has led to an increase in police violence, the

4 Foreign Affairs. *The real crisis of global order: Illiberalism on the rise.* December 14, 2021. Available at: https://www.foreignaffairs.com/articles/world/2021-12-14/illiberalism-real-crisis-global-order.

5 Coglianese, Cary; Mahboubi, Neysun A. Administrative law in a time of crisis: Comparing national responses to COVID-19. *Administrative Law Review*, v. 73, 2021, p. 12; Bolleyer, Nicole; Salát, Orsolya. Parliaments in times of crisis: COVID-19, populism, and executive dominance. *West European Politics*, v. 44, n. 5–6, 2021, p. 1103–1128.

6 Guasti, Petra. The impact of the Covid-19 pandemic in central and eastern Europe: The rise of autocracy and democratic resilience. *Democratic Theory*, v. 7, n. 2, 2020, p. 47–60.

7 Human Rights Watch. *Turkey: Covid-19 pandemic used to strengthen autocratic rule.* January 13, 2021. Available at: https://www.hrw.org/news/2021/01/13/turkey-covid-19-pandemic-used-strengthen-autocratic-rule.

persecution of minorities and political opponents, and an even greater concentration of power in the hands of executive leaders.[8] It is reckless that in several countries unilateral executive decrees have become daily tools for legislating and managing crises.

5.2 Good examples of judicial, legislative, and subnational checks on the executive

Despite these anti-democratic examples, it is important to note that several other countries, such as Germany, France, Holland, Switzerland, New Zealand, Austria, and Japan, managed to involve the other branches of government and subnational entities in their response to the crisis. Tom Ginsburg and Mila Versteeg made a survey of 106 countries up until July 2020 and found that in 64% of them, legislatures were directly involved in responding to the pandemic. They contributed by declaring or extending the state of emergency or by approving new legislation. In 45% of countries, legislatures drafted entire new laws specifically to deal with the pandemic.[9]

In addition, in 52% of the countries surveyed by Ginsburg and Versteeg, the legislature was involved in the pandemic response on a permanent basis. When only democratic regimes were analyzed, 68% of them ensured this role for the legislature. The permanent control could include extending or renewing the constitutional declaration of emergency, passing temporary legislation that needed to be renewed periodically, or establishing some type of parliamentary oversight committee. These data indicate that, in democratic countries, legislatures have not been completely sidelined. The authors also point out that the judiciary and subnational governments exercised some kind of control. Courts were involved in the response to the pandemic in 55% of democratic countries. In turn, subnational units showed some resistance to central government action in 40% of democracies.[10]

It should be noted, however, that this data does not capture the quality and intensity of the involvement of courts, parliaments, and subnational entities. According to the authors, the control exercised by the judiciary in Germany during COVID-19 does not even compare to the involvement of the judiciary in a country like the Philippines, where the involvement of the Supreme Court was limited to the release of prisoners to contain the spread of the virus in prisons. But both countries were included in the database as having judicial involvement in the response to the pandemic.

8 Ginsburg, Tom; Versteeg, Mila. *The bound executive: Emergency powers during the pandemic. Op. cit.*, p. 1.527–1.530.
9 Ginsburg, Tom; Versteeg, Mila. *The bound executive: Emergency powers during the pandemic. Op. cit.*, p. 1.517.
10 Ginsburg, Tom; Versteeg, Mila. *The bound executive: Emergency powers during the pandemic. Op. cit.*, p. 1.517.

Similarly, there is a significant difference in legislative involvement between a country like Sweden, where the legislature passed new laws and developed a new oversight mechanism to review emergency regulations, and a country like Namibia, where the legislature merely passed and extended the state of emergency. However, the legislatures of both countries were classified in the survey as poles of "continuous" control of the executive.[11]

For these reasons, concerns raised throughout this book on the dangers of executive dominance remain valid. Legislative oversight should not be limited to declaring or extending a state of emergency. Courts that decide only one case during the crisis should not be considered active or participatory. On the contrary, both branches should exercise active and persistent control over the executive's actions.

5.3 Strategies for legislative oversight of the executive branch during the pandemic

What was the role of parliaments during the pandemic? What oversight strategies were commonly used to control the executive? The following sections will attempt to address these questions in light of the democratic importance of the legislature. Among public institutions, parliaments are most closely associated with popular representation, as they create laws and oversee government actions. As John Locke said in 1690, "[T]he Legislative cannot transfer the power of making laws to any other hands. For being but a delegated power for the people, they, who have it, cannot pass it over to others".[12]

During the pandemic, legislature sessions in democratic nations were not interrupted or were interrupted only for a limited period. Throughout 2020 and 2021, parliaments in countries such as Germany and France did not change their production capacity or activity levels.[13] In effect, legislators had to make several decisions in a short period of time before the declaration of a public health emergency. They had to decide whether to hold face-to-face meetings or to resort to virtual formats, and how to adopt mechanisms capable of ensuring the proper functioning of the legislative work. All this had to be done while overcoming technical and legal obstacles, given the urgency of such an exceptional context.[14] As Alan Greene explains, the parliaments that

11 Ginsburg, Tom; Versteeg, Mila. *The bound executive: Emergency powers during the pandemic. Op. cit.*

12 Locke, John. Second treatise. In: *Two treatises of government.* Indianapolis: Hackett Publishing, Chapter XI, § 141.

13 Ginsburg, Tom; Versteeg, Mila. *The bound executive: Emergency powers during the pandemic. Op. cit.*, p. 1.526–1.528.

14 Alcántara, Manuel; Barragán, Mélany; Montero, Mercedes García. Latin American legislatures during the pandemic. In: Llanos, Mariana; Marsteintredet, Leiv (Eds.). *Latin America in times of turbulence: Presidentialism under stress.* New York: Routledge, 2023, p. 123; Bar-Siman-Tov, Ittai. Covid-19 meets politics: The novel coronavirus as a novel challenge for legislatures. *The Theory and Practice of Legislation*, v. 8, n. 1–2, 2020, p. 11–48.

could resort to virtual sessions "demonstrated that technological solutions can be developed to ensure that parliaments can sit during a pandemic or other emergency, without substantial impact on the legislative functions of passing laws and holding the government to account".[15]

It is important to note that parliamentary oversight was able to improve both the quality and the effectiveness of anti-crisis measures.[16] Legislators provided feedback to the executive; identified potentially problematic measures; and pointed out gaps, inconsistencies, and other shortcomings in the executive measures.[17] Legislative sessions were the best available alternative for reviewing and debating emergency policies. Because of their visibility and media coverage, they provided an important chance for the opposition to confront the executive's acts and to voice the concerns of the population.[18]

In this sense, some legislatures have played an active role in responding to the crisis by (i) enacting specific new laws, (ii) amending previous laws to adapt them to the new emergency, and (iii) conducting continuous and intensive oversight of executive actions, particularly through parliamentary committees set up specifically to oversee the crisis response. Another function of the legislature was to declare and extend a state of emergency. According to the study by Ginsburg and Versteeg, 73% of democratic constitutions in force require parliament to declare a state of emergy.[19]

In addition, countries such as France, New Zealand, the United Kingdom, and Brazil set up *ad hoc* committees specifically to monitor the executive during the pandemic.[20] These committees made extensive use of fact-finding oversight mechanisms: government ministers had to appear in person before parliament to answer questions, provide information, and give explanations and justifications. A variety of oversight tools were used: hearings, commissions of inquiry, and oral evidence sessions.[21]

15 Greene, Alan. *Emergency powers in a time of pandemic*. Bristol: Bristol University Press, 2020, p. 117.

16 Grogan, Joelle. 'Extraordinary or extralegal responses? COVID-19 and the rule of law in Europe'. *Democracy Reporting International*, 2021, p. 15. Available at: https://democracy-reporting.org/en/office/EU/publications/extraordinary-or-extralegal-responses-covid-19-and-the-rule-of-law-in-the-eu.

17 Petrov, Jan. The COVID-19 emergency in the age of executive aggrandizement: What role for legislative and judicial checks? *The Theory and Practice of Legislation*, v. 8, n. 1–2, 2020, p. 71–92.

18 Petrov, Jan. The COVID-19 emergency in the age of executive aggrandizement: What role for legislative and judicial checks? *Op. cit.*, p. 79–80.

19 Ginsburg, Tom; Versteeg, Mila. The bound executive: Emergency powers during the pandemic. *Op. cit.*, p. 1.507.

20 Ginsburg, Tom; Versteeg, Mila. The bound executive: Emergency powers during the pandemic. *Op. cit.*, p. 1.528.

21 Griglio, Elena. Parliamentary oversight under the Covid-19 emergency: Striving against executive dominance. *The Theory and Practice of Legislation*, v. 8, n. 1–2, 2020, p. 49–70; Brazil. Federal Senate. *Final report of the Covid investigation*. 2021. Available at: https://legis.senado.leg.br/comissoes/mnas?codcol=2441&tp=4.

These committees had several objectives: to provide parliamentarians with firsthand information on the management of the crisis, to anticipate the government's orientations for future policymaking, to summon the executive to explain the handling of the pandemic, and to review the results achieved so far. They also promoted debate between parliamentarians and members of the government on key anti-crisis measures and provided policy guidance to the cabinet. They thus acted as transparency providers: their investigative prerogatives, together with their rules on public access, ensured that civil society had access to a wide range of information relevant to policymaking.[22]

In Brazil, a Parliamentary Commission of Inquiry (CPI) held numerous hearings with executive ministers and issued a report calling for the criminal conviction of numerous members of the Bolsonaro government (including the president) for corruption and omissions during the pandemic.[23] The charges were related to the denial of the emergency risks, to the suspicion of corruption in the negotiations for the purchase of vaccines by the ministry of health, and to the deaths that have been caused by the use of unscientific treatments against COVID-19.[24]

Also, in France, the National Assembly set up a fact-finding committee on the impact, management, and consequences of the crisis. It gave priority to a general and crosscutting mandate in which the various parliamentary groups and committees would be represented. The president of the National Assembly was appointed chairman and general rapporteur. The committee heard the prime minister, the minister of health, and other members of the government, such as the director general of health or the chairman of the Scientific Council.[25] The Belgian Chamber of Deputies, in its turn, set up a standing committee on COVID-19 to review the implementation of the laws granting special powers to the executive. In the same vein, committees of the British Parliament launched new inquiries into COVID-related aspects of policymaking

22 Alcántara, Manuel; Barragán, Mélany; Montero, Mercedes García. Latin American legislatures during the pandemic. *Op. cit.*, p. 123; Bar-Siman-Tov, Ittai. Covid-19 meets politics: The novel coronavirus as a novel challenge for legislatures. *Op. cit.*, p. 11–48; Griglio, Elena. Parliamentary oversight under the Covid-19 emergency: Striving against executive dominance. *Op. cit.*, p. 49–70.

23 Brazil. Federal Senate. *Final report of the Covid investigation*. 2021. Available at: https://legis.senado.leg.br/comissoes/mnas?codcol=2441&tp=4.

24 Brazil. Federal Senate. *CPI da Pandemia: principais pontos do relatório*. Available at: https://www12.senado.leg.br/noticias/materias/2021/10/20/cpi-da-pandemia-principais-pontos-do-relatorio.

25 Derosier, Jean-Philippe; Toulemonde, Gilles. The French parliament in the time of coronavirus. A parliament on life support. In: *Parliament in the time of coronavirus*. Robert Schuman Foundation, 2020, p. 9. Available at: https://old.robert-schuman.eu//en/doc/ouvrages/FRS_French_Parliament_Covid-19.pdf.

that fell within their remit. In doing so, they have all increased the accountability of the executive.[26]

Moreover, the legislatures of several countries, including the United Kingdom, Belgium, and Brazil, enacted entirely new laws that were specifically directed at the pandemic. The expiry dates of these laws ensured an ongoing role for parliamentarians: when the legislation expired, they had to renew it.[27] In countries such as Germany, existing infectious disease legislation has been amended several times to address the unique challenges of the COVID-19 emergency.[28] With these new laws or amendments, parliaments were able to actively engage in wide-ranging and heated debates about the ideal response. Legislative sessions were also closely followed by the media and general public, as they should be in a constitutional democracy.

The deliberative spirit, new laws, and committees with broad oversight competences were essential tools for a successful response to the pandemic. In the words of Alan Greene, courts are not the only institutions to take rights seriously; this duty can

> feed into legislative responses to a pandemic and also in legislatures' duties in holding governments to account for their decisions. Here, again, we see why the idea of a culture of justification is important, when determining the protection to be afforded to human rights.[29]

Indeed, a "pandemic clearly does not justify the complete suspension of legislative activity".[30]

Finally, it is important to mention that legislation granting additional powers to the executive during a crisis can be enacted in anticipation (*ex-ante*) or after the crisis begins (*ex-post*). *Ex-ante* legislation allows administrators to assume additional powers if and when an emergency arises. It is usually drafted with more time, calm, discussion, and analysis because it is conceived in times of normality, when parliamentary debates are not conducted in the heat of the moment. *Ex-post* legislation, on the other hand, has the advantage of ensuring

26 Griglio, Elena. Parliamentary oversight under the Covid-19 emergency: Striving against executive dominance. *Op. cit.*, p. 67.

27 Ginsburg, Tom; Versteeg, Mila. The bound executive: Emergency powers during the pandemic. *Op. cit.*, p. 1.517.

28 Kaiser, Anna-Bettina; Hensel, Roman. Federal Republic of Germany: Legal response to Covid-19. In: *The Oxford compendium of national legal responses to Covid-19*. April 2021. Available at: https://oxcon.ouplaw.com/view/https://doi.org/10.1093/law-occ19/law-occ19-e2; Kaiser, Anna-Bettina. The state of exception under German law and the current pandemic: Comparative models and constitutional rights. *e-Pública*, v. 7, n. 3, 2020, p. 4–15.

29 Greene, Alan. *Emergency powers in a time of pandemic*. Bristol: Bristol University Press, 2020, p. 49.

30 Greene, Alan. *Emergency powers in a time of pandemic*. *Op. cit.*, p. 117.

legislative involvement in the actual emergency and allows for adaptation to the specific needs of the moment.[31]

Hastily drafted legislation adopted in the heat of an emergency can also be problematic, especially if it remains in force after the crisis has passed. In such cases, a sunset clause is essential to reduce the risk of permanent restrictions on rights. It is important that, given the scenario of uncertainty and chaos in which the new laws are drafted, greater care is taken to protect fundamental rights and the founding principles of a constitutional democracy. For example, some of the anti-terrorist laws drafted in the United States after the attacks of September 11, 2001, infringed on the Universal Declaration of Human Rights (UDHR) precisely because, in the name of public security, they violated the right to human dignity, the right to nondiscriminatory treatment, and the right to a fair trial.[32] These laws submerged in a climate of chaos and popular outcry for answers, and ended up relativizing several fundamental rights of citizens, both American and foreign, in often disproportionate and inappropriate ways.[33]

In conclusion, crisis scenarios pose great challenges to legislatures. Certainly, an active approach by this branch of government is essential to successfully prevent the executive from taking undemocratic steps. Although laws must be debated and voted on quickly during a crisis – and many mistakes can be made in the process – there is no doubt about the importance of primary legislative production. Any unconstitutional legislation could later be invalidated by the courts, in a salutary system of checks and balances.

5.4 Strategies for judicial oversight of the executive branch during the pandemic

In countries where the executive has been significantly constrained, the courts have played three distinct roles: (i) they have reviewed the procedural legitimacy of the state of emergency declarations; (ii) they have engaged in substantive review of restrictions on fundamental rights, balancing them against public health concerns; and (iii) in some cases, they have demanded that the government take more active and effective measures to combat the virus and its effects, particularly in cases of administrative inaction.[34]

31 Ginsburg, Tom; Versteeg, Mila. The bound executive: Emergency powers during the pandemic. *Op. cit.*, p. 1.504.

32 United Nations. *Universal declaration of human rights*. Available at: https://www.un.org/en/about-us/universal-declaration-of-human-rights.

33 Whidden, Michael J. Unequal justice: Arabs in America and United States antiterrorism legislation. In: *Bioterrorism: The history of a crisis in American society*. New York: Routledge, 2020, p. 253–282; Brasch, Walter M. *America's unpatriotic acts: The federal government's violation of constitutional and civil rights*. Lausanne: Peter Lang, 2005; Margulies, Joseph. *Guantanamo and the abuse of presidential power*. New York: Simon and Schuster, 2007.

34 Ginsburg, Tom; Versteeg, Mila. The bound executive: Emergency powers during the pandemic. *Op. cit.*, p. 1.518–1.526.

First, when the state of emergency has been invoked, some courts have examined whether all constitutional requirements have been met, such as the requirement that parliament must authorize and extend the use of emergency powers. The court of El Salvador, for example, invalidated the executive's extension of the state of emergency because of a lack of parliamentary approval.[35] Similarly, in countries where the executive has taken action without a legal basis, courts have requested the legislature to approve primary legislation.[36]

Local courts in countries such as Germany and Italy have also highlighted the importance of a clear legal basis for executive acts. These decisions even led the German national parliament to promote a legislative reform in November 2020, precisely to include a more detailed and specific delegation in the German Infectious Diseases Protection Act (Infektionsschutzgesetz, IfSG).[37] For its part, various regional courts in Italy have declared the illegality of the Prime Ministers' Decrees (DPCMs) and ordered their non-application for violation of the principle of legality.[38] Only in 2021, in a widely criticized decision, did the Italian Constitutional Court uphold the constitutionality of these decrees.[39]

The second role of the courts was the judicial review of restrictions on fundamental rights. In Germany, the Constitutional Court has examined several cases of conflicts between the right to public health and the freedoms of movement, assembly, worship, expression, and so on. In these cases, the court had to balance rights in light of the principles of reasonableness and proportionality.[40] In cases involving the cities of Stuttgart and Giessen, for example, the Constitutional Court held that the right of citizens to protest

35 Ginsburg, Tom; Versteeg, Mila. The bound executive: Emergency powers during the pandemic. *Op. cit.*, p. 1.519.

36 Ginsburg, Tom; Versteeg, Mila. The bound executive: Emergency powers during the pandemic. *Op. cit.*

37 Germany. *Gesetz zur Verhütung und Bekämpfung von Infektionskrankheiten beim Menschen (Act on the Prevention and Control of Infectious Diseases in Humans)*. Available at: https://www.gesetze-im-internet.de/ifsg/index.html.

38 Italy. Tribunale di Reggio Emilia. Sentenza 27 gennaio 2021, n. 54; Tribunale di Pisa. Sentenza 17 marzo 2021, n. 419. *See also* Claudiani, Simona. Brevi Note Sui DPCM: Tra Emergenza e Stabilizzazione. In: Morana, Donatella; Mabellini, Stefania (Eds.). *L'emergenza pandemica e l'impatto sul diritto pubblico: innovazione e prospettive future. Quaderni del Dottorato di Ricerca in Diritto Pubblico dell'Università degli Studi di Roma "Tor Vergata"*. Milan: Wolters Kluwer, 2022, p. 67.

39 Italian Constitutional Court. *Sentenza n. 198/2021, published on October 27, 2021*. Available at: https://www.cortecostituzionale.it/actionSchedaPronuncia.do?anno=2021&numero=198.

40 Kaiser, Anna-Bettina; Hensel, Roman. Federal Republic of Germany: Legal response to Covid-19. In: *The Oxford compendium of national legal responses to Covid-19*. April 2021. Available at: https://oxcon.ouplaw.com/view/https://doi.org/10.1093/law-occ19/law-occ19-e2; Ginsburg, Tom; Versteeg, Mila. The bound executive: Emergency powers during the pandemic. *Op. cit.*, p. 1.520.

should be preserved if the requirements of social distance were met.[41] It also invalidated the general ban on worshipping in mosques, on the grounds that less-restrictive measures, such as social distancing, could be applied.[42] In this sense, in times of crisis, the judiciary can evaluate executive measures through the filter of constitutional principles.[43]

Finally, the third role of the courts arises when the executive fails to address the emergency. They can demand that governments take effective measures in order to fulfill their constitutional obligations. There are several cases in which the courts have required the government and private actors to take active measures to combat the COVID-19 pandemic. Brazil was an infamous example. As already highlighted, the country's former president, Jair Bolsonaro, did not issue any social distancing orders or lockdowns. As a result of inaction at the federal level, various Brazilian courts were asked to impose lockdowns on cities with precarious public health systems. On April 30, 2020, the city of São Luís, in the state of Maranhão, became the first city in Brazil to be placed under complete lockdown by a judicial order. The local court established a lockdown for a minimum of ten days, suspending all nonessential activities and limiting public gatherings of any kind, because the city's public health system had collapsed.[44]

The Brazilian Supreme Court, for its part, banned the Bolsonaro government's propaganda against social distancing and demanded that the government provide scientific information about the pandemic. It also ordered the government to disclose all available data about the death toll, based on the principle of transparency, and to create a plan to protect the Indigenous

41 Germany. Bundesverfassungsgericht (BVerfG) (German Federal Constitutional Court). *Beschluss der 1. Kammer des Ersten Senats vom 15. April 2020 - 1 BvR 828/20 -, Rn. 1–19.* Available at: https://www.bverfg.de/e/rk20200415_1bvr082820.html; *Beschluss der 1. Kammer des Ersten Senats vom 17. April 2020 - 1 BvQ 37/20 -, Rn. 1–32.* Available at: http://www.bverfg.de/e/qk20200417_1bvq003720.html.

42 Germany. Bundesverfassungsgericht (BVerfG) (German Federal Constitutional Court). *Beschluss der 2. Kammer des Ersten Senats vom 29. April 2020 - 1 BvQ 44/20 -, Rn. 1–19.* Available at: http://www.bverfg.de/e/qk20200429_1bvq004420.html.

43 Hestermeyer, Holger. *Coronavirus lockdown-measures before the German constitutional court.* April 30, 2020. Available at: http://constitutionnet.org/news/coronavirus-lockdown-measures-german-constitutional-court; Eichler, Jessika; Sonkar, Sumit. Challenging absolute executive powers in times of corona: Re-examining constitutional courts and the collective right to public contestation as instruments of institutional control. *Review of Economics and Political Science*, v. 6, n. 1, 2021, p. 3–23.

44 O Globo (Brazilian Newspaper). *'Lockdown' na Grande São Luís começa nesta terça: saiba o que funciona durante bloqueio para conter a pandemia do coronavirus.* May 5, 2020. Available at: https://g1.globo.com/ma/maranhao/noticia/2020/05/05/lockdown-na-grande-sao-luis-comeca-nesta-terca-saiba-o-que-funciona-durante-bloqueio-para-conter-a-pandemia-do-coronavirus.ghtml. *See also* Ginsburg, Tom; Versteeg, Mila. The bound executive: Emergency powers during the pandemic. *Op. cit.*, p. 1.523.

population.[45] In other Latin American countries, the courts also (i) ordered the release of inmates who were at risk of being infected by the virus inside overcrowded prisons and (ii) urged the executive to make greater investments in hiring health care professionals and equipment.[46]

All of these decisions demonstrate the extreme importance of judicial involvement in emergency response. Courts can effectively constrain executive excesses or omissions and make it clear that the chief executive is acting illegally. In Brazil, if the judiciary had remained inactive, the response to the pandemic would have been even more disastrous, with official government propaganda spreading misleading information about COVID-19. In fact, if Posner and Vermeule's "unbound executive" theory had been taken literally in Brazil during the pandemic, the death toll and humanitarian tragedy would have been even more alarming.

5.5 Supervision and oversight by subnational governments

Subnational governments and local authorities also played an important role in responding to the pandemic. In Brazil, states and municipalities had to take the lead in enacting various measures, such as restricting movement and requiring the wearing of masks, to prevent the collapse of the public health system.[47] In Germany, each state (*Länder*) passed its own regulations, considering the specificities and transmission rates of the virus in each area. Despite the federal government's efforts to ensure a unified response, restrictions were at times more severe in some *Länder* than in others.[48] Indeed, the involve-

45 Pinheiro, Victor Marcel; Ilarraz, Marcelo; Mestriner, Melissa Terni. The impacts of the COVID-19 crisis on the Brazilian legal system–a report on the functioning of the branches of the government and on the legal scrutiny of their activities. *Op. cit.*; Teixeira, Carmen Fontes, Santos, Jamilli Silva. Análise estratégica da atuação do governo federal brasileiro na pandemia de COVID-19: 2020–2021. *Op. cit.*, p. 1278; Inácio, Magna; Recch, Filipe; Valencia, Carolina Guerrero. The Power of the administrative decisions of Latin American presidents. *Op. cit.*, p. 75–105.

46 Ginsburg, Tom; Versteeg, Mila. The bound executive: Emergency powers during the pandemic. *Op. cit.*, p. 1.524; Inácio, Magna; Recch, Filipe; Valencia, Carolina Guerrero. The power of the administrative decisions of Latin American presidents. In: Llanos, Mariana; Marsteintredet, Leiv (Eds.). *Latin America in times of turbulence: Presidentialism under stress.* New York: Routledge, 2023, p. 75–105.

47 Ramos, Edith Maria Barbosa; Ramos, Paulo Roberto Barbosa; Costa, Laísse Lima Silva. Pandemia e Federalismo: Reflexões sobre as decisões do Supremo Tribunal Federal na apreciação de conflitos de competência entre os entes federativos no enfrentamento à Covid-19. *Revista de Ciências Jurídicas e Sociais-IURJ*, v. 1, n. 1, 2020, p. 46–61.

48 Kuhlmann, Sabine; Franzke, Jochen. Multi-level responses to COVID-19: Crisis coordination in Germany from an intergovernmental perspective. *Local Government Studies*, v. 48, n. 2, 2022, p. 312–334; Kuhn, Katharina; Morlino, Irene. Decentralisation in times of crisis: Asset or liability? The case of Germany and Italy during Covid-19. *Swiss Political Science Review*, v. 28, n. 1, 2022, p. 105–115; Kropp, Sabine; Schnabel, Johanna. Germany's response to COVID-19: Federal coordination and executive politics. In: Chattopadhyay, Rupak et al.

ment of local authorities has the virtue of controlling government excesses or "taking the reins" when the executive is inactive. It is also important to adapt measures to local specificities, demonstrating that a uniform response is not always the best solution.

Despite these virtues, some potential pragmatic and democratic problems may arise when local executives are asked to manage crises. Controversies can emerge over the distribution of competences and the relationship between local and central legislation. Uncertainties about the division of responsibilities can lead to a "blame game" that plagues decision-making in many emergency management scenarios.

In Brazil, for example, the Supreme Court reaffirmed that states had the authority to manage the crisis in their specific areas. The court's intent was to make clear that the federal executive, governed by Bolsonaro, could not interfere with local decisions or try to block states and municipalities from enacting restrictive measures, such as lockdowns. However, Bolsonaro's government misinterpreted this decision as a legal basis to continue to be inactive in the face of the crisis. In this blame game, the central government left all responsibility for managing the crisis to the states, which contributed to a chaotic and completely disorganized response. Uncertainty and lack of coordination at the federal level can thus undermine the effectiveness of a national response to a pandemic. The resulting inconsistencies can be disastrous in the long run.[49]

In other words, despite the importance of the participation of subnational governments, the anti-crisis policy must not be uncoordinated. Leaving everything in the hands of the states, regions, or municipalities can be a bad option, especially because of (i) a lack of resources, since the central unit is usually the one that collects the most taxes; (ii) poor institutional management; and (iii) the possible prevalence of patronage and corruption.[50] A lesson for future approaches should be to balance the benefits of local knowledge and experience with the resources and coordination capacity of national governments.

In Germany, for example, although each *Länder* had the prerogative to choose different restrictive measures during the pandemic, the federal government promoted several national agreements to harmonize the country's response to COVID-19. Although these agreements were not binding, the federal and state governments usually abided by them. As a result, there was a high degree of standardization and harmonization during the emergency.[51]

(Eds.). *Federalism and the response to COVID-19: A comparative analysis.* New York: Routledge, 2022, p. 162.

49 Grogan, Joelle. COVID-19, the rule of law and democracy. Analysis of legal responses to a global health crisis. *Hague Journal on the Rule of Law*, v. 14, n. 2–3, 2022, p. 349–369.

50 Grogan, Joelle. COVID-19, the rule of law and democracy. Analysis of legal responses to a global health crisis. *Op. cit.*

51 Kuhn, Katharina; Morlino, Irene. Decentralisation in times of crisis: Asset or liability? The case of Germany and Italy during Covid-19. *Swiss Political Science Review*, v. 28, n. 1, 2022, p. 105–115.

Ultimately, what may be most effective is a nationally coordinated response informed by this kind of dialogue and the participation of local units.

5.6 Deliberative democracy and social participation

In summary, responses to crises of any kind should be guided by the oversight and active participation of parliaments, the judiciary, subnational entities, the media, and other social groups. Also, there must be legitimacy at all stages of the legislative process, including transparency, respect for the principle of legality, consultation of experts by legislators, protection of the system of checks and balances, and respect for human rights.

Participatory governance and public debate are undoubtedly the best tools for dealing with crises that do not require secrecy. Because it affects different groups of citizens in different ways, the government must respond to their different needs and be constantly scrutinized by an attentive media. Public consultation is extremely important: institutional checks and balances can produce more legitimate and informed responses than the executive acting alone.[52] Deliberative and participatory democracy can bring the best answers.[53]

Indeed, cooperation, contestation, and dialogue are the best options in crises. Different actors with different epistemic bases and institutional advantages can help identify blind spots in the emergency response. Legislatures can serve as the arena for policy debate and as the ultimate *locus* of democratic legitimacy. The judiciary can protect the rule of law and the fundamental rights of citizens. And subnational governments, for their part, have the exclusive ability to calibrate policies according to local needs, conditions, and preferences. The best response comes from the contribution of different sources.[54]

For example, when the courts impose or lift a restriction on rights, when the legislature refuses to grant certain powers to the executive, or when subnational entities define their own response to the crisis to the detriment of the national government, a more qualified response can emerge in terms of both effectiveness and legitimacy. The participation of nongovernmental organizations (NGOs) and other private actors can also bring new solutions and align government action with the needs of citizens. With no public debate or consultation, there is a greater likelihood of errors in the design of policies, particularly in how they affect underrepresented groups and minorities.

52 Rosenberg, Shawn W. (Ed.). *Deliberation, participation and democracy*. London: Palgrave Macmillan, 2007, *passim*.
53 Habermas, Jürgen. *Between facts and norms: Contributions to a discourse theory of law and democracy*. New York: John Wiley & Sons, 2018, *passim*.
54 Ginsburg, Tom; Versteeg, Mila. The bound executive: Emergency powers during the pandemic. *Op. cit.*, p. 1.533.

Also, public participation is an established right under the International Covenant on Civil and Political Rights.[55] In accordance with international law, states should always invite the general public and external experts to provide feedback and constructive criticism on the measures.[56] In the words of Alan Greene,

> Constitutions, international treaties and the fundamental values they espouse – such as democracy, human rights and the rule of law – do not need to be jettisoned in response to such a crisis. Instead, at these moments, their true value is revealed.[57]

In short, there is no infallible institution, just as there is no institutional arrangement that alone guarantees a just political regime. Public administration, parliament, and the judiciary make mistakes, and history bears witness to this. These are bodies made up of real men and women, with their incentives and prejudices. It is better to place one's hopes for control in the dynamics and interaction between different powers, taking concrete account of their institutional capacities, than to believe in a single institution.

Bibliography

Alcántara, Manuel; Barragán, Mélany; Montero, Mercedes García. Latin American legislatures during the pandemic. In: Llanos, Mariana; Marsteintredet, Leiv (Eds.). *Latin America in times of turbulence: Presidentialism under stress.* New York: Routledge, 2023, p. 123.

Bar-Siman-Tov, Ittai. Covid-19 meets politics: The novel coronavirus as a novel challenge for legislatures. *The Theory and Practice of Legislation*, v. 8, n. 1–2, 2020, p. 11–48.

Bolleyer, Nicole; Salát, Orsolya. Parliaments in times of crisis: COVID-19, populism, and executive dominance. *West European Politics*, v. 44, n. 5–6, 2021, p. 1103–1128.

Brasch, Walter M. *America's unpatriotic acts: The federal government's violation of constitutional and civil rights.* Lausanne: Peter Lang, 2005; Margulies, Joseph. *Guantanamo and the abuse of presidential power.* New York: Simon and Schuster, 2007.

55 International Covenant on Civil and Political Rights.

> Article 25. Every citizen shall have the right and the opportunity, without any of the distinctions mentioned in article 2 and without unreasonable restrictions: (a) To take part in the conduct of public affairs, directly or through freely chosen representatives; (b) To vote and to be elected at genuine periodic elections which shall be by universal and equal suffrage and shall be held by secret ballot, guaranteeing the free expression of the will of the electors; (c) To have access, on general terms of equality, to public service in his country.

56 Grogan, Joelle. Extraordinary or extralegal responses? COVID-19 and the rule of law in Europe. *Democracy Reporting International*, 2021, p. 17.

57 Greene, Alan. *Emergency powers in a time of pandemic.* Bristol: Bristol University Press, 2020, p. 166.

Claudiani, Simona. Brevi Note Sui DPCM: Tra Emergenza e Stabilizzazione. In: Morana, Donatella; Mabellini, Stefania (Eds.). *L'emergenza pandemica e l'impatto sul diritto pubblico: innovazione e prospettive future. Quaderni del Dottorato di Ricerca in Diritto Pubblico dell'Università degli Studi di Roma "Tor Vergata"*. Milan: Wolters Kluwer, 2022, p. 67.

Coglianese, Cary; Mahboubi, Neysun A. Administrative law in a time of crisis: Comparing national responses to COVID-19. *Administrative Law Review*, v. 73, 2021, p. 12.

Cormacain, Ronan; Bar-Siman-Tov, Ittai. Legislatures in the time of Covid-19. *The Theory and Practice of Legislation*, v. 8, n. 1–2, 2020, p. 8; Grogan, Joelle. 'Extraordinary or extralegal responses? COVID-19 and the rule of law in Europe'. *Democracy Reporting International*, 2021, p. 9.

Derosier, Jean-Philippe; Toulemonde, Gilles. The French parliament in the time of coronavirus. A parliament on life support. In: *Parliament in the time of coronavirus*. Robert Schuman Foundation, 2020, p. 9. Available at: https://old.robert-schuman.eu//en/doc/ouvrages/FRS_French_Parliament_Covid-19.pdf.

Eichler, Jessika; Sonkar, Sumit. Challenging absolute executive powers in times of corona: Re-examining constitutional courts and the collective right to public contestation as instruments of institutional control. *Review of Economics and Political Science*, v. 6, n. 1, 2021, p. 3–23.

Ginsburg, Tom; Versteeg, Mila. The bound executive: Emergency powers during the pandemic. *Op. cit.*, p. 1.527–1.530.

Greene, Alan. *Emergency powers in a time of pandemic*. Bristol: Bristol University Press, 2020, p. 117.

Griglio, Elena. Parliamentary oversight under the Covid-19 emergency: Striving against executive dominance. *The Theory and Practice of Legislation*, v. 8, n. 1–2, 2020, p. 49–70.

Grogan, Joelle. Extraordinary or extralegal responses? COVID-19 and the rule of law in Europe. *Democracy Reporting International*, 2021, p. 15. Available at: https://democracy-reporting.org/en/office/EU/publications/extraordinary-or-extralegal-responses-covid-19-and-the-rule-of-law-in-the-eu.

Grogan, Joelle. COVID-19, the rule of law and democracy. Analysis of legal responses to a global health crisis. *Hague Journal on the Rule of Law*, v. 14, n. 2–3, 2022, p. 349–369.

Guasti, Petra. The impact of the Covid-19 pandemic in central and eastern Europe: The rise of autocracy and democratic resilience. *Democratic Theory*, v. 7, n. 2, 2020, p. 47–60.

Habermas, Jürgen. *Between facts and norms: Contributions to a discourse theory of law and democracy*. New York: John Wiley & Sons, 2018, *passim*.

Hestermeyer, Holger. *Coronavirus lockdown-measures before the German constitutional court*. April 30, 2020. Available at: http://constitutionnet.org/news/coronavirus-lockdown-measures-german- constitutional-court.

Inácio, Magna; Recch, Filipe; Valencia, Carolina Guerrero. The power of the administrative decisions of Latin American presidents. In: Llanos, Mariana; Marsteintredet, Leiv (Eds.). *Latin America in times of turbulence: Presidentialism under stress*. New York: Routledge, 2023, p. 75–105.

Kaiser, Anna-Bettina. The state of exception under German law and the current pandemic: Comparative models and constitutional rights. *e-Pública*, v. 7, n. 3, 2020, p. 4–15.

Kaiser, Anna-Bettina; Hensel, Roman. Federal Republic of Germany: Legal response to Covid-19. In: *The Oxford compendium of national legal responses to Covid-19*. April 2021. Available at: https://oxcon.ouplaw.com/view/https://doi.org/10.1093/law-occ19/law-occ19-e2

Kropp, Sabine; Schnabel, Johanna. Germany's response to COVID-19: Federal coordination and executive politics. In: Chattopadhyay, Rupak et al. (Eds.). *Federalism and the response to COVID-19: A comparative analysis.* New York: Routledge, 2022, p. 162.

Kuhlmann, Sabine; Franzke, Jochen. Multi-level responses to COVID-19: Crisis coordination in Germany from an intergovernmental perspective. *Local Government Studies*, v. 48, n. 2, 2022, p. 312–334.

Kuhn, Katharina; Morlino, Irene. Decentralisation in times of crisis: Asset or liability? The case of Germany and Italy during Covid-19. *Swiss Political Science Review*, v. 28, n. 1, 2022, p. 105–115.

Locke, John. *Second treatise. Two treatises of government.* Indianapolis: Hackett Publishing, Chapter XI, § 141.

Petrov, Jan. The COVID-19 emergency in the age of executive aggrandizement: What role for legislative and judicial checks? *The Theory and Practice of Legislation*, v. 8, n. 1–2, 2020, p. 71–92.

Pinheiro, Victor Marcel; Ilarraz, Marcelo; Mestriner, Melissa Terni. The impacts of the COVID-19 crisis on the Brazilian legal system–a report on the functioning of the branches of the government and on the legal scrutiny of their activities. *Op. cit.*

Ramos, Edith Maria Barbosa; Ramos, Paulo Roberto Barbosa; Costa, Laísse Lima Silva. Pandemia e Federalismo: Reflexões sobre as decisões do Supremo Tribunal Federal na apreciação de conflitos de competência entre os entes federativos no enfrentamento à Covid-19. *Revista de Ciências Jurídicas e Sociais-IURJ*, v. 1, n. 1, 2020, p. 46–61.

Rosenberg, Shawn W. (Ed.). *Deliberation, participation and democracy.* London: Palgrave Macmillan, 2007, *passim.*

Roth, Kenneth. How authoritarians are exploiting the Covid-19 crisis to grab power. *Human Rights Watch*, v. 3, 2020, p. 15.

Teixeira, Carmen Fontes, Santos, Jamilli Silva. Análise estratégica da atuação do governo federal brasileiro na pandemia de COVID-19: 2020–2021. *Op. cit.*, p. 1278.

Whidden, Michael J. Unequal justice: Arabs in America and United States antiterrorism legislation. In: *Bioterrorism: The history of a crisis in American society.* New York: Routledge, 2020, p. 253–282.

6 Constitutional limits of decrees in times of emergency

The exigencies of modern states have led legislators to transfer much of their lawmaking powers to administrators. The complexities of government require the creation of an even greater body of regulations, as the state cannot properly function solely through primary laws. It has become one of the major tasks of constitutional and administrative law to control this power, ensuring that delegated legislation carries sufficient democratic legitimation.[1] A representative government implies that legislative norms achieve validation and legitimacy through the expression of consent in the legislature itself. The executive branch may exercise such legislative powers only when specifically delegated by parliament.

In previous chapters, we have emphasized the importance of checks and balances on a dominant executive and the dangers of excessive issuance of decrees without a clear legal basis. At this point, we will try to establish the parameters for identifying which infra-legal acts should be declared unconstitutional under the principle of legality. Despite the profound differences between legal systems, the aim is to construct a general criterion for recognizing when secondary legislation does not meet the requirements of the rule of law. To this end, we will examine the German "theory of materiality", also called "theory of essentialness" (*Wesentlichkeitstheorie*), which requires that essential questions of a particular political, social, or economic matter be decided by an act of parliament.[2]

It is important to note that the considerations in the next topic are mainly directed to the regulatory activity of the president, prime minister, and government ministers, who represent eminently political and nontechnical authorities. The issue of independent regulatory agencies, which have

1 Pünder, Hermann. Democratic legitimation of delegated legislation: A comparative view on the American, British, and German law. *International & Comparative Law Quarterly*, v. 58, n. 2, 2009, p. 353–378.

2 Staupe, Júrgen. *Parlamentsvorbehalt und Delegationsbefugnis – Zur "Wesentlichkeitstheorie" und zur Reichxveite legislativer Regelungskompetenz, insbesondere im Schulrecht*. Berlin: Duncker & Humblot, 1985, p. 24.

DOI: 10.4324/9781003610816-7

qualified expertise in certain matters, will not be discussed in depth. This is because these agencies have strategic institutional mechanisms to make highly technical and scientific decisions, so there are important reasons related to their expertise that justify greater discretion.

6.1 What does the "faithful execution" of laws mean?

The public administration can clarify, detail, and facilitate the application of laws and ensure their faithful execution. Through secondary legislation, it can add details that the legislator did not see necessary to provide directly in the law and clarify dubious or controversial aspects. This leaves a considerable margin of discretion to the executive. Indeed, it would be inconvenient or even impossible for parliament to anticipate and deal with all the details of a law's implementation.

Different constitutions may express the principle of legality in different ways. For example, the German Constitution (Basic Law) stipulates that

> the Federal Government, a Federal Minister or the Land governments may be authorized by law to issue statutory instruments. The content, purpose and scope of the authority conferred shall be specified in the law. Each statutory instrument shall contain a statement of its legal basis.[3]

For its part, the Brazilian Federal Constitution states that the president has the power to "issue decrees and regulations" for the "faithful execution" of the laws.[4] Also, the Constitution of the Italian Republic establishes that "the exercise of the legislative function may not be delegated to the Government

3 Basic Law for the Federal Republic of Germany.

> Article 80 [Issuance of statutory instruments] (1) The Federal Government, a Federal Minister or the Land governments may be authorised by a law to issue statutory instruments. The content, purpose and scope of the authority conferred shall be specified in the law. Each statutory instrument shall contain a statement of its legal basis. If the law provides that such authority may be further delegated, such subdelegation shall be effected by statutory instrument. (2) Unless a federal law otherwise provides, the consent of the Bundesrat shall be required for statutory instruments issued by the Federal Government or a Federal Minister regarding fees or basic principles for the use of postal and telecommunication facilities, basic principles for levying of charges for the use of facilities of federal railways or the construction and operation of railways, as well as for statutory instruments issued pursuant to federal laws that require the consent of the Bundesrat or that are executed by the Länder on federal commission or in their own right. (3) The Bundesrat may submit to the Federal Government drafts of statutory instruments that require its consent. (4) Insofar as Land governments are authorised by or pursuant to federal laws to issue statutory instruments, the Länder shall also be entitled to regulate the matter by a law.

4 Brazilian Federal Constitution of 1988. "Art. 84. The President of the Republic has the exclusive power to: (. . .) IV – sanction, promulgate and publish laws, as well as issue decrees and regulations for their faithful execution".

unless principles and criteria have been established and then only for a limited time and for specified purposes".[5]

As many administrative law scholars point out, it is difficult to determine exactly what subjects should be fully covered by laws and what the normative density of delegating law should be. Sometimes, the discretionary space is filled by regulatory decrees that go beyond the hermeneutic limits inherent in primary legislation. The ambiguity in some legal terms can end up providing a semantic opening in which the executive can expand its powers.

Regarding the regulations issued by presidents and prime ministers, one may argue that because of their very broad democratic legitimacy, they would be free to give their political guidelines to the regulatory activity, interpreting the provisions of laws with wide discretion. Given that a primary law will never be absolutely clear, they could clarify the ambiguous points and implement it according to their political will. This is the argument often used by the Brazilian Federal Public Prosecutor's Office in lawsuits against decrees issued by presidents.[6]

However, this broad interpretation of regulatory power does not seem to be the best option. The other branches may not be able to control secondary legislation effectively, which may end up being used as instruments to undermine the principle of separation of powers and democracy itself. We defend that a constitutional system imposes a duty of "strict" execution on presidents, prime ministers, and ministers of the government, who must confine themselves to the provisions of the law.

This understanding, it should be made clear, is not the same as an orthodox understanding of the principle of legality. These authorities do, of course, have a margin of discretion since they are direct enforcers of the Constitution, not just the law. The view that "Congress makes the laws, and the administration's job doesn't involve any normative thinking" is obsolete in light of the intense de-legalization process underway.[7] But we argue that executive action must

5 Constitution of the Italian Republic. "Art. 76. The exercise of the legislative function may not be delegated to the Government unless principles and criteria have been established and then only for a limited time and for specified purposes".

6 Petition filed by the Federal Attorney General's Office in the files of the following lawsuits submitted to the Federal Supreme Court: ADIs n. 6.119, 6.139, 6.134 and ADPFs n. 581 e 586. June 5, 2019. Available at: https://www.conjur.com.br/dl/agu-defende-stf-decreto-armas-bolsonaro.pdf.

7 In the words of Hermann Pünder,Constitutional purists may complain about the shift of law-making authority from the

> legislative to the executive branch. It is at odds with the idea of the separation of powers, an idea that is considered a major guarantee for freedom. The constitutional purist may also mourn that the authority shift departs from the basic principle that "delegatus non potest delegare". As John Locke said in 1690: "The Legislative cannot transfer the Power of Making Laws to any other hands. For being but a delegated Power for the People, they, who have it, cannot pass it over to others.' These considerations, however, have long been bypassed by the need for administrative institutions to exercise lawmaking authority (. . .) The separation of powers was originally rooted in the fear of tyranny. However, these concerns have

always be consistent with legality, the system of principles and rules outlined in the Constitution, and above all, with fundamental rights. It must be compatible with a literal, teleological, systematic, or historical interpretation of the law.

Furthermore, it is true that laws can have different normative densities, leading to regulations with more or less creative/discretionary content. Laws can have (i) exhaustive normative density, (ii) high normative density, or (iii) low normative density.[8] Laws of exhaustive normative density are those which, in principle, seek to exhaust the discipline of a given subject. They are formulated as completely as possible, leaving practically no room for discretionary judgments. They are usually enacted in matters such as the establishment of taxes, crimes, and the corresponding penalties.

Nevertheless, it is important to mention that even in these cases it is unrealizable to exclude all subjectivity on the part of the law enforcer. The large number of doctrinal and judicial disagreements in tax and criminal matters, with different legal positions, proves the impossibility of a single interpretation. Laws, however much they try to seek absolute completeness, cannot do so to the point of leaving no margin of appreciation.

Laws of high normative density, in its turn, go as far as to initiate, without pretending to exhaust, the regulation of a certain issue in a very detailed manner. In this case, the executive is given the space to specify the content of an obligation or right already established by law. As an example, the German Infectious Diseases Protection Act (Infektionsschutzgesetz, IfSG),[9] as amended in November 2020, set clear and limited parameters for executive regulations, which constrained the public administration. The law identified the specific "content, purpose, and scope" of the restrictive measures that the executive could implement.

Finally, there are laws of low normative density, which establish only very general parameters of regulation to be carried out by the executive. These are the so-called *lois-cadre* or "framework laws", specific to matters of great technical complexity or susceptible to constant change.[10] These laws do not provide the administrator with essential elements to guide his actions or regulations but refer in general terms to moral, political, and economic values existing in society (public health, public utility, market competition, etc.). Their

---

in the meantime lost their significance, as the executive branch itself carries democratic legitimation".

(Pünder, Hermann. Democratic legitimation of delegated legislation – a comparative view on the American, British and German law. International & Comparative Law Quarterly, v. 58, n. 2, 2009, p. 353–378.)

8 Aragão, Alexandre Santos de. Princípio da legalidade e poder regulamentar no Estado contemporâneo. *Revista de Direito Administrativo*, v. 225, 2001, p. 109–130.

9 Germany. *Gesetz zur Verhütung und Bekämpfung von Infektionskrankheiten beim Menschen (Act on the Prevention and Control of Infectious Diseases in Humans)*. Available at: https://www.gesetze-im-internet.de/ifsg/index.html.

10 Aragão, Alexandre Santos de. Princípio da legalidade e poder regulamentar no Estado contemporâneo. *Op. cit.*, p. 123.

purpose is precisely to introduce a vagueness that makes it possible to deal with social phenomena that are too transient to be captured in a precise rule.[11] This was the case with the "decree-laws" (*decreti-legge*) enacted in Italy during the COVID-19 pandemic, which stated in general terms that the restrictive measures applied by the executive had to meet a criteria of "adequacy and proportionality". The law did not specify what these criteria were, leaving the administration a wide margin of discretion.[12]

In all these cases, and regardless of the degree of legal normative density, we argue that executive regulatory activity must be subject to the following material limits: (i) the text of the law, (ii) the purpose and scope defined in the delegating law, and (iii) the constitutional-legal system that governs the regulated sector. In this sense, the chief executive and his ministers must adopt specific hermeneutical guidelines in secondary regulation, such as grammatical, teleological, historical, or systematic interpretation. They should never take into account only their political-ideological will to realize a certain electoral promise. Regulatory activity must always comply with and complement the spirit and content of the legislative act.[13]

First, the regulatory decree cannot, as a rule, go against, below, or beyond the text of the law itself.[14] Acts aimed at regulating laws cannot (i) create new rights or obligations; (ii) extend, limit, or modify rights or obligations contained in the law; (iii) prescribe or prohibit what the law does not prescribe or prohibit; (iv) authorize or prohibit in a manner different from that prescribed by law; (v) extinguish or annul rights created by law; (vi) create new or different principles; (vii) change the form that the law requires the regulation to take; or (viii) change the text or spirit of the law in any way.[15] For example, if the law prescribes a list of beneficiaries of a certain right, it is not up to the

11 Aragão, Alexandre Santos de. Princípio da legalidade e poder regulamentar no Estado contemporâneo. *Op. cit.*

12 Italy. Decree-Law 25 of March 2020, n. 19

> (*Decreto-Legge* 25 marzo 2020, n. 19).(. . .) 2. Pursuant to and for the purposes of paragraph 1, one or more of the following measures may be adopted, in accordance with the principles of adequacy and proportionality to the actual risk in certain parts of the national territory or in the entire national territory (a) restriction of the movement of persons, including by providing for limitations on the possibility of moving away from one's residence, domicile, or abode except for individual movements limited in time and space or motivated by work requirements, situations of necessity or urgency, health reasons, or other specific reasons; (. . .).

13 Cyrino, André Rodrigues. *O poder regulamentar autônomo do Presidente da República: a espécie regulamentar criada pela EC n. 32/2001*. Belo Horizonte: Fórum, 2005, p. 91.

14 Brandão, Rodrigo; Capecchi Nunes, Daniel. *Poder regulamentar e 'jogo duro constitucional': o caso dos decretos de armas*. *Jota*. July 10, 2019. Available at: https://www.jota.info/opiniao-e-analise/artigos/poder-regulamentar-e-jogo-duro-constitucional-o-caso-dos-decretos-de-armas-10072019.

15 Ráo, Vicente. *O direito e a vida dos direitos*. São Paulo: Editora Revista dos Tribunais, 1991, p. 354.

executive regulation to expand it unless the law expressly states that this list is only illustrative.

In the same way, regulatory decrees must be issued ***secundum legem*** since they cannot create new obligations but can only develop those that already exist in the law. All legal interpretation, including that of the chief executive, must start from the text of the rule, revealing the semantic content of the words.[16] Grammatical interpretation often provides the guides and boundaries of meaning. Even when there is doubt and the legal rule is vague and of low normative density, the text remains relevant. It acts as one of several elements to be taken into account by the interpreter in the search for the most appropriate answer to the question posed. In other words, it is necessary to respect the framework defined by the legal text itself.[17]

Second, the executive must not disregard the very purposes for which the laws were enacted. Regulatory interpretation must be conducted with fundamental regard for the spirit and purpose of the delegating statute.[18] Laws are designed to meet specific needs and must be interpreted in a way that best serves the purpose for which they were created.[19] The exercise of regulatory power cannot be in direct contradiction with the objectives expressed in the delegating law. It is essential that the use of the normative powers of the chief executive be expressly in line with the objectives that explicitly and implicitly guided the legal text. The regulation cannot point in a direction contrary to the law it is intended to regulate.[20]

In this sense, decrees must give the laws a "faithful execution", reasonably shaped to the legal objectives.[21] The term "faithful" means (i) trust and loyalty, (ii) zeal and devotion, (iii) honesty, (iv) faith in someone or something, and (v) accuracy and rigor.[22] The executive interpretation of legislative acts must be loyal, honest, in good faith, and demonstrate accuracy and rigor in relation to the text of the rule. As Zachary Price points out, allowing the president or

16 Barroso, Luís Roberto. *Interpretação e aplicação da Constituição: fundamentos de uma dogmática constitucional transformadora.* São Paulo: Saraiva, 2009, p. 131.

17 Souza Neto, Cláudio Pereira de; Sarmento, Daniel. *Direito constitucional: teoria, história e métodos de trabalho.* Belo Horizonte: Fórum, 201, p. 336.

18 Barroso, Luís Roberto. *Interpretação e aplicação da Constituição*: fundamentos de uma dogmática constitucional transformadora. *Op. cit.*, p. 143.

19 Barroso, Luís Roberto. *Interpretação e aplicação da Constituição*: fundamentos de uma dogmática constitucional transformadora. *Op. cit.*, p. 131.

20 Brandão, Rodrigo; Capecchi Nunes, Daniel. *Poder regulamentar e 'jogo duro constitucional': o caso dos decretos de armas. Jota.* July 10, 2019. Available at: https://www.jota.info/opiniao-e-analise/artigos/poder-regulamentar-e-jogo-duro-constitucional-o-caso-dos-decretos-de-armas-10072019.

21 Bellia, Patricia L. Faithful execution and enforcement discretion. *University of Pennsylvania Law Review*, v. 164, 2015, p. 1.753–1.800.

22 Cambridge Dictionary. 2024. Available at: https://dictionary.cambridge.org/dictionary/english/faithful.

prime minister to disregard the underlying meaning of primary laws means, after all, "giving him a new veto possibility".[23]

Third, the executive's regulatory power must take a systematic and structural view of the system as a whole. The delegating law must be considered in conjunction with all the others, not in isolation. The "system" is a hermeneutic construction, supported above all by fundamental constitutional principles.[24] Thus, in this exercise, the chief executive cannot disregard the Constitution and the other laws that deal with the same matter. In the words of Pontes de Miranda, a renowned Brazilian jurist, "regulation is more difficult than making the law itself, it requires full knowledge of the scope of the legal rules and of the branch of law in which the legislation is immersed".[25]

Indeed, care and fidelity in the exercise of the regulatory activity require compliance with best practices in interpretation and implementation. The executive's actions do not take place in a legal or historical *vacuum*. Fidelity means remaining faithful to past practices and precedents, as well as maintaining continuity with other existing laws. It is necessary to consider history in order to form a coherent view of its purpose and content. When interpreting, the executive must seek the best possible meaning that makes sense of past practice and provides a coherent fit with current policies.[26]

In addition, the executive may rely on other methods of interpretation, such as the historical method. On this basis, it can examine the *occasio legis* (the reasons that led to the enactment of the law), the explanatory *memorandum*, and the parliamentary debates in order to determine the will of the legislator on a given subject. In this way, it will be able to create a regulation that respects the will of the parliamentarians expressed during the discussion of the law. Also, the greater the possibility that the regulation will restrict fundamental rights, the more can be demanded of the legislator, who must be clearer about his intentions. Restrictions of rights must be subject to the legislative process and expressed in laws with a high normative density, which are essential to limit arbitrariness. In short, the executive cannot issue a regulation that completely departs from the legal framework and does not have the slightest relevance to the spirit of the law.

An infamous example of a regulation that simultaneously violates the grammatical, teleological, and systematic limits of a law is the Decree n. 10.344/2020, issued by former Brazilian president Jair Bolsonaro, which classified beauty salons and gyms as "essential activities" during the COVID-19

23 Price, Zachary S. Enforcement discretion and executive duty. *Vanderbilt Law Review*, v. 67, 2014.

24 Souza Neto, Cláudio Pereira de; Sarmento, Daniel. *Direito constitucional: teoria, história e métodos de trabalho*. Belo Horizonte: Fórum, 2012, p. 336.

25 Miranda, Francisco Cavalcanti Pontes de. *Comentários à Constituição de 1946. VI*, 2. ed. Max Limonad: São Paulo, 1953, p. 411.

26 Crocker, T. P. Presidential power and constitutional responsibility. *Boston College Law Review*, n. 52, 2011, p. 1578–1579.

pandemic. Despite the importance of these activities to some, it is clear that the former president has made a largely unreasonable interpretation of Law n. 13.979/2020, which provides for measures to deal with the coronavirus public health emergency.

A systematic interpretation would already indicate the need to consider the list of essential activities contained in another piece of legislation – Federal Law n. 7.783/1989, which "defines essential activities and regulates the satisfaction of the community's unavoidable needs":

> Art. 10 The following are considered essential services or activities:
>
> I – water treatment and supply; production and distribution of electricity, gas, and fuels;
> II – medical and hospital care;
> III – distribution and marketing of medicines and foodstuffs;
> IV – funeral directors;
> V – public transport;
> VI – sewage and waste collection and treatment;
> VII – telecommunications;
> VIII – safekeeping, use, and control of radioactive substances, equipment and nuclear materials;
> IX – data processing linked to essential services;
> X – air traffic control and air navigation; (Edited by Law No. 13.903, of 2019)
> XI – bank clearing;
> XII – medical-expert activities related to the general social security system and social assistance; (Included by Law No. 13.846, of 2019)
> XIII – medical and forensic activities related to the characterization of the physical, mental, intellectual or sensory impairment of people with disabilities, through the integration of multi-professional and interdisciplinary teams, for the purpose of recognizing the rights provided for by law, in particular in Law No. 13.146, of July 6, 2015 (Statute of People with Disabilities); and (Included by Law No. 13.846, of 2019)
> XIV – other medical-expert services of the Federal Medical Expert career that are indispensable to meet the community's unavoidable needs. (Included by Law No. 13.846, of 2019)
> XV – port activities. (Included by Provisional Measure No. 945, of 2020).

However, the former president chose to ignore the aforementioned list, which was already established in a law passed by Congress and explicitly defined what essential activities are. In addition to the lack of systematic interpretation, Bolsonaro also disregarded the limits of the legal text itself and its objectives since the law that the decree sought to regulate (Federal Law n. 13.979/2020) was enacted to protect the population from the spread of the virus. In this scenario, it is certain that the classification of beauty salons and gyms as essential activities manifestly violates the spirit of the primary legislation.

6.2 Restrictions on fundamental rights by normative acts of the executive branch

Fundamental rights are not absolute, and their exercise may be restricted by acts of public authority. The restriction may originate in an abstract norm or be the product of interpretation by the judiciary,[27] when it operates at a concrete and individual level and has repercussions on the subjective dimension of fundamental rights.[28] This section will analyze restrictions established by abstract normative acts that modify the content of fundamental rights. These acts have disadvantageous or negative consequences for the actual or potential holders of the respective right. In this context, we will discuss whether secondary legislation can establish restrictions on fundamental rights.[29]

According to J. J. Gomes Canotilho, fundamental rights encounter the following explicit and implicit limitations in the text of constitutions: (i) direct or immediate constitutional limitations, which are those established by the constitutional rules themselves; (ii) limitations established by laws; and (iii) limitations resulting from the resolution of conflicts between colliding rights, when there is a balancing of values that enjoy equal constitutional protection.[30]

In all these cases, normative restrictions on fundamental rights must meet certain conditions of legitimacy, usually referred to as "limits of limits". Some constitutions explicitly establish these requirements: the Portuguese

27 *See* Novais, Jorge Reis. *As restrições aos Direitos Fundamentais não expressamente autorizadas pela Constituição.* Coimbra: Coimbra Editora, 2003; Pereira, Jane Reis Gonçalves. *Interpretação constitucional e direitos fundamentais.* São Paulo: Saraiva Educação, 2018; Abrahão, Marcela da Rosa. *As Restrições aos Direitos Fundamentais por Ato Normativo do Poder Executivo.* São Paulo: Almedina, 2017; Alexy, Robert. *Teoría de los derechos fundamentales.* Madrid: Centro de Estudios Constitucionales, 1993; Moncada, Luís Cabral de. *Lei e regulamento.* Coimbra: Ed. Coimbra, 2002; Voronoff, Alice. *Direito administrativo sancionador no Brasil.* Belo Horizonte: Fórum, 2018; Staupe, Júrgen. *Parlamentsvorbehalt und Delegationsbefugnis - Zur "Wesentlichkeitstheoríe" und zur Reichxveite legislativer Regelungskompetenz, insbesondere im Schulrecht.* Berlin: Duncker & Humblot, 1985; Di Giovine, Alfonso et al. *Introduzione allo studio della riserva di legge nell'ordinamento costituzionale italiano.* Torino: G. Giappichelli, 1969, p. 65.

28 Pereira, Jane Reis Gonçalves. *Interpretação constitucional e direitos fundamentais,* 2. ed. São Paulo: Saraiva Educação, 2018, p. 234–235.

29 Novais, Jorge Reis. *As restrições aos Direitos Fundamentais não expressamente autorizadas pela Constituição.* Coimbra: Coimbra Editora, 2003, p. 227.

30 Canotilho, José Joaquim Gomes. *Direito Constitucional e Teoria da Constituição,* 7. ed. Coimbra: Almedina, 2003, p. 1.276.

Constitution, for example, states in article 18 that "all laws limiting rights, freedoms, and guarantees must be general and abstract in nature and must not have a retroactive effect or diminish the extent and scope of the essential content of the constitutional provisions".[31] For its part, the German Constitution, in its article 19, expressly states that when a basic right is restricted by or pursuant to a law, such law must "apply generally and not merely to a single case. In addition, the law must specify the basic right affected and the Article in which it appears". It also states that "in no case may the essence of a basic right be affected".[32] In its turn, article 53 of the Spanish Constitution also states that the exercise of rights and freedoms "may be regulated only by law, which must, in any case, respect their essential content".[33]

It is then possible to extract some requirements for a legitimate restriction of basic rights. The first of these "limits of limits" is precisely the *principle of the rule of law*. It is generally accepted that fundamental rights can only be limited by primary legislation approved by the parliament.[34] The executive cannot adopt measures restricting these rights without a clear legal basis. The justification for this is precisely the greater democratic legitimacy of the parliament and the gains in transparency, pluralism, participation, and integration that the parliamentary legislative process offers compared to legislation emanating from the executive branch.

Indeed, legislative bodies remain the central "forum" for debating and weighing the commitments and needs of citizens. The plural composition of legislatures, the direct election of its members, the existence of representation for minority groups, and the transparency of the legislative process are arguments that reinforce the reservation of parliamentary law for the restriction of fundamental rights.[35]

Nevertheless, one must ask whether the principle of legality implies the absolute impossibility of infra-legal rules dealing with fundamental rights. Although it is widely accepted that the principle of legal reserve is fully applicable in the context of restrictions on fundamental rights, it is not easy to

31 Constitution of the Portuguese Republic of 1976. Available at: https://www.parlamento.pt/Legislacao/paginas/constituicaorepublicaportuguesa.aspx. Accessed on: October 20, 2020.

32 Basic Law of the Federal Republic of Germany of 1949. Available at: https://www.btg-bestellservice.de/pdf/80208000.pdf.

33 Spanish Constitution of 1978. Available at: https://www.tribunalconstitucional.es/es/tribunal/normativa/Normativa/CEportugu%C3%A9s.pdf.

34 Novais, Jorge Reis. *As restrições aos Direitos Fundamentais não expressamente autorizadas pela Constituição*. Coimbra: Coimbra Editora, 2003, p. 227; Staupe, Júrgen. *Parlamentsvorbehalt und Delegationsbefugnis – Zur "Wesentlichkeitstheorie" und zur Reichxveite legislativer Regelungskompetenz, insbesondere im Schulrecht*. Berlin: Duncker & Humblot, 1985; Abrahão, Marcela da Rosa. *As Restrições aos Direitos Fundamentais por Ato Normativo do Poder Executivo. Op. cit.*, p. 272–273.

35 Novais, Jorge Reis. *As restrições aos Direitos Fundamentais não expressamente autorizadas pela Constituição*. Coimbra: Coimbra Editora, 2003, p. 878.

determine the scope of legitimate administrative action in this area.[36] The following questions arise: should everything concerning fundamental rights be regulated by the ordinary legislator? Can the executive branch issue regulations that impact fundamental rights, or is it entirely prohibited from doing so? Must any law restricting rights have an "exhaustive normative density" and thus leave no room for executive discretion?

In answering these questions, it is first necessary to distinguish between "limitations" and "configurations" of fundamental rights. The purpose of "configurations" is simply to concretize, develop, or densify rights. In these cases, the provision is a fundamental prerequisite for adequate and effective protection, improving or enabling the conditions for the exercise of the right. Restrictions, on the other hand, have a constricting, suppressive, and limiting effect on the faculties and legal positions covered by the rights, creating obstacles to their exercise.[37]

Part of the literature holds that the requirement of a primary law does not prevent the executive from protecting, safeguarding, and implementing a fundamental right. Thus, the executive cannot restrict or limit fundamental rights, but it can act to promote and protect them regardless of the existence of a law. It is only when the executive's rule generates limitations, restrictions, or obstacles that a prior legal basis is required.

It's important to note, however, that even rules enacted with the intention of "configuring" and "concretizing" may end up generating restrictions on its exercise or on the exercise of other rights. In some situations, by shaping the right, the legislator may end up indirectly creating "adverse effects" and limiting it. It is perfectly possible that, on the basis of apparently harmless and merely regulatory measures, the exercise of a fundamental right is severely restricted. What appears to be a mere regulation may, in fact, be a restriction.[38]

As a solution, jurists such as Robert Alexy believe that all legislative interventions that may constitute obstacles to rights should be understood as restrictions, even if they are, at the same time, configurations.[39] In his words, "When something is restrictive from some point of view, it remains restrictive, even if from some other point of view it is a configuration".[40] Thus, the distinction

36 Pereira, Jane Reis Gonçalves. *Interpretação constitucional e direitos fundamentais. Op. cit.*, p. 348.

37 Abrahão, Marcela da Rosa. *As Restrições aos Direitos Fundamentais por Ato Normativo do Poder Executivo. Op. cit.*, p. 272–273 and Novais, Jorge Reis. *As restrições aos Direitos Fundamentais não expressamente autorizadas pela Constituição. Op. cit.*, p. 227.

38 Silva, Virgílio Afonso da. *Direitos fundamentais: Conteúdo essencial, restrições e eficácia*. São Paulo: Malheiros, 2009, p. 102.

39 Pereira, Jane Reis Gonçalves. *Interpretação constitucional e direitos fundamentais. Op. cit.*, p. 243.

40 Alexy, Robert. *Teoría de los derechos fundamentales.* Madrid: Centro de Estudios Constitucionales, 1993, p. 323: "When something is restrictive from some point of view, it remains restrictive, even when from some other point of view it is configuring".

between configuration and restriction does not take on dichotomous and exclusive contours. Whenever there is any degree of restriction of a fundamental right, the requirement of prior parliamentary legislation must prevail.[41]

It is also necessary to analyze the degree of normative density of a law restricting rights. In this area, the German "theory of materiality" or "theory of essentialness" (*Wesentlichkeitstheorie*) states that parliament must make basic or essential decisions on all issues – especially in the area of fundamental rights.[42] The parliament is constitutionally required to define the "content, purpose and scope" of legislative powers that are delegated to the executive.[43] If the delegating statutes do not fulfill these criteria, the secondary regulation is void. This guarantees that the parliament elected by the people bears political responsibility for all restrictions of rights, including those created by the executive.[44] Indeed, the rule of law requires that all essential decisions of the state be made by the legislature itself.[45]

In this regard, the German Federal Constitutional Court, together with the doctrine, created the figure of the *Bestimmheitsgebot*, that is, the requirement of determinability that the delegating law must meet, which avoids the granting of unlimited normative competence (a *carte blanche*) to the executive. The normative discipline established by the law must not be so summary, so simple,

41 Pereira, Jane Reis Gonçalves. *Interpretação constitucional e direitos fundamentais. Op. cit.*, p. 243.

42 Pünder, Hermann. Democratic legitimation of delegated legislation – a comparative view on the American, British and German law. *International & Comparative Law Quarterly*, v. 58, n. 2, 2009, p. 353–378:

> (. . .) the legislator is required to make a substantive decision and where the legitimation of executive delegated legislation is primarily a question of its basis in statutes. This also corresponds to the German constitutional history, which in the context of the Weimar disaster (characterised by extensive use of 'Notverordnungen', emergency rules, by the Reichspra¨sident) and national socialist dictatorship (which was originally based on the extremely far reaching 'Erma¨chtigungsgesetz' 1936) is coloured by a conscious turning away from unlimited delegation powers of the legislature. Parliament is elected by the people and should not without good cause be relieved of its responsibility for substantive legislation. Statutes as 'central regulatory instruments' form a basic model which is worthy of preservation.

43 Basic Law of the Federal Republic of Germany of 1949. *Art 80 paragraph 1 sentence 2.* Available at: https://www.btg-bestellservice.de/pdf/80208000.pdf. *See also* Umbach, Dieter C.; Clemens, Thomas; Dollinger, Franz-Wilhelm. *Bundesverfassungsgerichtsgesetz: Mitarbeiterkommentar e Manual.* Heidelberg: CF Müller GmbH, 2005.

44 Pünder, Hermann. Democratic legitimation of delegated legislation – a comparative view on the American, British, and German law. *International & Comparative Law Quarterly*, v. 58, n. 2, 2009, p. 353–378.

45 *See* German Constitutional Court. *Bundesverfassungsgericht - BVerfG, order of the first senate of November 19, 2021 - 1 BvR 781/21 -, paras. 1–306.* Available at: https://www.bundesverfassungsgericht.de/SharedDocs/Entscheidungen/EN/2021/11/rs20211119_1bvr078121en.html;jsessionid=8167C5E8EDD7A42DC32D922EE0B73900.internet992.

that its complementation can lead to any result.[46] Thus, what is essential must be decided by parliament, the democratically legitimized source of primary legislation.[47]

According to the German "theory of materiality", a decision is considered "essential" if it is relevant to the realization of fundamental rights or if it is politically controversial. In other words, issues concerning the restriction of rights, which are the subject of dissent in society, must be decided through the ordinary legislative process.[48] The criterion of essentiality, therefore, refers to the fundamental and innovative decisions in the relationship between the state and the individuals, involving the preservation and promotion of human dignity and affecting the fundamental ethical values of life in society.[49] Decisions that may constitute or trigger serious threats to individual liberty and equality should be fully submitted to parliament. Controversial decisions require the legitimacy, participation, pluralistic debate, and transparency that only the parliamentary legislative process can provide.[50]

The executive branch, on the other hand, can regulate the secondary details of a given restriction, regulating noncontroversial situations.[51] In other words, the executive may issue regulations that do not fully innovate in the legal system.[52] There will be no need for a primary law for (i) regulating details or purely marginal aspects of fundamental rights or (ii) regulating a restriction on the right that does not involve controversy or political importance.[53]

46 German Constitutional Court. Bundesverfassungsgericht - BVerfG 47, 46–85, Beschluss vom 21. Dezember 1977, 1 BvL 1/75, 1 BvR 147/75, Sexualerziehung in der Schule. In: Schwabe, Jürgen. *Cincuenta años de jurisprudencia del Tribunal Constitucional Federal Alemán*. Translated by Marcela Anzola Gil. Colombia: Gustavo Ibáñez, 2003, p. 180.

47 Novais, Jorge Reis. *As restrições aos Direitos Fundamentais não expressamente autorizadas pela Constituição. Op. cit.*, p. 852.

48 Critics claim, however, that the main problem with the theory of essentiality lies in the absence of indisputable criteria for distinguishing the essential from the nonessential, so that, ultimately, the essential ends up being whatever the Constitutional Court says it is. Due to its fluid and imprecise nature, the critics argue that it does not provide reliable parameters for determining in advance which aspects of a given matter are or are not essential. This opens the door to judicial decisionism, since it will always be the Constitutional Court that ultimately assesses the essentiality of the issue in controversy. *See* Staupe, Júrgen. *Parlamentsvorbehalt und Delegationsbefugnis - Zur "Wesentlichkeitstheorie" und zur Reichxveite legislativer Regelungskompetenz, insbesondere im Schulrecht*. Berlin: Duncker & Humblot, 1985, p. 114–117.

49 Novais, Jorge Reis. *As restrições aos Direitos Fundamentais não expressamente autorizadas pela Constituição. Op. cit.*, p. 879–880.

50 Novais, Jorge Reis. *As restrições aos Direitos Fundamentais não expressamente autorizadas pela Constituição. Op. cit.*, p. 879–880.

51 Moncada, Luís Cabral de. *Lei e regulamento*. Coimbra: Ed. Coimbra, 2002, p. 1.029–1.040.

52 Abrahão, Marcela da Rosa. *As Restrições aos Direitos Fundamentais por Ato Normativo do Poder Executivo. Op. cit.*, p. 218 and Novais, Jorge Reis. *As restrições aos Direitos Fundamentais não expressamente autorizadas pela Constituição. Op. cit.*, p. 876–879.

53 Novais, Jorge Reis. *As restrições aos Direitos Fundamentais não expressamente autorizadas pela Constituição. Op. cit.*, p. 878.

What the legislator may not do, however, is to delegate powers to the executive in the form of "blank" or "hidden" delegations. The law must define the criteria to be used by the administration to comply with the concepts set forth in the law and provide elements that will later enable the judiciary to assess the legitimacy of the administrative action. The law must seek to define standards, parameters, or examples that can guide the administration. Even if the restrictive law does not exhaust the rules on the matter, it must outline comprehensible principles that can guide the respective application and control. Therefore, although the use of general clauses is permissible in order to allow the administration to take into account the circumstances of particular cases, there must be "an identifiable link that makes the regulation a product of the law rather than an independent creation".[54] In short, executive actions in the fundamental rights field must always be guided by a legal authority that has made the essential decisions.

An example of this paradigm is the decision of the German Constitutional Court on the limits and possibilities of sex education in schools. In this case, the Court stated that sex education creates tension between the rights of parents, the rights of children, and the competence of the state to teach and educate. Faced with this clash of constitutional rights, the Court found that the legislator should "determine the functions of schools in educational matters" and the public administrator could only fix the "details of teaching and learning methods":

> According to the Constitution, all forms of sex education must be regulated by a primary law (. . .). In particular, the educational functions of schools must be defined by a parliamentary legislation. (. . .) [But] the details of teaching and learning methods cannot in principle be reserved for primary legislation, since the structure of the class must leave room for adaptation to specific situations.[55]

In another example, the German Constitutional Court, ruling on professional freedom in the medical field, made it clear that it is not possible to impose substantial restrictions on fundamental rights without specific legal authorization. The decision concerned the competence of medical chambers to regulate the way in which medical specialties are practiced in the absence of laws on the subject. In this case, medical chambers decided that specialists should limit their activities to the field of their specialty and refrain from treating patients requiring medical care of a different nature. In its decision, the

54 Voronoff, Alice. *Direito administrativo sancionador no Brasil*. Belo Horizonte: Fórum, 2018, p. 246.

55 German Constitutional Court. Bundesverfassungsgericht - BVerfG 47, 46–85, Beschluss vom 21. Dezember 1977, 1 BvL 1/75, 1 BvR 147/75, Sexualerziehung in der Schule. In: Schwabe, Jürgen. *Cincuenta años de jurisprudencia del Tribunal Constitucional Federal Alemán*. Translated by Marcela Anzola Gil. Colombia: Gustavo lbáiíez, 2003, p. 183.

Court ruled that "the characteristic of a specialist cannot be left exclusively to the regulation of the statutes of the medical chambers. At the very least, the restrictions must be determined by the legislature itself".[56]

Indeed, since 1972, the German Court recognizes that only parliament could create new rules that significantly impact on fundamental rights. One of the first cases presented before the Court concerned the introduction of a *Förderstufe* (an additional year of compulsory schooling) in schools in Hesse. The issue involved complex questions about the right of parents to choose their children's education and the freedom of the administration to set educational levels and goals for public school students. In its decision, the Court clarified that "the essential characteristics of an additional requirement of compulsory schooling must be created by primary law".[57]

More recently, in September 2003, a decision on freedom of religion in schools confirmed the importance of the Court's jurisprudence. In the case, the applicant, a Muslim candidate for a state school teaching post in Baden-Württemberg, had been rejected by a decision of the Stuttgart Higher School Board because she had declared the intention to wear a headscarf at school during lessons. The School Board argued that wearing a headscarf was an expression of cultural segregation and therefore not only a religious but also a political symbol. According to the Board, the effect of cultural disintegration caused by wearing a headscarf was incompatible with state neutrality.[58]

In its decision, the Court held that every citizen has the right to access public services, regardless of his or her religious beliefs, and that wearing a headscarf falls under the protection of freedom of religion. It ruled that state neutrality does not mean a rigid separation between state and religion but rather an open and inclusive attitude that allows freedom of belief for all. Therefore, schools should be open to other religious and philosophical values in order to maintain state neutrality. The Court also stated that in a society of religious diversity, there is no right to remain untouched by the actions, rituals, or religious symbols of other faiths.[59]

The Court further clarified that only the legislature could decide on the tension between a teacher's positive freedom of belief and the state's obligation of confessional neutrality. An *a priori* restriction on the wearing of religious symbols or clothing by teachers required a legal basis. In the case, it held that there was no such legal basis. But it stated that, in the future, social

56 German Constitutional Court. *Bundesverfassungsgericht - BVerfG 33, 125, de 09.05.1972.* Available at: http://www.oefre.unibe.ch/law/dfr/bv033125.html.

57 German Constitutional Court. *Bundesverfassungsgericht - BVerfG 34, 165, de 06.12.1972.* Available at: http://www.oefre.unibe.ch/law/dfr/bv034165.html.

58 German Constitutional Court. *Bundesverfassungsgericht - BVerfG, 2 BvR 1436/02, de 24.09.2003.* Available at: http://www.bverfg.de/entscheidungen/rs20030924_2bvr143602.html.

59 German Constitutional Court. *Bundesverfassungsgericht - BVerfG, 2 BvR 1436/02, de 24.09.2003. Op. cit.*

changes and growing religious pluralism could eventually give the legislator cause to review the limits of religious expression in schools.[60]

Finally, another relevant example of rights restriction by an executive act came from the Brazilian Supreme Court, which declared null and void a decree issued by a governor restricting the right of assembly. In the case, the governor of the Federal District issued a decree that sought to regulate the exercise of the right of assembly in the following terms: "Art. 1º. It is forbidden to hold public demonstrations with the use of vehicles, devices, and sound objects in the Praça dos Três Poderes, Esplanada dos Ministérios and Praça do Buriti and adjacent streets". The purpose of the decree, according to its preamble, was to discipline the exercise of freedom of assembly "so that mutual respect is always present, without violating the basic postulates of democracy".[61] At the time of the ruling, the Court stated that it was unacceptable that a secondary legislation, under the pretext of regulating a fundamental right, should end up emptying its essential core, making its exercise impossible. According to the opinion of Judge Gilmar Mendes, the matter could not be regulated by decree since any conflict that justifies the restriction of the freedom of demonstration and assembly requires prior legislation.[62]

Therefore, it can be concluded that the delegating laws must be accompanied by substantive standards, normative guidelines, and a defined scope and purpose that limit executive action. The law cannot give a blank check. There can be no full de-legalization in the area of restrictions on fundamental rights, and it is not possible for the primary legislation to leave room for arbitrary, unlimited, and uncontrolled administrative action.[63]

Bibliography

Abrahão, Marcela da Rosa. *As Restrições aos Direitos Fundamentais por Ato Normativo do Poder Executivo*. São Paulo: Almedina, 2017.

Alexy, Robert. *Teoría de los derechos fundamentales*. Madrid: Centro de Estudios Constitucionales, 1993.

Aragão, Alexandre Santos de. Princípio da legalidade e poder regulamentar no Estado contemporâneo. *Revista de Direito Administrativo*, v. 225, 2001, p. 109–130.

Barroso, Luís Roberto. *Interpretação e aplicação da Constituição: fundamentos de uma dogmática constitucional transformadora*. São Paulo: Saraiva, 2009, p. 131.

Bellia, Patricia L. Faithful execution and enforcement discretion. *University of Pennsylvania Law Review*, v. 164, 2015, p. 1.753–1.800.

60 German Constitutional Court. *Bundesverfassungsgericht - BVerfG, 2 BvR 1436/02, de 24.09.2003. Op. cit.*

61 *See* Brazilian Federal Supreme Court. ADI n. 1.969, Rel. Min. Ricardo Lewandowski, published on August 31, 2007.

62 Brazilian Federal Supreme Court. ADI n. 1.969, Rel. Min. Ricardo Lewandowski, published on August 31, 2007.

63 Osório, Fábio Medina. *Direito administrativo sancionador*. São Paulo: Revista dos Tribunais, 2019, p. 238–245.

Brandão, Rodrigo; Capecchi Nunes, Daniel. *Poder regulamentar e 'jogo duro constitucional': o caso dos decretos de armas. Jota.* July 10, 2019. Available at: https://www.jota.info/opiniao-e-analise/artigos/poder-regulamentar-e-jogo-duro-constitucional-o-caso-dos-decretos-de-armas-10072019.

Canotilho, José Joaquim Gomes. *Direito Constitucional e Teoria da Constituição*, 7. ed. Coimbra: Almedina, 2003, p. 1.276.

Crocker, T. P. Presidential power and constitutional responsibility. *Boston College Law Review*, n. 52, 2011, p. 1578–1579.

Cyrino, André Rodrigues. *O poder regulamentar autônomo do Presidente da República: a espécie regulamentar criada pela EC n. 32/2001.* Belo Horizonte: Fórum, 2005, p. 91.

Di Giovine, Alfonso et al. *Introduzione allo studio della riserva di legge nell'ordinamento costituzionale italiano.* Torino: G. Giappichelli, 1969, p. 65.

Miranda, Francisco Cavalcanti Pontes de. *Comentários à Constituição de 1946. VI*, 2. ed. Max Limonad: São Paulo, 1953, p. 411.

Moncada, Luís Cabral de. *Lei e regulamento.* Coimbra: Ed. Coimbra, 2002.

Novais, Jorge Reis. *As restrições aos Direitos Fundamentais não expressamente autorizadas pela Constituição.* Coimbra: Coimbra Editora, 2003.

Osório, Fábio Medina. Direito administrativo sancionador. *São Paulo, Revista dos Tribunais*, 2019, p. 238–245.

Pereira, Jane Reis Gonçalves. *Interpretação constitucional e direitos fundamentais.* São Paulo: Saraiva Educação, 2018.

Price, Zachary S. Enforcement discretion and executive duty. *Vanderbilt Law Review*, v. 67, 2014.

Pünder, Hermann. Democratic legitimation of delegated legislation: A comparative view on the American, British, and German law. *International & Comparative Law Quarterly*, v. 58, n. 2, 2009, p. 353–378.

Ráo, Vicente. *O direito e a vida dos direitos.* São Paulo: Editora Revista dos Tribunais, 1991, p. 354.

Schwabe, Jürgen. *Cincuenta años de jurisprudencia del Tribunal Constitucional Federal Alemán.* Translated by Marcela Anzola Gil. Colombia: Gustavo lbáiíez, 2003, p. 180.

Silva, Virgílio Afonso da. *Direitos fundamentais: Conteúdo essencial, restrições e eficácia.* São Paulo: Malheiros, 2009, p. 102.

Souza Neto, Cláudio Pereira de; Sarmento, Daniel. *Direito constitucional: teoria, história e métodos de trabalho.* Belo Horizonte: Fórum, 201, p. 336.

Staupe, Júrgen. *Parlamentsvorbehalt und Delegationsbefugnis – Zur "Wesentlichkeitstheorie" und zur Reichxveite legislativer Regelungskompetenz, insbesondere im Schulrecht.* Berlin: Duncker & Humblot, 1985, p. 24.

Voronoff, Alice. *Direito administrativo sancionador no Brasil.* Belo Horizonte: Fórum, 2018.

7 The legal responses to COVID-19 in Italy, Brazil, and Germany

Italy, Brazil, and Germany gave significantly different responses to the COVID-19 pandemic. In these countries, there was a gradation between the levels of involvement of the legislative and judicial branches in the fight against the emergency. In Italy, the participation of the other branches can be classified as a "weak-form review" since they exercised only a rare and weak oversight over executive actions.[1] The parliament, in practice, limited itself to converting the decree-laws, which in turn entrusted the adoption of containment measures to the prime ministers, without parliamentary scrutiny.[2] The Italian Constitutional Court, for its part, issued few rulings on the crisis and generally recognized the validity of the prime minister's decrees.[3]

In Brazil, the other branches of government played an intermediary role. The National Congress passed numerous laws specifically related to COVID-19 and formed a Parliamentary Inquiry Commission (CPI) to investigate allegations of corruption and omissions on the part of the federal executive, headed by then-president Jair Bolsonaro.[4] The Brazilian Supreme Court, for its part, has published thousands of decisions related to the pandemic, invalidating a series of executive acts that contradicted World Health Organization (WHO) guidelines. However, this intense judiciary and legislative oversight coexisted

1 Claudiani, Simona. Brevi Note Sui DPCM: Tra Emergenza e Stabilizzazione. In: Morana, Donatella; Mabellini, Stefania (Eds.). *L'emergenza pandemica e l'impatto sul diritto pubblico: innovazione e prospettive future. Quaderni del Dottorato di Ricerca in Diritto Pubblico dell'Università degli Studi di Roma "Tor Vergata"*. Milan: Wolters Kluwer, 2022, p. 69.

2 *See, e.g.*, Guzzetta, Giovanni. DPCM e Costituzione anche alla luce della sent. 198/2021 della Corte costituzionale. *Op. cit.*; Trabucco, Daniele. Il "virus" nel sistema delle fonti: decreti-legge e dpcm al tempo del Covid-19: tra principio di legalità formale e principio di legalità sostanziale. *Op. cit.*; Musella, Fortunato. I poteri di emergenza nella Repubblica dei Presidenti. *Op. cit.*; Cavino, Massimo et al. Covid-19. Una prima lettura dei provvedimenti adottati dal Governo, *Op. cit.*

3 *See* Italian Constitutional Court. *Sentenze* March 12, 2021, n. 37; January 14, 2021, n. 4; December 23, 2020, n. 278; November 24, 2020, n. 245.

4 Brazilian Federal Senate. *CPI da Pandemia: principais pontos do relatório.* Available at: https://www12.senado.leg.br/noticias/materias/2021/10/20/cpi-da-pandemia-principais-pontos-do-relatorio.

DOI: 10.4324/9781003610816-8

with the regulatory protagonism of local administrations, which issued thousands of decrees, ordinances, and regulations without a clear legal basis. Thus, considering that the other branches have not been silent, but, simultaneously, there has been a chaotic profusion of secondary legislation, Brazil can be considered an example of a "mid-term review" of executive actions.

Finally, in Germany, other political actors were constantly active and performed a "strong-form review". Federal and local legislators passed several anti-COVID laws, which were continually updated and rediscussed by parliamentarians. At the same time, the German Infectious Diseases Protection Act (IfSG),[5] as amended in November 2020, set clear and defined parameters for executive regulations, limiting the content, purpose, and scope of administrative acts. In the same vein, the German judiciary actively shaped the contours of what was permitted and prohibited during this period, ruling on several lawsuits that debated restrictions on rights.[6]

This chapter will analyze these three types of approaches to a crisis. From the outset, it should be noted that we defend the so-called strong-form review approach. As in Germany, which is the highest-ranked country in Europe for its COVID-19 response,[7] all institutional actors should be involved in the control of the executive branch. Administrators must have some discretion to manage emergencies, but always within a very clear and specific legal basis.

7.1 Italy: "weak-form review"

Italy[8] had one of the highest mortality rates from COVID-19 in Europe and was one of the first countries to introduce restrictive policies. The initial

5 *German Act on the prevention and control of infectious diseases in humans ("Gesetz zur Verhütung und Bekämpfung von Infektionskrankheiten beim Menschen")*. Available at: https://www.gesetze-im-internet.de/ifsg/index.html.

6 Kaiser, Anna-Bettina; Hensel, Roman. Federal Republic of Germany: Legal response to Covid-19. In: *The Oxford compendium of national legal responses to Covid-19*. May 2022. Available at: https://oxcon. ouplaw.com/view/https://doi.org/10.1093/law-occ19/law-occ19-e2; Kaiser, Anna-Bettina. The state of exception under German law and the current pandemic: Comparative models and constitutional rights. *e-Pública*, v. 7, n. 3, 2020, p. 4–15. *See also* German Federal Constitutional Court (Bundesverfassungsgericht). *Constitutional complaints (BvR) – 2020 to 2022*. Available at: https://www.bundesverfassungsgericht.de/SiteGlobals/Forms/Suche/EN/Entscheidungensuche_Formular.html?nn=5403310&facettedYear=2021&language_=en.

7 Euronews. *Germany is the highest-ranked country in Europe for its COVID-19 response, new survey reveals*. October 7, 2020. Available at: https://www.euronews.com/2020/10/07/germany-is-the-highest-ranked-country-in-europe-for-its-covid-19-response-new-survey-revea. *See also* ISGlobal (Barcelona Institute for Global Health). *COVID-19: Scientific updates*. Available at: https://www.isglobal.org/en/archivo-novedades-cientificas-covid19.

8 Italy is a parliamentary unitary republic. The parliament is bicameral and consists of the Chamber of Deputies and the Senate. Both chambers must approve the same text of each bill in order for it to become law. The president of the republic appoints the prime minister, also called the "President of the Council of Ministers", after consulting the parties in Parliament.

measures differed at local, regional, and national levels and were introduced so quickly and haphazardly that they created a "regulatory and legal chaos".[9] The pandemic was mainly managed through decrees of the president of the Council of Ministers (*Decreti del Presidente del Consiglio dei Ministri*, DPCM), a type of administrative act.[10] The centrality of this instrument reflected the eclipse of parliament, which in practice surrendered its normative power to the executive.

Indeed, Italian legal literature has noted with surprise and criticism the profound inertia of the national legislature during the pandemic, which (i) limited itself to converting decree-laws (*decreti-legge*)[11] and (ii) did not actively react to the adoption of containment measures through DPCMs, acts exempt from parliamentary scrutiny.[12] In practice, the legislature was a spectator to the combative actions of the executive. The central body of the democratic system

---

By convention, the president of the republic appoints ministers based on a proposal from the prime minister (Guzzetta, Giovanni; Marini, Francesco Saverio. *Diritto pubblico italiano ed europeo*. Torino: G Giappichelli Editore, 2022, *passim*).

9 Grogan, Joelle. Analyzing global use of emergency powers in response to COVID-19. *European Journal of Law Reform*, v. 4, 2020, p. 345; Matteucci, Stefano Civitarese et al. Italy: Legal response to Covid-19. In: *The Oxford compendium of national legal responses to Covid-19*. May 2022. Available at: https://oxcon.ouplaw.com/display/10.1093/law-occ19/law-occ19-e11; Beqiraj, Julinda. Italy's Coronavirus legislative response: Adjusting along the way. *Verfassungsblog*. April 8, 2020. Available at: https://verfassungsblog.de/italys-coronavirus-legislative- response-adjusting-along-the-way/.

10 The legal nature of DPCMs is the subject of extensive debate in Italy, which will be explored later. For now, it should be noted that the Italian Constitutional Court has classified them as a type of administrative act endowed with generality and abstraction. *See* Italian Constitutional Court. *Sentenza* n. 198/2021, published in October 27, 2021; Italian Constitutional Court. *Sentenza* n. 2831, published on May 4, 2020.

11 The legislative delegation in Italy was made by decree-laws, legislative acts for times of urgency and necessity, which have the force of law and are considered primary legislation. *See* article 77 of the Constitution of the Italian Republic:

> The Government may not, without an enabling act from the Houses, issue decrees having the force of ordinary law. When in extraordinary cases of necessity and urgency the Government adopts provisional measures having the force of law, it must on the same day present said measures for confirmation to the Houses which, even if dissolved, shall be summoned especially for this purpose and shall convene within five days. The decrees lose effect from their inception if they are not confirmed within sixty days from their publication. The Houses may however regulate by law legal relationships arising out of not confirmed decrees.

12 Guzzetta, Giovanni. DPCM e Costituzione anche alla luce della sent. 198/2021 della Corte costituzionale. *Op. cit.*; Guzzetta, Giovanni. Le fonti dell'emergenza alla prova della pandemia. *Op. cit.*; Trabucco, Daniele. Il "virus" nel sistema delle fonti: decreti-legge e dpcm al tempo del Covid-19: tra principio di legalità formale e principio di legalità sostanziale. *Op. cit.*; Musella, Fortunato. I poteri di emergenza nella Repubblica dei Presidenti. *Op. cit.*; Cavino, Massimo et al. Covid-19. Una prima lettura dei provvedimenti adottati dal Governo. *Op. cit.*; Claudiani, Simona. Brevi Note Sui DPCM: Tra Emergenza e Stabilizzazione, In: Morana, Donatella; Mabellini, Stefania (Eds.). *L'emergenza pandemica e l'impatto sul diritto pubblico: innovazione e prospettive future. Quaderni del Dottorato di Ricerca in Diritto Pubblico dell'Università degli Studi di Roma "Tor Vergata"*. Milan: Wolters Kluwer, 2022, p. 70.

didn't even meet on a weekly basis to discuss the impact of the pandemic; in March 2020, when the number of COVID-19 cases increased exponentially in Italy, plenary sessions were convened only twice a month.[13]

These prime minister's decrees (DPCMs) are not governed by a uniform legal discipline or classification.[14] Before the pandemic, they focused mainly on bureaucratic issues, generally aimed at disciplining internal sectors of the public administration. Part of the Italian doctrine considered them as a kind of secondary normative source.[15-16] Another strand, endorsed by the Italian Constitutional Court, argued that such decrees are a type of administrative act endowed with generality and abstraction.[17] The legal basis of the anti-COVID DPCMs was exclusively based on decree-laws adopted during the emergency itself: the Decree-Law n. 6 of February 23, 2020, and Decree-Law n. 19 of March 25, 2020. These acts, which have the force of primary law, gave the prime minister the power to create, modify, and extinguish subjective legal relations. They also (i) set out the possible measures that a DPCM could adopt

13 In March, November, and December 2020, the full Chamber of Deputies of Italy met only twice a month. In March 2020, when the number of Covid-19 cases increased exponentially, the entire Chamber of Deputies met only on March 5 and March 25, 2020. Despite knowing the difficulties of adapting to the telematic environment, this number of meetings is insufficient in the face of a crisis as serious as the pandemic. Available at: https://www.camera.it/leg18/76. Romanelli, Rinaldo. Costituzione calpestata dai DPCM di Conte, uomo solo al comando. *Il Riformista*, March 31, 2020. Available at: https://www.ilriformista.it/costituzione-calpestata-dai-dpcm-di-conte-uomo-solo-al-comando-72541/?refresh_ce; Open Polis. *Coronavirus, il parlamento è il grande assente*. September 9, 2020. Available at: https://www.openpolis.it/coronavirus-il-parlamento-e-il-grande-assente/.

14 On the "*Decreto del Presidente del Consiglio dei Ministri DPCM*", *see* Labriola, Silvano. Decreto del Presidente del Consiglio. *Enciclopedia del diritto*, v. 11, 1988, p. 281; Luciani, Massimo et al. Il sistema delle fonti del diritto alla prova dell'emergenza. *Rivista Aic*, n. 2, 2020, p. 109–141; Morbidelli, Giuseppe et al. Delle ordinanze libere a natura normativa. *Diritto amministrativo*, v. 24, n. 1–2, 2016, p. 33–70.

15 *See* Luciani, Massimo et al. Il sistema delle fonti del diritto alla prova dell'emergenza. *Rivista Aic*, v. 2020, n. 2, 2020, p. 109–141; Guzzetta, Giovanni. DPCM e Costituzione anche alla luce della sent. 198/2021 della Corte costituzionale. *Op. cit.*

16 In that sense, the DPCMs would be comparable to the ministerial decrees provided for in article 17, paragraph 3, of the law of August 23, 1988, n. 400, which states: "Regulations may be adopted by ministerial decree in matters that fall within the competence of the minister or of authorities subordinate to the minister, when the law expressly confers such power (. . .)" Law of August 23, 1988, n. 400. In the original: Art. 17 (Regolamenti) (. . .) 3. By ministerial decree, regulations may be adopted on matters

> within the minister's competence or that of authorities subordinate to the minister, when the law expressly confers such power. Such regulations, for matters falling within the competence of more ministers, may be adopted with inter-ministerial decrees, leaving the need for the necessary authorization from the law. Ministerial and inter-ministerial regulations cannot contain rules contrary to those of the regulations issued by the Government. They must be communicated to the President of the Council of Ministers before they are issued (. . .).

17 Italian Constitutional Court. *Sentenza* n. 198/2021, published on October 27, 2021; Italian Constitutional Court. *Sentenza* II, May 4, 2020, n. 2831.

during the pandemic and (ii) defined the process for the creation of a DPCM, establishing the obligation of prior consultation of the relevant ministers and regional governments.

In particular, article 1 of Decree-Law n. 19/2020 provided for a list of 31 possible and different "contents" of DPCMs, which could cover a very wide range of legal situations and impose restrictions on fundamental freedoms of movement, assembly, religion expression, and so on. In other words, the scope of DPCMs was significantly expanded during the pandemic, which is a highly questionable fact from the perspective of democratic legitimacy and the principle of legality.

Against this background, the next section will try to answer the following questions: is the frequent use of premier's decrees to deal with an emergency constitutional? Is this instrument adequate and appropriate for the objectives pursued? Is it constitutionally acceptable for a decree-law to delegate so many powers to the prime minister?[18]

7.1.1 *Criticism of the use of prime minister's decrees (DPCM) during the pandemic: violation of the principle of legality and the democratic principle*

The centrality of the prime minister's decrees during the COVID-19 crisis has provoked great criticism because the DPCMs do not represent a primary normative source. These acts were the product of an excessively vague and imprecise legislative delegation.[19] Critics rightly claim that the principle of legality established in Article 13 of the Italian Constitution has not been respected.[20] In light of this perspective, several regional courts have declared the DPCMs illegal and ruled that they should not be applied because of the violation of

18 Italian Constitutional Court. *Sentenza* II, May 4, 2020, n. 2831, p. 16.

19 Guzzetta, Giovanni. DPCM e Costituzione anche alla luce della sent. 198/2021 della Corte costituzionale. *Op. cit.*; Guzzetta, Giovanni. *Le fonti dell'emergenza alla prova della pandemia. Op. cit.*, p. 74; Cavino, Massimo et al. Covid-19. Una prima lettura dei provvedimenti adottati dal Governo. *Op. cit.*, p. 9; Clementi, Francesco et al. Il lascito della gestione normativa dell'emergenza: tre riforme ormai ineludibili. *Osservatorio costituzionale*, n. 3, 2020, p. 1–15.

20 Constitution of the Italian Republic.

> Art. 13 Personal liberty is inviolable. No one may be detained, inspected, or searched nor otherwise subjected to any restriction of personal liberty except by order of the Judiciary stating a reason and only in such cases and in such manner as provided by the law. In exceptional circumstances and under such conditions of necessity and urgency as shall conclusively be defined by the law, the police may take provisional measures that shall be referred within 48 hours to the Judiciary for validation and which, in default of such validation in the following 48 hours, shall be revoked and considered null and void. Any act of physical and moral violence against a person subjected to restriction of personal liberty shall be punished. The law shall establish the maximum duration of preventive detention.

the principle of the rule of law.[21] Among the various legal deficiencies, courts claimed that the delegating primary legislation (i.e., the decree-laws) did not sufficiently specify the conditions, scope, content, and purpose of the DPCMs.

Professors such as Giovanni Guzzetta,[22] Fortunato Musella,[23] and Massimo Cavino[24] published articles arguing that these prime minister's decrees are not the correct and legitimate instrument for dealing with emergencies. In their view, the Italian Constitution has identified the "decree-laws" as the primary normative source for such moments of urgency and necessity. Article 76 of the Italian Constitution establishes that "the exercise of the legislative function cannot be delegated to the Government except with the determination of directive principles and criteria and only for a limited time and for defined subjects".[25] In the same vein, article 77 states that "the Government may not, without delegation from the Chambers, issue decrees that have the effect of ordinary law". The government may adopt decree-laws "only in extraordinary cases of necessity and urgency" and must present them "on the same day for conversion to the Chambers".[26] Thus, any crisis that cannot be subsumed under the special cases provided for in articles 78, 87, and 126 of the Italian Constitution[27] (i.e., war aggression or a regional emergency) should be

21 Italy. Tribunale di Reggio Emilia. Sentenza 27 gennaio 2021, n. 54; Tribunale di Pisa. Sentenza 17 marzo 2021, n. 419. *See also* Claudiani, Simona. Brevi Note Sui DPCM: Tra Emergenza e Stabilizzazione, *Op. cit.*, p. 67.

22 Guzzetta, Giovanni. DPCM e Costituzione anche alla luce della sent. 198/2021 della Corte costituzionale. *Op. cit.*; Guzzetta, Giovanni. *Le fonti dell'emergenza alla prova della pandemia. Op. cit.*, p. 74.

23 Musella, Fortunato. I poteri di emergenza nella Repubblica dei Presidenti. *Op. cit.*

24 Cavino, Massimo et al. Covid-19. Una prima lettura dei provvedimenti adottati dal Governo. *Op. cit.*

25 Constitution of the Italian Republic. In the original, "*Articolo 76. L'esercizio della funzione legislativa non può essere delegato [cfr. art. 72 c. 4] al Governo se non con determinazione di principi e criteri direttivi e soltanto per tempo limitato e per oggetti definiti*".

26 Constitution of the Italian Republic. In the original,

> Articolo 77. Il Governo non può, senza delegazione delle Camere [cfr. art. 76], emanare decreti che abbiano valore di legge ordinaria. Quando, in casi straordinari di necessità e di urgenza, il Governo adotta, sotto la sua responsabilità, provvedimenti provvisori con forza di legge, deve il giorno stesso presentarli per la conversione alle Camere che, anche se sciolte, sono appositamente convocate e si riuniscono entro cinque giorni [cfr. artt. 61 c. 2, 62 c. 2]. I decreti perdono efficacia sin dall'inizio, se non sono convertiti in legge entro sessanta giorni dalla loro pubblicazione. Le Camere possono tuttavia regolare con legge i rapporti giuridici sorti sulla base dei decreti non convertiti.

27 Constitution of the Italian Republic.

> Art. 78 Parliament has the authority to declare a state of war and vest the necessary powers into the Government;Art. 87 The President of the Republic is the Head of the State and represents national unity. The President may send messages to Parliament. (. . .) The President is the commander-in-chief of the armed forces, shall preside over the Supreme Council of Defence established by law, and shall make

included in the prescriptive scope of article 77 of the Constitution and then be addressed by the executive branch only through decree-laws.

These instruments have no spatial or temporal limits and can be used for situations that persist over time, in particular when the circumstances that justified the initial intervention are subsequently aggravated.[28] Such legislation would, therefore, be perfectly suited to the efforts to combat the COVID-19 pandemic, which required a rapid and flexible response from the government.

7.1.2 Prime minister's decrees (DPCMs) versus decree-laws

Despite these criticisms, one could argue that there are justifications that theoretically support the use of DPCMs to manage crises. The COVID-19 emergency would have been so urgent that even decree-laws would not have been fast enough to deal with it. The government needed an even quicker tool. It would also have been difficult to convene the Italian legislature, which has not been quick to embrace digital tools as an alternative to the traditional legislative process based on physical presence.[29] Furthermore, DPCMs could be considered an alternative source of legislation for crisis scenarios. From this point of view, article 77 of the Italian Constitution, which provides for the possibility of issuing decree-laws in cases of urgency and necessity, would not be an exhaustive list, but only an exemplary one.[30]

> declarations of war as have been agreed by Parliament. The President shall preside over the High Council of the Judiciary. The President may grant pardons and commute punishments. The President shall confer the honorary distinctions of the Republic; Art. 126 The Regional Council may be dissolved and the President of the Executive may be removed with a reasoned decree of the President of the Republic in the case of acts in contrast with the Constitution or grave violations of the law. The dissolution or removal may also be decided for reasons of national security. Such decree is adopted after consultation with a committee of Deputies and Senators for regional affairs which is set up in the manner established by a law of the Republic. The Regional Council may adopt a reasoned motion of no confidence against the President of the Executive that is undersigned by at least one-fifth of its members and adopted by roll call vote with an absolute majority of members. The motion may not be debated before three days have elapsed since its introduction. The adoption of a no confidence motion against a President of the Executive elected by universal and direct suffrage, and the removal, permanent inability, death or voluntary resignation of the President of the Executive entail the resignation of the Executive and the dissolution of the Council. The same effects are produced by the simultaneous resignation of the majority of the Council members.

28 Guzzetta, Giovanni. DPCM e Costituzione anche alla luce della sent. 198/2021 della Corte costituzionale. *Op. cit.*, p. 19.

29 Lupo, Nicola et al. Come evitare l'auto-emarginazione del Parlamento nell'emergenza attuale. *Osservatorio Costituzionale*, n. 6, 2020, p. 7–28; Bar-Siman-Tov, Ittai. Legislatures in the time of Covid-19. *The Theory and Practice of Legislation*, v. 8, n. 1–2, 2020, p. 8.

30 Constitution of the Italian Republic.

> Art. 77 The Government may not, without an enabling act from the Houses, issue a decree having force of law. When the Government, in case of necessity and urgency, adopts under its own responsibility a temporary measure, it shall introduce such measure to Parliament

This book, however, argues that these arguments are not compatible with a textual, teleological, systematic, and historical interpretation of the Italian Constitution. If the Constitution had not considered decree-laws to be quick enough, it would have expressly provided for an even quicker solution. Decree-laws have a special nature and have been singled out as the unique normative source reserved for the executive in times of emergency. In practice, the procedure established for the DPCMs issued during the pandemic was highly complex, and it is not possible to say that they were approved extremely quickly or easily. DPCMs required the approval of the prime minister on the proposal of the minister of health after hearing the minister of the interior, the minister of defense, the minister of economy and finance, and other relevant ministers.[31] Moreover, telematic channels that allowed for virtual meetings of the Council of Ministers could have been used to quickly discuss and approve decree-laws.

Finally, the ultimate justification for this very broad delegation of normative power to the executive would be the need for technical and scientific discretion. As already explored, some argue that the executive has more *expertise* and technical capacity in certain areas, such as public health. In this perspective, only the prime minister and the minister of health could know the best measures to control the virus.

Nevertheless, we argue that experts should always work both in the executive and legislative branches, assisting not only the enactment of administrative regulations but also actively participating in the shape of the content of primary legislation. Scientific reports indicating, for example, the level of contamination that justifies a complete lockdown should also be distributed to parliamentarians – especially those responsible for drafting the laws that will be discussed in the plenary sessions. During COVID-19, it was not only the cabinet or Council of Ministers that should have been supported by experts in infectious diseases, microbiology, and pandemic management – but also the parliament itself, especially through its committees. The importance of parliamentary involvement requires that experts in these fields also help the legislators to pass laws based on scientific data.

In this scenario, Giovanni Guzzetta lists at least six constitutional advantages of using decree-laws over DPCMs. The decree-law (i) is expressly provided for in the Constitution for emergencies; (ii) is a collegial act of the Council of Ministers; (iii) is subject to parliamentary control at the time of its conversion into a law and eventually amended; (iv) involves the participation of the president of the republic, formally allowing the head of state to exercise

for transposition into law. During dissolution, Parliament shall be convened within five days of such introduction. 20 Such a measure shall lose effect from the beginning if it is not transposed into law by Parliament within sixty days of its publication. Parliament may regulate the legal relations arisen from the rejected measure.

31 Italy. *Decree-Law 25 of March 2020, n. 19 (Decreto-Legge 25 marzo 2020, n. 19)*. Available at: https://faolex.fao.org/docs/pdf/ita194206.pdf.

the interim control granted to him by the Constitution; (v) can be submitted to citizen control by means of a referendum; and (vi) can be submitted to the Constitutional Court for abstract judicial review.[32]

In its turn, the prime minister's decrees are not subject to control by the president of the republic or the parliament, and do not even require formal approval by the entire Council of Ministers. There is no control by different institutional sources, which increases the risk of authoritarian deviations and disproportionate suppression of fundamental freedoms. In short, unilateral acts such as DPCMs should be rare and punctual exceptions to the broad and intensive normative production of the legislature. One-man rule should often be avoided, especially in times of crisis.

7.1.3 Is the broad delegation of normative power to the Italian prime minister constitutional?

In theory, prime minister's decrees should be hierarchically subordinate to the primary legislation from which they extract their basis of validity. But, during the pandemic, the relationship between the DPCMs and their legal basis, the Decree-Law n. 6 of February 23, 2020, and the Decree-Law n. 19 of March 25, 2020, did not follow the principles of a typical delegation. There was an extremely broad delegation – almost a "blank check"[33] – with the use of undetermined legal terms that did not detail the limits of regulatory activity. When the Italian primary legislator was supposed to create legal certainty and a minimum of predictability for a crisis situation, it simply transferred a very broad normative power to the prime minister. All this in a scenario of extreme instability, complexity, and difficult choices.

As mentioned, the decree-laws listed a number of measures that could be taken to fight the pandemic. These measures ranged from a complete lockdown to a curfew. The decision was left to the discretion of the prime minister, after consulting the relevant ministers. There was no legal requirement as to "when" or "why" one or the other restrictive measure should be taken.[34]

32 Guzzetta, Giovanni. DPCM e Costituzione anche alla luce della sent. 198/2021 della Corte costituzionale. *Op. cit.*, *passim*. *See also* Zagrebelsky, Gustavo et al. *La Giustizia costituzionale. I. Storia, principi, interpretazioni*. Imola: Il mulino, 2018, p. 101–108; Mortati, Costantino. *Istituzioni di diritto pubblico*. Padova: Cedam, Tomos 1 e 2, 1976, p. 700–715; Paladin, Livio. *Diritto Costituzionale*. Padova: Cedam, 1995, p. 191–195.

33 The delegation of legislative authority should not be "blank", that is, unaccompanied by mandatory parameters, standards, and guidelines established by the legislature in the primary delegating law. *See* Marchetti, Gloria et al. *La delegazione legislativa tra Parlamento e Governo: studio sulle recenti trasformazioni del modello costituzionale*. Milano: Giuffrè, 2016, *passim* and Coglianese, Cary. Dimensions of delegation. *University of Pennsylvania Law Review*, v. 167, n. 7, 2019, p. 1849–1889.

34 Decree-Law 25 of March 2020, n. 19 ("*Decreto-Legge Marzo 25, 2020, n. 19*").

> Emergency measures to prevent the spread of COVID-19 1. In order to contain and counteract the health risks arising from the spread of the COVID-19 virus in certain parts of the national territory or, if necessary, in the entire national territory, one or more of the

For example, there were no general parameters, criteria, or guidelines in the decree-law that could justify the adoption of a complete lockdown. The prime minister had a bouquet of solutions at his disposal and a very wide power of choice, being able to choose the alternative that he considered the most "adequate and proportional".[35]

In times of crisis, it is questionable whether the president of the Council should have such powers to decide how to intervene without a clearly defined legal framework. Especially in scenarios of technical unpredictability, it is hard to decide which measure is appropriate for each moment or stage of the emergency. Leaving so much power in the hands of the chief executive alone could be extremely risky and harmful to the democratic system and also to the crisis response. Parliament cannot delegate to a secondary source the decisions that it is supposed to make. In the words of Giovanni Guzzetta, "Transferring from the primary act to the secondary act the function of fulfilling the legal requirements circumvents the logic of the system".[36]

Fortunately, during the pandemic, the Italian Council of Ministers was presided over by politicians who respected the opinion of experts on the subject and were committed to enforce restrictive measures. In theory, however, the prime minister could have been a denialist politician who would always take

---

measures listed in paragraph 2 may be adopted, in accordance with the provisions of this Decree, for predetermined periods of no more than thirty days each, which may be repeated and modified several times until July 31, 2020, the end of the state of emergency declared by the resolution of the Council of Ministers of January 31, 2020, with the possibility of modulating its application upwards or downwards according to the epidemiological evolution of the said virus. 2. Pursuant to and for the purposes of paragraph 1, one or more of the following measures may be adopted, in accordance with the principles of adequacy and proportionality to the actual risk in certain parts of the national territory or in the entire national territory (a) restriction of the movement of persons, including by providing for limitations on the possibility of moving away from one's residence, domicile, or abode except for individual movements limited in time and space or motivated by work requirements, situations of necessity or urgency, health reasons, or other specific reasons; (b) closure to the public of urban roads, parks, playgrounds, villas and public gardens, or other public spaces; (. . .) 3. For the duration of the emergency referred to in paragraph 1, may be imposed the performance of activities not subject to suspension as a result of the application of measures referred to in this article, where this is absolutely necessary to ensure its effectiveness and public utility, by order of the prefect taken after hearing, without formality, the social partners concerned.

35 Decree-Law 25 of March 2020, n. 19 ("*Decreto-Legge Marzo 25, 2020, n. 19*").

Emergency measures to prevent the spread of COVID-19 1. In order to contain and counteract the health risks arising from the spread of the COVID-19 virus in certain parts of the national territory or, if necessary, in the entire national territory, one or more of the measures listed in paragraph 2 may be adopted, in accordance with the provisions of this Decree, (. . .). 2. Pursuant to and for the purposes of paragraph 1, one or more of the following measures may be adopted, in accordance with the principles of adequacy and proportionality to the actual risk in certain parts of the national territory or in the entire national territory.

36 Guzzetta, Giovanni. DPCM e Costituzione anche alla luce della sent. 198/2021 della Corte costituzionale. *Op. cit.*, p. 24.

the most lenient of the measures listed in the decree-law. In other words, the premier could have taken extremely soft measures, even in the face of a high level of contamination, without ever imposing any kind of curfew or lockdown, which have proven to be essential in the pandemic. Without a framework or well-defined normative limits in the delegating law, the executive's discretion becomes very broad, with serious risks for public safety and also for the constitutional system.[37]

In addition to the weak legal basis, the use of DPCMs during the pandemic has been also criticized for deficiencies in the deliberative process. The monocratic and non-collegial nature of this instrument is reprehensible in light of the importance of democratic deliberation. As already mentioned, the participation of parliament in important decisions is not a mere formality: the legislature is the place that best reflects the different political forces in society. Its debates between different parties bring together plural points of view, which enriches the formulation of solutions, even and especially in times of crisis. Emergencies should not be an excuse to create an administrative leviathan. They do not justify a radical transfer of normative power from the legislature to the executive. In the future, crises must be addressed by collegial, pluralistic bodies, not by the pen of the chief executive.

Finally, it is important to emphasize that, during the pandemic, the premier's decrees were reinterpreted to have a broader scope. Previously, DPCMs focused on eminently administrative issues with an organizational scope within the administrative bureaucracy. But since 2020, they have been used to impose restrictions on the essential core of fundamental rights, far beyond the boundaries of public administration. All this without a solid constitutional or legal basis. For this reason, DPCMs can be included in the typology of "paraconstitutional initiatives", presented by Matthew Shugart and John M. Carey, which refers to "decrees of purely presidential initiative that are not clearly delineated in the Constitution".[38]

At this point, it is important to give an example of the wide areas of incidence of these acts. On February 23, 2020, a DPCM established restrictions on freedom of movement and banned any form of assembly in 11 municipalities in two northern regions (Lombardy and Veneto). Two weeks later, on March 8, the premier extended these measures to the entire region of Lombardy and to 14 municipalities in three northern and central regions (Emilia-Romagna, Piedmont, and Marche). The sudden escalation of the virus led then-premier Giuseppe Conte to issue a new DPCM on March 9, 2020, establishing a nationwide lockdown. Two days later, the DPCM of March 11, 2020, specified which essential services and strategic industrial sectors could

37 Guzzetta, Giovanni. DPCM e Costituzione anche alla luce della sent. 198/2021 della Corte costituzionale. *Op. cit.*

38 Carey, John M.; Shugart, Matthew Soberg. Calling out the tanks or filling out the forms? In: Carey, John M.; Shugart, Matthew Soberg (Org.). *Executive decree authority*. Cambridge: Cambridge University Press, 1998, p. 1–29.

remain open during the lockdown. Until the end of 2021, dozens of these decrees introduced or modified other measures, always unilaterally and without parliamentary control.[39]

7.1.4 Criticism of the decision of the Italian Constitutional Court n. 198 of October 22, 2021

In the first year of the pandemic, the Italian Constitutional Court did not hear the merits of the cases brought against the prime minister's decrees related to anti-COVID measures. It was not until October 2021, with the *Sentenza* n. 198, that the constitutionality of the DPCMs was examined.[40] The case was originally brought against a fine of 400 euros imposed on a citizen for failing to comply with the ban – imposed by a prime minister's decree – on leaving home without a valid reason. According to the local judge, the penalty imposed was the final product of a flawed chain of legislative delegation carried out by a decree-law in favor of "mere administrative acts" of the government. In his opinion, the interlocution between the decree-law and the DPCM had violated the principle of typicality of primary sources of law.

When the case reached the Italian Constitutional Court, it classified the DPCMs as administrative acts, stating that their role was limited to the implementation of laws that anticipate their content. The Court distinguished these acts from *ordinanze di necessità* (ordinances of necessity), which "are capable of assuming different contents in order to adapt to changing situations".[41] According to the decision, the DPCMs (i) respected the typology of measures listed in the Decree-Law n. 19/2020 and (ii) followed the criteria and guidelines established by the decree-law. The Court found that the DPCMs had complied with the "principles of adequacy and proportionality to the actual risk in certain parts of the national territory or throughout the country", a requirement laid down in article 1(2) of D.L. n. 19/2020. Thus, the prime minister simply gave effect to the primary legislation "by means of sufficiently specific administrative acts".[42]

39 Rullo, Luigi. The COVID-19 pandemic crisis and the personalization of the government in Italy. *International Journal of Public Leadership*, v. 17, n. 2, 2021, p. 199.

40 Corte Costituzionale italiana (Italian Constitutional Court). *Sentenza n. 198 of October 22, 2021*. Available at: https://www.cortecostituzionale.it/actionSchedaPronuncia.do?anno=2021&numero=198.

41 Corte Costituzionale italiana (Italian Constitutional Court). *Sentenza n. 198 of October 22, 2021*. Available at: https://www.cortecostituzionale.it/actionSchedaPronuncia.do?anno=2021&numero=198. Specifically on *ordinanze di necessità*, *see* Morrone, Andrea. Le ordinanze di necessità e urgenza, tra storia e diritto. In: Vignudelli, Aljs (Ed.). *Istituzioni e dinamiche del diritto. I confini mobili della separazione dei poteri*. Milan: Giuffrè, 2009, p. 133–184.

42 Corte Costituzionale italiana (Italian Constitutional Court). *Sentenza n. 198 of October 22, 2021*. Available at: https://www.cortecostituzionale.it/actionSchedaPronuncia.do?anno=2021&numero=198.

Based on these arguments, the Italian Constitutional Court ruled that the DPCMs issued during the pandemic were valid and in conformity with the constitutional system, since they drew their source of validity from a primary rule with the force of law – the decree-laws. In the Court's view, the essential decisions regarding crisis management were already determined by these primary rules, so that the DPCMs only served to give them applicability. The decrees issued by the president of the Council were then created within a fixed normative framework and could not go beyond its limits. According to the ruling, the primary legislative source had already listed the measures to be applied in the fight against the emergency, and it was up to the DPCMs to determine, moment by moment and place by place, those that were most necessary and effective. Therefore,

> Decree-Law n. 19 of 2020, far from conferring legislative power on the President of the Council of Ministers, in violation of Articles 76 and 77 of the Constitution, only authorizes him to implement the specific measures established in the Decree-Law.[43]

In this context, several questions arise: can the mere expression "principles of adequacy and proportionality to the actual risk in certain parts of the national territory or in the whole country", as stated in Decree-Law n. 19/2020, be considered a sufficient parameter for legislative delegation? In other words, are "principles of adequacy and proportionality" sufficient elements to recognize the minimum legal basis required by the principle of substantive legality? Or are they too imprecise, vague, and general guidelines? Can a law of such low normative density allow core restrictions on fundamental rights by executive acts?

In effect, it is surprising that the Italian Constitutional Court considered such a vague and imprecise criterion as sufficient to meet the requirements of normative delegation. As mentioned earlier, Decree-Law n. 19/2020 provided for a variety of possible "adequate and proportionate" measures without defining the level of risk to be addressed by each of them. The delegation was characterized by an excessive degree of vagueness, attributable not only to the use of generic terms but also to the absence of a clear definition of the type and level of risk associated with each measure.

In contrast, the legislative delegations that occurred in Germany during the COVID-19 pandemic anticipated the specific scope and purpose of restrictive measures. The power of choice was not openly delegated to the executive. The German Infectious Diseases Protection Act (Infektionsschutzgesetz, IfSG) served as the base law for acts restricting fundamental rights during the emergency. After listing all the possible measures, from lockdowns to the obligation

43 Corte Costituzionale italiana (Italian Constitutional Court). *Sentenza n. 198 of October 22, 2021. Op. cit.*

to wear masks, the section 5, § 28a of the Infectious Diseases Act established detailed parameters to guide the executive in applying the restrictions. It specified that "protective measures shall be taken considering the respective regional and supra-regional incidence of infection with the aim of avoiding an imminent overload of regional and supra-regional inpatient care".[44] The Infectious Diseases Act, a law with a clearly high normative density, even described in detail how to obtain data on the contamination rate. In a long paragraph, which is worth transcribing here, the German legislator provided clear details for the administrative measures:

German Infectious Diseases Protection Act (Infektionsschutzgesetz, IfSG)

Section 5, § 28a. Special protective measures to prevent the spread of coronavirus disease 2019 (COVID-19) in the event of an epidemic situation of national significance.

(1) Necessary protective measures within the meaning of Section 28 (1) sentences 1 and 2 to prevent the spread of the coronavirus disease 2019 (COVID-19) may, in particular, be the following for the duration of the declaration of an epidemic situation of national significance pursuant to Section 5 (1) sentence 1 by the German Bundestag:

1. Arrangement of a distance requirement in public spaces,
2. Obligation to wear a mouth-nose cover (mask obligation),

(. . .)

(3) Decisions on protective measures to prevent the spread of coronavirus disease 2019 (COVID-19) (. . .) shall be based in particular on the protection of life and health and the functioning of the health care system; foreseeable changes in the incidence of infection due to more contagious virus variants that place a greater

44 Gesetz zur Verhütung und Bekämpfung von Infektionskrankheiten beim Menschen (Act on the Prevention and Control of Infectious Diseases in Humans). In original:

(. . .) Wesentlicher Maßstab für die weitergehenden Schutzmaßnahmen ist insbesondere die Anzahl der in Bezug auf die Coronavirus-Krankheit-2019 (COVID-19) in ein Krankenhaus aufgenommenen Personen je 100 000 Einwohner innerhalb von sieben Tagen. Weitere Indikatoren wie die unter infektionsepidemiologischen Aspekten differenzierte Anzahl der Neuinfektionen mit dem Coronavirus SARS-CoV-2 je 100 000 Einwohner innerhalb von sieben Tagen, die verfügbaren intensivmedizinischen Behandlungskapazitäten und die Anzahl der gegen die Coronavirus-Krankheit-2019 (COVID-19) geimpften Personen sollen bei der Bewertung des Infektionsgeschehens berücksichtigt werden. Die Landesregierungen können im Rahmen der Festlegung der Schutzmaßnahmen unter Berücksichtigung der jeweiligen stationären Versorgungskapazitäten in einer Rechtsverordnung nach § 32 Schwellenwerte für die Indikatoren nach den Sätzen 4 und 5 festsetzen; entsprechend können die Schutzmaßnahmen innerhalb eines Landes regional differenziert werden (. . .).

Available at: https://www.gesetze-im-internet.de/ifsg/index.html.

> burden on the health care system shall be taken into account. In particular, the protective measures referred to in points 1, 2, 3, 5, and 18 of paragraph 1 may be taken to prevent infection. Further, protective measures shall be taken considering the respective regional and supra-regional incidence of infection with the aim of avoiding an imminent overload of regional and supra-regional inpatient care. The main indicator for further protective measures is the number of cases of coronavirus disease 2019 (COVID-19) per 100,000 population hospitalized within seven days. Other indicators, such as the number of new SARS-CoV-2 coronavirus infections per 100,000 population within seven days, differentiated according to aspects of the epidemiology of the infection, the available intensive care capacity, and the number of persons vaccinated against coronavirus disease 2019 (COVID-19), should be taken into account when assessing the incidence of infection. When determining the protective measures, the Land governments may set threshold values for the indicators pursuant to sentences 4 and 5 in an ordinance pursuant to § 32, taking into account the respective inpatient treatment capacities; accordingly, the protective measures may be differentiated regionally within a Land. The Robert Koch Institute shall publish on the Internet at https://www.rki.de/ covid-19-trends daily data on the indicators pursuant to sentences 4 and 5, broken down by age group and relating at least to individual Länder and to the territory of the Federal Republic of Germany. The Länder may also use the indicators pursuant to sentences 4 and 5 as a benchmark for the Land or the respective region instead of in relation to 100,000 inhabitants, differentiated by Land or region (. . .).[45]

All these details differ significantly from the text of the Italian Decree-Law n. 19 of March 25, 2020, which has a low normative density:

> (. . .) 1. To contain and counteract the health risks posed by the COVID-19 virus in certain parts of the national territory, or the entire parts of the national territory or, if necessary, in the entire national territory, one or more in accordance with the provisions of this Decree, one or more of the measures one or more of the measures referred to in paragraph 2, for predetermined periods of no more than thirty days each, which may be repeated and modified and may be modified several times until July 31, 2020, the date on which the end of the state of emergency

45 *German Act on the prevention and control of infectious diseases in humans (Gesetz zur Verhütung und Bekämpfung von Infektionskrankheiten beim Menschen - Infektionsschutzgesetz - IfSG).* Available at: https://www.gesetze-im-internet.de/ifsg/index.html.

declared by resolution of the Council of Ministers on of January 31, 2020, and with the possibility of modulating its application according to the epidemiological evolution of the said virus.

2. Pursuant to and for the purposes of paragraph 1, one or more of the following measures may be adopted, in accordance with the principles of adequacy and proportionality to the actual risk in certain parts of the national territory or in the entire national territory (a) restriction of the movement of persons, including by providing for limitations on the possibility of moving away from one's residence, domicile, or abode except for individual movements limited in time and space or motivated by work requirements, situations of necessity or urgency, health reasons, or other specific reasons; b) the closure to the public of urban streets, parks, playgrounds, villas and public gardens or other public places; c) the restriction or prohibition of entry and exit to and from municipal, provincial, regional and national territory; d) the application of precautionary quarantine measures to persons who have been in close contact with confirmed cases of the contagious and contagious spreading disease or who return from areas outside the Italian territory; (. . .) For technical and scientific aspects, as well as to assess adequacy and proportionality, the procedures referred to in this subparagraph will be generally adopted only after consultation with the Scientific Technical Committee (*il comitato tecnico scientifico*) referred to in the ordinance by the Head of the Civil Protection Department of 3 February 2020, n. 630.[46]

As noted in the previous chapters, the legislatures should not permit the exercise of administrative regulatory power based on vague parameters. Substantive legality does not tolerate such uncertainty, since excessive openness allows for decisions based on mere political will. As already mentioned, in the Italian case, former prime ministers Giuseppe Conte and Mario Draghi fortunately used their discretionary powers during COVID-19 in a way that was attentive to scientific guidelines, using severe measures such as lockdowns to prevent high mortality rates. But in practice what would happen if the cabinet were headed by a politician who undermined pandemic risks, such as Jair Bolsonaro or Donald Trump? Such a delegation could have been disastrous, leading to a humanitarian tragedy and the loss of millions of lives, as happened in Brazil, the United States, and several other countries whose executive leaders ignored World Health Organization (WHO) guidelines.

Moreover, the *Sentenza* n. 198 of 2021 differs from the usual jurisprudence of the Italian Constitutional Court, which had already established that the exercise of administrative discretion must be determined in advance in terms

46 Decree-Law 25 of March 2020, n. 19 (Decreto-Legge 25 marzo 2020, n. 19).

of its "content" and "nature, modality".[47] According to a previous ruling (*Sentenza* n. 115 of April 7, 2011), especially when it comes to restrictions on fundamental rights, it should be avoided a "blank delegation, generically guided by a principle-value, without specifying or detailing the content and methods of administrative action".[48]

Finally, in *Sentenza* n. 198, the Court affirmed that the validity of this delegation was justified by (i) the temporary nature of the DPCMs, (ii) the regular reports from the cabinet to parliament on pandemic management, and (iii) the obligation of the executive to consult a Scientific and Technical Committee (*il comitato tecnico scientifico*).[49] It stressed that the DPCMs could only be adopted for predetermined periods and could only be renewed until the end of the state of emergency. The decision also pointed out that the Decree-Law n. 19/2020, established that "[t]he President of the Council of Ministers or a Minister delegated by him shall present a report to the Chambers on the measures adopted pursuant to this decree".[50] The Court then found that the decree-law provided for sufficient technical and scientific specifications and assessments of adequacy and proportionality, since the DPCMs were issued after consultation of the Technical and Scientific Committee.

However, we argue that the temporary nature of the restrictive measures does not justify an open delegation without detailed parameters. Despite their limited duration, the DPCMs have had a very significant impact during their period of validity, affecting fundamental freedoms and having legal, social, and economic consequences that went beyond the pandemic. Also, the mere sending of reports and communications by the cabinet to parliament about the measures adopted is not sufficient to constitute substantive legislative control. Such provisions do not reflect effective parliamentary oversight, but mere communication without any supervisory force. This situation is very different from what happens with decree-laws at the moment they are converted, when there is extensive parliamentary discussion, with the possibility of amendments, exclusions, or even nonconversion. In this case, there is real control

47 Corte Costituzionale italiana (Italian Constitutional Court). *Sentenza n. 115 of April 7, 2011*. Available at: https://www.cortecostituzionale.it/actionPronuncia.do.

48 Corte Costituzionale italiana (Italian Constitutional Court). *Sentenza n. 115 of April 7, 2011. Op. cit.*

49 Decree-Law n. 19 of March 25, 2020 (Decreto-Legge 25 marzo 2020, n. 19):

> (. . .) For technical and scientific aspects, as well as to assess adequacy and proportionality, the procedures referred to in this subparagraph will be generally adopted only after consultation with the Scientific Technical Committee (il comitato tecnico scientifico) referred to in the ordinance by the Head of the Civil Protection Department of February 3, 2020, n. 630 (. . .).

50 Decree-Law 25 of March 2020, n. 19 (Decreto-Legge 25 marzo 2020, n. 19). In original:

> *Art. 2, comma 1. (. . .) Il Presidente del Consiglio dei ministri o un Ministro da lui delegato illustra preventivamente alle Camere il contenuto dei provvedimenti da adottare ai sensi del presente comma, al fine di tenere conto degli eventuali indirizzi dalle stesse formulati (. . .).*

and enforcement of checks and balances. Similarly, the imposition of a general obligation for hearing the Scientific and Technical Committee cannot be considered a sufficient legal framework. As in the German case, the law itself must provide clear parameters and basic decisions related to which measures can be taken according to each risk level.

In short, the Italian jurists' concern about the legal instruments of the anti-COVID measures is not a mere formal concern or a legalistic caprice. On the contrary, the centrality of primary normative sources corresponds to an essential logic of constitutional design. Fundamental decisions in the public interest must originate in the choices made by the people's representatives, in the heart of the democratic circuit that is parliament. The principle of legality requires that normative instruments imposing restrictions on rights should follow a hierarchical system typical of the organization of a democratic state. Decrees cannot claim to regulate significant parts of citizens' lives in a preventive and general manner without parliamentary control. Thus, the DPCMs should not have been the instrument for fundamental political decisions during the COVID-19 emergency, but rather the decree-laws.

7.1.5 *The Italian Constitutional Court during the pandemic*

Between 2020 and 2021, the Italian Constitutional Court clearly adopted an attitude of deference to the decisions of the executive and the legislature. In addition to *Sentenza* n. 198, several other decisions reflected this judicial posture. In the *Sentenza* n. 213 of November 11, 2021, for example, the Court recognized the validity of decree-laws, converted into law, prohibiting evictions during the pandemic. It found that, in the exceptional situation of a public health emergency, the legislator's discretion in designing measures to combat the pandemic is wider than in normal circumstances. In the light of that greater discretion, the Court stated that the contested measures were not manifestly unreasonable, but instead reflected a legitimate balancing of the protection of the interests and rights at stake. It also pointed out that this sacrifice for the landlords could only be temporary: once the emergency was over, the normal rules on eviction would apply.[51]

For its part, in *Sentenza* n. 37 of March 12, 2021, the Court resolved a question related to the distribution of powers between the state and the regions, interpreted in the light of the public interest in the protection of public health. It ruled that the region of Valle D'Aosta did not have the competence to adopt a specific law on measures to limit the spread of the coronavirus in social and economic activities. The regional law provided for the reopening

51 Corte Costituzionale italiana (Italian Constitutional Court). *Sentenza n. 213 of November 11, 2021.* Available at: https://www.cortecostituzionale.it/actionSchedaPronuncia.do?anno=2021&numero=213.

of many activities in the regional territory and established measures that were less restrictive than the national ones.[52]

According to the Constitutional Court, the regional law violated the exclusive competence of the state in the field of international public health. The pandemic was an international crisis that required centralized organization and management. Thus, national security and the prevention of public health should prevail over local autonomy. The Court also affirmed that the implementation of the regional act could cause "the risk of serious and irreparable damage to the public interest" as well as "the risk of serious and irreparable damage to the rights of citizens". As a result, the law was annulled.[53]

In the end of 2020, the Court declared that the postponement of the hearings and the suspension of the terms in criminal procedures were compatible with the reasonable duration of the trial and was justified by the aim of protecting public health.[54] It maintained that the challenged decree-laws, converted into laws, were justified in terms of reasonableness and proportionality by the need to protect public health in the face of the COVID-19 pandemic. It therefore decided that, in the balance of fundamental rights, the right to life and health should take precedence during emergencies.

It can be seen that these decisions have generally recognized the validity of executive acts, especially decree-laws that were later converted into laws. In contrast to the German and Brazilian Supreme Courts, there was generally no opposition to administrative measures or special protection for regional autonomy. In addition to the small number of cases judged, the trials did not promote changes in the policies set by the national executive. Despite some lower courts' rulings against the prime minister's decrees,[55] the data point to a deferential approach and low judicial interventionism.

7.1.6 The concentration of power in the hands of the prime minister: the personalization of politics in Italy

The active role of the prime minister in the pandemic response is closely linked to the process of *personalization* of politics in Italy. The emergency has accelerated and deepened the growing *presidentialization* of this parliamentary

52 Corte Costituzionale italiana (Italian Constitutional Court). *Sentenza n. 213 of November 11, 2021.* Available at: https://www.cortecostituzionale.it/actionSchedaPronuncia.do?anno=2021&numero=37.

53 Corte Costituzionale italiana (Italian Constitutional Court). *Sentenza n. 37 of March 12, 2021.* Available at: https://www.cortecostituzionale.it/actionSchedaPronuncia.do?anno=2021&numero=37.

54 Corte Costituzionale italiana (Italian Constitutional Court). *Sentenza n. 278 of December 23, 2020.* Available at: https://www.cortecostituzionale.it/actionSchedaPronuncia.do?param_ecli=ECLI:IT:COST:2020:278.

55 Italy. Tribunale di Reggio Emilia. *Sentenza* n. 54 of January 27, 2021, and Tribunale di Pisa. Sentenza n. 419 of March 17, 2021.

system.[56] It reinforced the political and institutional trends that already existed before the crisis and served as a favorable condition for the Italian prime ministers to introduce new practices and to expand their normative power. In fact, there was a growing dominance of the executive and the verticalization and concentration of decision-making powers. All this led to a consolidation of the prime minister's force at the expense of parliament.

The Italian political regime has been historically characterized by a highly personalized nature of government. The country is accustomed to radical shifts of power from the legislature to the executive, as the traditional form of collegial government has often given way to monocratic rule, as in the fascist regime of Benito Mussolini.[57] Currently, Italy is a prime example of the international phenomenon of the *presidentialization* of parliamentary political systems. Prime ministers have become "the main driving force of government and the focus of mass expectations".[58]

During the COVID-19 emergency, then-prime ministers Giuseppe Conte and Mario Draghi made significant changes to the government's decision-making process, demonstrating an increasingly centralized control of the state, particularly through the expansion of the use of DPCMs. They also became a public presence in the media, especially on digital platforms. The importance of their online publications was evidenced by the "institutional use" of the Facebook and Twitter platforms and the exponential growth in the number of followers. These platforms became important tools for communicating official decisions to citizens and for announcing the content of decrees even before they were published in the Official Gazette.[59]

The pandemic has further intensified (i) the direct relationship between the prime ministers and the citizens and (ii) their centrality within the structure of the executive branch. The chief executive was primarily responsible for coordinating and defining public policies and served as a point of reference for Italian citizens. The eyes of the country were focused on the ministerial decrees. As

56 Rullo, Luigi. The COVID-19 pandemic crisis and the personalization of the government in Italy. *Op. cit.*, p. 197.

57 Romanelli, Raffaele (Ed.). *Storia dello Stato italiano dall'Unità a oggi.* Roma: Donzelli editore, 1995, *passim*; Calise, Mauro. Personalization of politics. In: Badie, Bertrand; Berg-Schlosser, Dirk; Morlino, Leonardo (Eds.). *International encyclopedia of political science.* London: Sage, 2011, p. 88; Calise, Mauro et al. The personalization of power. *Studia Politica. Romanian Political Science Review*, v. 10, n. 4, 2010, p. 617–622; Rahat, Gideon; Kenig, Ofer. *From party politics to personalized politics? Party change and political personalization in democracies.* Oxford University Press, 2018 and De Luca, Marino. The Italian style: Giuseppe Conte's 'half-populist'leadership during Covid-19. *LSE European Politics and Policy (EUROPP) blog*, 2020. Available at: https://blogs.lse.ac.uk/europpblog/2020/06/08/the-italian-style-giuseppe-contes-half-populist-leadership-during-covid-19/.

58 Musella, Fortunato. *Political leaders beyond party politics.* London: Palgrave Macmillan, 2018, p. 97.

59 Rullo, Luigi. The COVID-19 pandemic crisis and the personalization of the government in Italy. *Op. cit.*, p. 197.

already discussed, the DPCMs represented an instrument for the premiers to gain more power and autonomy: the escalation of these acts underlined the lack of institutional dialogue between the government branches in the face of the crisis.[60]

In particular, former prime minister Giuseppe Conte established a kind of direct and emotional relationship with the public.[61] Using catchy slogans ("If you love Italy, keep your distance"),[62] famous quotes ("Let's keep our distance today so we can hug each other more warmly tomorrow"),[63] and reassuring messages ("We are in the same boat, whoever is at the helm has the duty to show the course, we have to make an extra effort, we have to do it together"),[64] Conte enjoyed growing public support during the pandemic.[65] According to a poll published by Eurobarometer in May 2020, 58% of Italians had a high or fairly high level of trust in the former prime minister, and the general opinion of the measures taken by the government was very or fairly positive (69%).[66]

Indeed, Facebook and Twitter were the prime minister's main communication channels for promoting government policies and disseminating information to the public. Such technologies have radically changed the information environment in which the executive leaders operate, allowing them to reach a huge popular audience, in a phenomenon called "technopopulism".[67] On Face-

60 Rullo, Luigi. The COVID-19 pandemic crisis and the personalization of the government in Italy. *Op. cit.*, p. 197.

61 Rullo, Luigi. The COVID-19 pandemic crisis and the personalization of the government in Italy. *Op. cit.*

62 Italy. Ministero della Salute (Ministry of Health). *Conte firma dpcm per la fase 2: "Se ami l'Italia, mantieni la distanza"*. April 27, 2020. Available at: https://www.salute.gov.it/portale/news/p3_2_1_1_1.jsp?lingua=italiano&menu=notizie&p=null&id=4613; Ciammella, Fabio et al. Covid-19 e political meme. Approccio transmediale alla co-creazione del discorso politico sulle piattaforme social. In: *Saperi, Conoscenze ed Esperienze In Formazione Atti della V conferenza nazionale delle dottorande e dei dottorandi in Scienze Sociali*, 2021, p. 131–137.

63 Corriere della Sera. *Coronavirus, Conte: "Stiamo distanti oggi, per abbracciarci con più calore domani"*. March 11, 2020. Available at: https://video.corriere.it/cronaca/coronavirus-conte-stiamo-distanti-oggi-abbracciarci-piu-calore-domani/0ff97ab2–63e8–11ea-9cf4–1c175ff3bb7c.

64 La Reppublica. *Coronavirus, il messaggio di Conte al Paese: 'Dobbiamo fare uno sforzo in più e farlo assieme'*. March 4, 2020. Available at: https://www.repubblica.it/politica/2020/03/04/news/coronavirus_il_messagio_di_conte_al_paese-250268512/.

65 Rullo, Luigi. The COVID-19 pandemic crisis and the personalization of the government in Italy. *Op. cit.*, p. 200.

66 European Parliament. Schulmeister, P. M. *Public opinion monitoring at a glance in the time of COVID-19*. Head of Public Opinion Monitoring Unit, 2020. Available at: https://www.europarl.europa.eu/at-your-service/files/be-heard/eurobarometer/2020/covid19/en-public-opinion-in-the-time-of-covid19–20200512.pdf.

67 Bickerton, Christopher J.; Accetti, Carlo Invernizzi. 'Techno-populism' as a new party family: The case of the five star movement and Podemos. *Contemporary Italian Politics*, v. 10, n. 2, 2018, p. 132–150; Rullo, Luigi. The COVID-19 pandemic crisis and the personalization of the government in Italy. *Op. cit.*, p. 197.

book, Conte's followers increased from nearly one million in January 2020 to more than three million at the beginning of May 2020.[68]

This scenario created a symbiotic relationship between the prime minister and citizens, while the relevance of other political actors declined. Every Facebook post made by Conte has taken the nature of official decisions: there was a clear integration of the digital platform into his government. For example, in the late evening of March 21, 2020, Conte spoke about new lockdown measures exclusively through a direct broadcast on his personal Facebook page. It forced the national television RAI (Radiotelevisione Italiana) to connect to the private platform in order to cover the dramatic policy that was about to be adopted.[69]

In short, the former Italian prime minister demonstrated an atypical way of doing politics. Bypassing official protocols and procedures, his decisions were made public via social networks. As mentioned, Conte announced several decrees on Facebook before they were published in the official gazette. For example, the "Relaunch Italy" decree was announced on Facebook on May 13, 2020, and came into effect just six days later, sparking criticism and uncertainty. Whereas in the past a tweet or post about a presidential proposal marked the end of a long and deliberative process, in 2020 Twitter and Facebook have become the starting point for policymaking.[70]

7.1.7 *The normative authority of the minister of health. A third-degree delegation?*

At certain times during the pandemic, there was a "derived" or "third-degree" delegation of legislative authority. The decree-laws delegated very broad discretionary powers to the prime minister, who in turn delegated normative power to the minister of health. For example, article 2 of the DPCM n. 275, published on November 4, 2020, established that an ordinance by the minister of health could classify an entire region as a so-called red zone (*zona rossa*), with a whole series of consequences in terms of restrictions of fundamental rights such as the freedom of movement, work, and commercial activity. The ordinances did not allow for prior adaptation and organization on the part of citizens, coming into effect literally overnight without any prior democratic discussion.

Against this third-degree delegation, Italian jurists such as Giovanni Guzzetta have rightly pointed out that a DPCM cannot grant normative

68 Rullo, Luigi. The COVID-19 pandemic crisis and the personalization of the government in Italy. *Op. cit.*, p. 197.

69 Rullo, Luigi. The COVID-19 pandemic crisis and the personalization of the government in Italy. *Op. cit.*

70 Ansa.it. *Conte announces seven-point plan to relaunch Italy*. May 27, 2020. Available at: https://www.ansa.it/english/news/2020/05/27/conte-announces-seven-point-plan-to-relaunch-italy_e0d59a2e-9299-4572-8fe9-33fb975140bd.html.

power to the minister of health, since this delegation should be specified by law. An authority that receives normative power cannot delegate it to another. In Guzzetta's words,

> in order for an authority, including the Minister of Health, to exercise a power, there must be a law or an act with the force of law granting that power and specifying, at least in general terms, the manner in which it is to be exercised.[71]

In fact, the regulatory power of the minister of health in Italy is provided for and regulated in article 32 of Law 833/1978 and could not have been reshaped and expanded by a mere DPCM.

In short, there was no legal basis for the minister of health to decide the fate of entire regions without the consent of the regional governments themselves. Such fundamental decisions should not have been taken away from parliament and placed in the hands of a government minister.[72] Decisions based on technical assessments must be properly publicized and explained to the legislature and the public in the most understandable way possible to ensure participation and responsiveness. Experts should help inform the decisions of those in power by providing them with research and data – not make decisions on their own, without political deliberation.[73-74]

During the pandemic, for example, both parliament and the cabinet needed technical support to formulate effective policies, given the sensitivity of the issues at stake and the catastrophic prospects arising from the epidemiological risks. Experts have assisted in the drafting of delegating laws with a high normative density, as was the case with the German Infectious Diseases Act. In Germany, specialists have also advised on the drafting of secondary legislation, always with due respect for the choices made in primary legislation. In conclusion, while scientific experts can be involved in policymaking, the basic and essential decisions must always be taken by the legislature.

71 Guzzetta, Giovanni. L'ultimo Dpcm manda in soffitta la Costituzione e cancella il principio di legalità. *Ilriformista*. November 5, 2020. Available at: https://www.ilriformista.it/lultimo-dpcm-manda-in-soffitta-la-costituzione-e-cancella-il-principio-di-legalita-173453/?refresh_ce.

72 Guzzetta, Giovanni. L'ultimo Dpcm manda in soffitta la Costituzione e cancella il principio di legalità. *Op. cit.*

73 Windholz, Eric L. Governing in a pandemic: From parliamentary sovereignty to autocratic technocracy. *The Theory and Practice of Legislation*, v. 8, n. 1–2, 2020, p. 93–113.

74 Rullo, Luigi. The COVID-19 pandemic crisis and the personalization of the government in Italy. *Op. cit.*, p. 204.

7.2 Brazil: "mid-term review"

In April 2021, *Médecins Sans Frontières* (MSF) declared that Brazil's response to COVID-19 was the worst in the world.[75-76] The country has suffered a true humanitarian tragedy, with 708,739 deaths from COVID-19 and a total of 38,230,814 confirmed cases.[77] Brazil's failure to tackle the pandemic is associated with a multitude of factors, such as the omission of the federal executive, the denialist discourse propagated by former president Jair Bolsonaro, the regulatory chaos stemming from local authorities, the lack of coordination between spheres of government, the inefficient strengthening of the health system, and the insufficient social and economic support measures. In addition to the former president, several political authorities have minimized the seriousness of the pandemic, encouraged the continuation of all economic activities, spread false information, and maintained a position contrary to the scientifically based measures recommended by international health organizations.[78]

During the crisis, the federal executive's approach has been characterized by a lack of decision-making, delays in issuing relevant decrees, and paralysis in critical policy agencies. Bolsonaro's administration has actively blocked or sabotaged emergency policies enacted by Congress and state governments to fill the vacuum left by his presidential inaction. As already mentioned, Brazil is an infamous example of federal executive underreach.[79] Between April and

75 The Guardian. *Brazil's Covid-19 response is worst in the world, says Médecins Sans Frontières.* April 15, 2021. Available at: https://www.theguardian.com/world/2021/apr/15/brazil-coronavirus-medecins-sans-frontieres-bolsonaro.

76 Brazil is a presidential federal republic divided into a federal union, a federal district, states, and municipalities, all of which are autonomous. The federal, state, and municipal executives are headed by a president, governors, and mayors, all of whom are directly elected by the people every four years, with the right to run for reelection once. Each of these federal units has a legislature, which is also directly elected by the people every four years. The federal legislature (National Congress) is bicameral, consisting of a lower house (Chamber of Deputies) and a senate (National Senate) representing each state. State and municipal legislatures are unicameral. In addition to the Federal Supreme Court, there are federal and state courts that have the power to invalidate legislation and administrative acts that do not comply with the Constitution or laws. *See, e.g.*, Mendes, Gilmar Ferreira; Branco, Paulo Gustavo Gonet. *Curso de direito constitucional*, 9. ed. São Paulo: Saraiva, 2014. Moraes, Alexandre de. Federação brasileira: necessidade de fortalecimento das competências dos Estados-membros. In: Tavares, André Ramos et al. (Eds.). *Estado constitucional e organização do poder*. São Paulo: Saraiva, 2010.

77 Brazilian Ministry of Health. *Painel Coronavírus.* April 23, 2024. Available at: https://covid.saude.gov.br/.

78 Ferraz, Octávio Luiz Motta; Rached, Danielle; Ventura, Deisy; Hubner Mendes, Conrado; Alberto, Marco Antônio Moraes. Brazil: Legal response to Covid-19. In: King, Jeff et al. (Eds.). *The Oxford compendium of national legal responses to Covid-19.* 2021. Available at: https://oxcon.ouplaw.com/display/10.1093/law-occ19/law-occ19-e16; Teixeira, Carmen Fontes; Santos, Jamilli Silva. Análise estratégica da atuação do governo federal brasileiro na pandemia de COVID-19: 2020–2021. *Ciência & Saúde Coletiva*, v. 28, 2023, p. 1277–1286.

79 Pozen, Davi; Scheppele, Kim L. Executive underreach, in pandemics and otherwise. *American Journal of International Law*, v. 114, 2020, p. 608–617.

June 2020, Bolsonaro dismissed two ministers of health whose recommendations were in line with the World Health Organization (WHO) guidelines. He also politicized the ministry by appointing a military officer, General Eduardo Pazzuello, as minister of health. Pazzuello had no medical or scientific qualifications and acted in accordance with the president's political positions, remaining in office for a year during the most critical period of the pandemic.[80] In the face of the federal executive's disastrous behavior, subnational governments, the federal Congress, and the judiciary have attempted to take measures to address the crisis, creating a broad opposition to Bolsonaro's government.[81]

Indeed, the National Congress and local governments made all the major decisions related to the pandemic. Because Brazil is a federalist democracy, states and municipalities have concurrent authority with the federal government in the area of public health. Therefore, they had the power to deal directly with the pandemic, hire health professionals, purchase equipment and medicines, and implement local restrictive measures. At the same time, Congress and the Supreme Court avoided any interruption in their activities through remote voting and live-streamed plenary sessions. Also, the Supreme Court issued hundreds of rulings emphasizing the importance of social distancing and forcing the government to take action in specific sectors.[82]

7.2.1 The role of the National Congress in managing the crisis

From March 2020 to December 2020, the National Congress passed more than 130 laws. Legislators took on the burden of proposing and passing laws that depend on supermajorities: they approved three constitutional amendments (related to the state budget) and five "complementary laws"[83] (related, for example, to the program to guarantee resources to federal entities, as well as the creation of emergency aid for the poor and unemployed).[84]

Congress enacted a series of new laws specifically aimed at the pandemic, providing for a wide range of preventive measures, such as the suspension of economic and social activities. Since the outbreak of the crisis, Congress has

80 BBC. *Who is Eduardo Pazuello, the general taking over the ministry of health on an interim basis?* May 16, 2020. Available at: https://www.bbc.com/portuguese/brasil-52686114.

81 Inácio, Magna; Recch, Filipe; Valencia, Carolina Guerrero. The power of the administrative decisions of Latin American presidents. In: Llanos, Mariana; Marsteintredet, Leiv (Eds.). *Latin America in times of turbulence: Presidentialism under stress.* New York: Routledge, 2023, p. 99–102.

82 Inácio, Magna; Recch, Filipe; Valencia, Carolina Guerrero. The power of the administrative decisions of Latin American presidents. *Op. cit.*

83 In Brazil, complementary laws differ from ordinary laws because they require the vote of a majority of the members of the Chamber of Deputies and the Federal Senate. They must be enacted to regulate specific matters, when expressly provided for in the Constitution of the Republic. *See* https://www4.planalto.gov.br/legislacao/portal-legis/legislacao-1/leis-complementares-1/todas-as-leis-complementares-1.

84 Inácio, Magna; Recch, Filipe; Valencia, Carolina Guerrero. The power of the administrative decisions of Latin American presidents. *Op. cit.*, p. 101.

adapted its deliberations to use a Remote Deliberation System (RDS) with extremely short deadlines. Following the recognition of the pandemic by the World Health Organization (WHO), several state legislatures have also announced the adoption of remote deliberation.[85] In several cases, it used its veto power against unilateral executive legislation: of the 108 *medidas provisórias* (provisional measures) issued by the president in 2020, 52 lost their effectiveness because members of Congress deliberately didn't put them to a vote.[86]

Among the various episodes of conflict between the former president and Congress, three were very significant. The first conflict concerned the social protection measures and the amount of emergency financial aid to be given to people without documented income due to unemployment, which increased significantly during the pandemic. The initial proposal of the Ministry of Economy of the federal executive was R$200 Brazilian reals per month (the equivalent of about 40 euros), but after pressure from Congress, the amount was increased to R$600 Brazilian reals (the equivalent of about 120 euros).[87]

Another confrontation involved Federal Law n. 1.142 of 2020, which dealt with social protection measures to prevent the spread of COVID-19 in Indigenous territories. Bolsonaro vetoed numerous provisions of this law, stating that social distancing measures were unnecessary. The veto was overridden by Congress a month later. Subsequently, there was a conflict over Federal Law n. 1.826 of 2020, which provided financial compensation by the federal government to health professionals and workers who became disabled as a result of treating patients affected by COVID-19. This law was vetoed in its entirety by the former president, but the veto was overridden by Congress on March 26, 2021.[88] Moreover, on several occasions, Bolsonaro tried to stop Congress from imposing restrictions on economic activity and social distancing. For example, the president vetoed provisions of a law that would have made it

85 Pinheiro, Victor Marcel; Ilarraz, Marcelo; Mestriner, Melissa Terni. The impacts of the COVID-19 crisis on the Brazilian legal system–a report on the functioning of the branches of the government and on the legal scrutiny of their activities. *The Theory and Practice of Legislation*, v. 8, n. 1–2, 2020, p. 195.

86 Pinheiro, Victor Marcel; Ilarraz, Marcelo; Mestriner, Melissa Terni. The impacts of the COVID-19 crisis on the Brazilian legal system – a report on the functioning of the branches of the government and on the legal scrutiny of their activities. *Op. cit.*

87 Teixeira, Carmen Fontes; Santos, Jamilli Silva. Análise estratégica da atuação do governo federal brasileiro na pandemia de COVID-19: 2020–2021. *Ciência & Saúde Coletiva*, v. 28, 2023, p. 1277–1286; Pinheiro, Victor Marcel; Ilarraz, Marcelo; Mestriner, Melissa Terni. The impacts of the COVID-19 crisis on the Brazilian legal system – a report on the functioning of the branches of the government and on the legal scrutiny of their activities. *Op. cit.*, p. 193.

88 Teixeira, Carmen Fontes; Santos, Jamilli Silva. Análise estratégica da atuação do governo federal brasileiro na pandemia de COVID-19: 2020–2021. *Op. cit.*; Pinheiro, Victor Marcel; Ilarraz, Marcelo; Mestriner, Melissa Terni. The impacts of the COVID-19 crisis on the Brazilian legal system – a report on the functioning of the branches of the government and on the legal scrutiny of their activities. *Op. cit.*

mandatory to wear masks to contain the virus. But Congress responded by again overriding the president's veto and keeping the requirement in place.

The Congress also established a Parliamentary Inquiry Commission (Comissão Parlamentar de Inquérito, CPI) to investigate allegations of crimes and unconstitutional omissions by the federal executive. This reflected the culmination of tensions between Bolsonaro's government and the national legislature. In Brazil, "Parliamentary Inquiry Commissions" are temporary committees installed in the National Congress, created at the request of at least one-third of the total number of deputies. Their purpose is to investigate facts of interest to public life and to the constitutional, legal, economic, or social order of the country. They have investigative powers equivalent to those of the judicial authorities, such as the power to take preventive measures, to question witnesses, to request information and documents from public administration bodies and institutions, to request hearings of deputies and ministers of state, to take testimony from federal, state, and municipal authorities, and to request the services of any authority, including the police. In addition, members of these committees may travel to any place in the national territory to conduct investigations and public hearings.[89]

After almost six months of work, the Brazilian Committee that was established to investigate the government actions and omissions during the COVID-19 pandemic concluded that "the Federal Government has been silent and has chosen to act in an unprofessional and careless manner in dealing with the new coronavirus pandemic, deliberately exposing the population to concrete risks of mass infection".[90] The Committee analyzed and systematized a body of evidence that revealed the implementation of an institutional strategy for the spread of the virus, promoted by the federal government under the leadership of former president Bolsonaro with the aim of implementing a "herd immunity".

In the final report, the Senate proposed criminal charges against the former president for the following crimes: malfeasance, charlatanism, epidemics resulting in death, violation of preventive health measures, irregular use of public funds, incitement to crime, forgery of private documents, crimes of responsibility (violation of social rights and incompatibility with the dignity, honor, and decorum of office), and crimes against humanity (in the form of extermination, persecution, and other inhumane acts).[91]

89 Brazil. Official Website of the Chamber of Deputies. *Comissões temporárias.* Available at: https://www2.camara.leg.br/atividade-legislativa/comissoes/comissoes-temporarias/parlamentar-de-inquerito.

90 Brazil. Official Website of the Federal Senate. *CPI da Pandemia: principais pontos do relatório.* Available at: https://www12.senado.leg.br/noticias/materias/2021/10/20/cpi-da-pandemia-principais-pontos-do-relatorio.

91 Brazil. Official Website of the Federal Senate. *CPI da Pandemia: principais pontos do relatório. Op. cit.*

Other government ministers, special advisors to the president, and members of parliament were also indicted by the Committee for crimes related to spreading false information about COVID-19, instigating disregard for social distance rules, and crimes of corruption in the purchase of vaccines and other medical supplies. The Senate also denounced Jair Bolsonaro's so-called parallel advisory cabinet, described in the report as an "intimate circle of advisors" with an "ideological attachment to chloroquine". These presidential advisors have been charged with the crime of epidemic resulting in death.[92]

In addition to the final report, the Committee was also extremely important in alerting the public to the importance of social distancing measures and the criminal omissions practiced by the former president. The meetings were televised and broadcast daily on major news channels. Hearings with Bolsonaro's ministers who couldn't answer simple questions about the management of the pandemic became internet "memes" and were widely shared on social media. The Committee was extremely important for disseminating scientific information to the population and served to reduce the popularity of the president of the republic.

This scenario is, therefore, an example of how the legislature can control the executive not only through the ordinary legislative process but also through special committees that draw the media's attention to unconstitutional executive deviations and omissions.[93] Indeed, members of Congress and political scientists have argued that the commission's investigation and accusations of corruption were one of the reasons Bolsonaro lost the subsequent presidential election in 2022.[94]

7.2.2 *Local governments and the pandemic: regulatory chaos and lack of coordination*

According to its Constitution, Brazil is a federal republic with three levels of government. The federal, state, and municipal governments have independent executive and legislative powers with broad and sometimes overlapping authority over public policy. In a wide range of social areas (including public health policy), these overlapping powers create tensions that are often not resolved by one-off judicial decisions, but by a political process of cooperation, dispute, and negotiation between the institutional actors involved.[95]

92 Brazil. Official Website of the Federal Senate. *CPI da Pandemia: principais pontos do relatório. Op. cit.*

93 OGLOBO. *Covid CPI and suspicions of corruption explain Bolsonaro's fall in popularity, say political scientists.* July 7, 2021. Available at: https://oglobo.globo.com/politica/cpi-da-covid-suspeitas-de-corrupcao-explicam-queda-de-popularidade-de-bolsonaro-dizem-cientistas-politicos-1-25101109.

94 Available at: https://noticias.uol.com.br/eleicoes/2022/10/03/omar-aziz-uol-news.htm.

95 Pinheiro, Victor Marcel; Ilarraz, Marcelo; Mestriner, Melissa Terni. The impacts of the COVID-19 crisis on the Brazilian legal system – a report on the functioning of the branches

Article 23, II, of the Brazilian Constitution establishes that "taking care of health and public assistance" is a "common competence" of all spheres of government. Article 24, XII, then establishes that "social security, health protection, and defense" is a concurrent legislative competence of the federal union and the states. The distribution of competences among the members of the federal state is guided by the general principle of predominance of interests. The union is responsible for matters and issues of predominant general interest, the states for matters of predominant regional interest, and the municipalities for matters of local interest.[96]

During the pandemic, most of the major public health measures were issued by local authorities. But state and municipal regulations to control the coronavirus have been inconsistent, with some states and municipalities banning all economic activities and others imposing almost no restrictions. The response has been fragmented and institutionally dispersed, with no single institution in charge of the anti-COVID policies. Federal, state, and municipal authorities have adopted partially conflicting policies, leading to political disputes, legal uncertainty, and concerns about the effectiveness of the crisis response.[97]

The governor of São Paulo (Brazil's most populous state, home to about 40% of the Brazilian population) was one of the first public authorities to issue an executive decree imposing a strict quarantine on nonessential businesses and suggesting the suspension of public gatherings. Also, the government of the state of Rio de Janeiro established the suspension of numerous activities, such as the holding of events and activities with public participation, visits to the beach, and so on. In other states and municipalities, however, there was not even an obligation to wear masks in public places.[98]

---

of the government and on the legal scrutiny of their activities. *Op. cit.*, p. 193; Vieira, Fabiola Sulpino; Servo, Luciana Mendes Santos. Covid-19 e coordenação federativa no Brasil: consequências da dissonância federal para a resposta à pandemia. *Saúde em debate*, v. 44, 2020, p. 100–113; da SP Néris, Eduardo Henrique Corrêa; Bedritichuk, Rodrigo Ribeiro. Brazilian federalism: Facing the COVID-19 pandemic. In: Chattopadhyay, Rupak et al. (Eds.). *Federalism and the response to COVID-19: A comparative analysis*. New York: Routledge, 2022, p. 59–65.

96 Ramos, Edith Maria Barbosa; Ramos, Paulo Roberto Barbosa; Costa, Laísse Lima Silva. Pandemia e Federalismo: Reflexões sobre as decisões do Supremo Tribunal Federal na apreciação de conflitos de competência entre os entes federativos no enfrentamento à Covid-19. *Revista de Ciências Jurídicas e Sociais-IURJ*, v. 1, n. 1, 2020, p. 46–61.

97 Pinheiro, Victor Marcel; Ilarraz, Marcelo; Mestriner, Melissa Terni. The impacts of the COVID-19 crisis on the Brazilian legal system – a report on the functioning of the branches of the government and on the legal scrutiny of their activities. *Op. cit.*, p. 193.

98 Ramos, Edith Maria Barbosa; Ramos, Paulo Roberto Barbosa; Costa, Laísse Lima Silva. Pandemia e Federalismo: Reflexões sobre as decisões do Supremo Tribunal Federal na apreciação de conflitos de competência entre os entes federativos no enfrentamento à Covid-19. *Revista de Ciências Jurídicas e Sociais-IURJ*, v. 1, n. 1, 2020, p. 46–61; Pinheiro, Victor Marcel; Ilarraz, Marcelo; Mestriner, Melissa Terni. The impacts of the COVID-19 crisis on the Brazilian legal system – a report on the functioning of the branches of the government and on the legal scrutiny of their activities. *Op. cit.*, p. 193; Vieira, Fabiola Sulpino; Servo, Luciana Mendes

Bolsonaro, for his part, constantly tried to block these restrictive actions by state and municipal governments. He responded by issuing a "provisional measure" (*medida provisória*) stating that the decisions on social distancing and economic restrictions should be subject to the approval of the federal authority. This decision was challenged and then partially annulled by the Supreme Court, as the states have the constitutional authority to make these decisions concurrently with the federal government. The Court found that the federal government could not invalidate social distancing measures established by local authorities.[99]

At the same time, decrees issued by Bolsonaro classified "beauty salons" and "gyms" as essential activities that should not be affected by restrictive regulations, in an open contradiction and delegitimization of the actions of subnational governments.[100] A large number of state governors simply refused to implement the decree, citing the mentioned Supreme Court ruling that confirmed their authority to adopt more restrictive measures than those proposed by the federal executive.[101]

In interviews and official statements, Bolsonaro has also blamed governors and mayors for the economic crisis and the rise in unemployment rates during the pandemic. He exhaustively declared: "I would like everyone to go back to work, but I'm not the one who decides that; it's the governors and the mayors",[102] and "Now there's a huge wave of unemployment coming. Informal workers as well as formal workers. Don't try to put it in my lap. It's up to the governors to solve this problem".[103]

Unfortunately, despite the attempts and efforts of numerous state and municipal governments to deal with the crisis, the normative acts were often simply ignored by the population. In Rio de Janeiro, for example, despite decrees prohibiting the use of beaches, they were always crowded at the peak of the state's COVID-19 rates. In addition, states and municipalities have less

Santos. Covid-19 e coordenação federativa no Brasil: consequências da dissonância federal para a resposta à pandemia. *Op. cit.*; da SP Néris, Eduardo Henrique Corrêa; Bedritichuk, Rodrigo Ribeiro. Brazilian federalism: Facing the COVID-19 pandemic. *Op. cit.*

99 Brazilian Supreme Federal Court (STF). ADPF 672 MC-Ref. Rel. Alexandre de Moraes, published on October 29, 2020.

100 Brazil. *Presidential Decree n. 10.344/2020.* Available at: https://www4.planalto.gov.br/legislacao/portal-legis/legislacao-1/decretos1/2020-decretos.

101 Ferraz, Octávio Luiz Motta; Rached, Danielle; Ventura, Deisy; Hubner Mendes, Conrado; Alberto, Marco Antônio Moraes. Brazil: Legal response to Covid-19. In: King, Jeff et al. (Eds.). *The Oxford compendium of national legal responses to Covid-19.* 2021. Available at: https://oxcon.ouplaw.com/display/10.1093/law-occ19/law-occ19-e16.

102 Available at: https://www.correiobraziliense.com.br/app/noticia/politica/2020/05/01/interna_politica,850397/bolsonaro-gostaria-que-todos-voltassem-a-trabalhar-mas-eu-nao-decido.shtml.

103 Available at: https://www.correiobraziliense.com.br/app/noticia/politica/2020/06/07/interna_politica,861854/nao-queiram-colocar-no-meu-colo-diz-bolsonaro-por-desemprego-na-pan.shtml.

economic power since the federal entity collects more taxes. Problems related to corruption by local entities in the purchase of medical supplies made the response to the pandemic even more difficult, which also contributed to the terrible outcome that occurred in the country.

7.2.3 Judicial oversight of executive actions

Between 2020 and 2021, the Brazilian Federal Supreme Court issued important decisions that limited the denialist and anti-scientific policies of Bolsonaro's federal government.[104] As the attacks on the Constitution and democracy intensified, the Supreme Court reacted more forcefully, containing the attempts by Bolsonaro and his supporters to weaken the democratic rule of law.[105]

Some of the important decisions of the Court during the pandemic include the ruling that (i) the president cannot prevent state and municipal authorities from adopting public health policies against the spread of the virus, (ii) the federal executive cannot reduce the transparency and publicity of administrative acts,[106] and (iii) it is prohibited to instruct or advertise to the population against scientifically approved measures such as quarantines and closures.[107] In most cases, these lawsuits were seen as a democratic brake on the deviations of the federal executive.

Indeed, the Court has played three fundamental roles: (i) a rational-scientific role, characterized by epistemic deference to science, recognizing the seriousness of the pandemic and relying on scientific data for decision-making; (ii) a mediating role, in which the court sought to mediate and balance horizontal and vertical tensions in policymaking, whether between different federal units or between different government institutions; and (iii) a protective role, characterized by effective mitigation and remediation of human rights violations, especially for social minorities.

In its rational-scientific role, the Court invalidated decisions by the federal executive that had no scientific basis and that spread false information about the pandemic. It also recognized the validity of laws that restricted fundamental rights due to the need for social distancing. Furthermore, given that

104 Vieira, Oscar Vilhena; Glezer, Rubens; Barbosa, Ana Laura Pereira. Supremocracia e Infralegalismo Autoritário: o comportamento do Supremo Tribunal Federal durante o governo Bolsonaro. *Novos estudos CEBRAP*, v. 41, 2023, p. 599.

105 Vieira, Oscar Vilhena; Glezer, Rubens; Barbosa, Ana Laura Pereira. Supremocracia e Infralegalismo Autoritário: o comportamento do Supremo Tribunal Federal durante o governo Bolsonaro. *Op. cit.*, p. 600.

106 Brazilian Supreme Federal Court (STF). ADI 6347 MC-Ref. Rel. Alexandre de Moraes, published on August 14, 2020; ADPF 690, Rel. Alexandre de Moraes, published on April 15, 2021.

107 Brazilian Supreme Federal Court (STF). ADPF 668. Rel. Roberto Barroso, monocratic decision published on May 11, 2020.

the judgments are televised, the Court has been able to promote a public debate on science and the importance of anti-COVID measures. To prevent Bolsonaro from starting a vaccine boycott, the Supreme Court ruled that vaccination is mandatory, establishing both that personal beliefs and convictions cannot prevent parents from vaccinating their children.[108] It also stated that states and municipalities can import and distribute vaccines, as long as they are in line with the federal vaccination plan.[109] The Court also ordered the federal government to disclose the order of preference among priority groups for vaccination against COVID-19.[110]

In its mediating role, the Supreme Court issued several rulings on the distribution of competences between the levels of government, always emphasizing the importance of local autonomy.[111] However, the public perception of these rulings was damaged by a misinterpretation, widely promoted by Bolsonaro, that the Court had given states and municipalities exclusive authority to deal with the pandemic. In this way, the decisions served to inflame passions and anti-institutional rhetoric that the federal government should remain inactive and that the humanitarian disaster that was occurring was the fault of state and local governments.

Finally, in its protective role, the Court required the executive branch to take active measures to deal with COVID-19 in Indigenous[112] and *quilombola* lands.[113] Based on extensive data, the judges found that the lethality of COVID-19 was greater among Indigenous and *quilombola* populations than among citizens living in urban areas, which should lead the federal government to adopt a series of measures for the special protection of these groups. The Court also sought to protect social minorities in police operations in the *favelas* (Brazilian slums), ruling that such operations should not be carried out during the pandemic, except in absolutely extraordinary cases, in which case it should be subject to sanitary precautions.[114] In addition, given the serious collapse of the health system in the state of Amazonas, the Court required

108 Brazilian Supreme Federal Court (STF). ADI 6586, Rel. Ricardo Lewandowski, published on April 7, 2021.

109 Brazilian Supreme Federal Court (STF). ADPF 770 MC-Ref. Rel. Min. Ricardo Lewandowski, published on February 24, 2021.

110 Brazilian Supreme Federal Court (STF). ADPF 754 TPI-segunda-Ref. Rel. Ricardo Lewandowski, published on March 11, 2021.

111 Brazilian Supreme Federal Court (STF). ADPF 672 MC-Ref. Rel. Alexandre de Moraes, published on October 29, 2020; ADI 6341 MC-Ref. Rel. Marco Aurélio, Relator(a) p/ Acórdão: Edson Fachin, Tribunal Pleno, published on November 13, 2020.

112 Brazilian Supreme Federal Court (STF). ADPF 709 MC-Ref. Rel. Roberto Barroso, published on October 7, 2020.

113 Brazilian Supreme Federal Court (STF). ADPF 742 MC, Rel. Marco Aurélio, Relator(a) p/ Acórdão: Edson Fachin, published on April 29, 2021.

114 Brazilian Supreme Federal Court (STF). ADPF 635 MC. Rel. Edson Fachin, published on December 15, 2021.

that the Federal Ministry of Health present a plan of strategies to deal with the crisis by sending a federal task force with doctors and equipment.[115]

Taken together, all of these cases demonstrate how active and combative the Supreme Court was during the pandemic. It did not remain silent in the face of Bolsonaro's anti-scientific and authoritarian speeches and actions. On the contrary, it served as an important center for transmitting truthful information and publicizing the importance of restrictive measures. Had it not been for the actions of the Supreme Court, legislators, and local governments, the wounds opened by the former president would have been even greater.

7.3 Germany: "strong-form" review

Germany is an example of a country where the institutional system of checks and balances remained solid during the COVID-19 crisis. Courts, legislators, and subnational governments played an active role in managing the pandemic and overseeing executive actions.[116] National and local legislatures enacted specific laws with a high normative density related to the emergency. The Act on the Prevention and Control of Infectious Diseases in Humans (Infektionsschutzgesetz)[117] was amended and adapted, allowing the federal and local governments to issue regulations with restrictive measures. Germany has managed to avoid autocratic tactics and remain true to its own principles of governance, while successfully containing the nation's viral infection rates.[118]

The German Federal Constitutional Court (Bundesverfassungsgericht, BVerfG) has also been actively involved in balancing fundamental rights with public health requirements. The Court ruled on cases involving freedom of movement and assembly, freedom of religious worship, freedom of speech,

115 Brazilian Supreme Federal Court (STF). ADPF 756 TPI-Ref. Rel. Ricardo Lewandowski, published on March 30, 2021.

116 Saurer, Johannes. Patterns of cooperative administrative federalism in the German response to COVID-19. *Administrative Law Review*, v. 73, n. 1, 2021, p. 139–163; Saurer, Johannes. COVID-19 and cooperative administrative federalism in Germany. *The Regulatory Review*. May 13, 2020. Available at: https://www.theregreview.org/2020/05/13/saurer-covid-19-cooperat ive-administrative-federalism-germany/.

117 Germany. *Gesetz zur Verhütung und Bekämpfung von Infektionskrankheiten beim Menschen (Act on the Prevention and Control of Infectious Diseases in Humans)*. Available at: https://www.gesetze-im-internet.de/ifsg/index.html.

118 Kuhlmann, Sabine; Franzke, Jochen. Multi-level responses to COVID-19: Crisis coordination in Germany from an intergovernmental perspective. *Local Government Studies*, v. 48, n. 2, 2022, p. 312–334; Kuhlmann, Sabine et al. Tracing divergence in crisis governance: Responses to the COVID-19 pandemic in France, Germany and Sweden compared. *International Review of Administrative Sciences*, v. 87, n. 3, 2021, p. 556–575; kuhn, Katharina; Morlino, Irene. Decentralisation in times of crisis: Asset or liability? The case of Germany and Italy during Covid-19. *Swiss Political Science Review*, v. 28, n. 1, 2022, p. 105–115; Kropp, Sabine; Schnabel, Johanna. Germany's response to COVID-19: Federal coordination and executive politics. In: Chattopadhyay, Rupak et al. (Eds.). *Federalism and the response to COVID-19: A comparative analysis*. New York: Routledge, 2022, p. 162.

and the right to privacy. Many of the laws and regulations enacted during the pandemic have been challenged on the basis of alleged violations of the principle of proportionality. Although most appeals were rejected, in some cases the Constitutional Court imposed changes to the legal framework. In lawsuits involving the cities of Stuttgart and Giessen, for example, the Court protected the right of citizens to protest as long as they complied with the requirements of social distancing. It also invalidated the general ban on worship in mosques, arguing that specific social distancing measures were followed in some temples.[119]

For these reasons, this section will first provide a brief overview of the German federal system and the normative powers of the executive branch. Then, the strategies used to maintain inter-branch dialogue during the pandemic will be analyzed. Despite some specific problems, the management of the pandemic in Germany can provide important lessons for future crisis management and serve as a model for how emergencies should be handled.

7.3.1 German federalism and the role of subnational governments

Germany is a parliamentary federal republic that comprises 16 constituent units called *Länder*, plus the federal government. It can be described as a prime example of cooperative and interlocking federalism.[120] At the federal level, the state is organized through the Federal Council (*Bundesrat*) and the parliament (*Bundestag*). The *Bundesrat* is made up of representatives of the *Länder*, who may be the heads of government themselves, or officials appointed by them. These subnational units have legislatures, executives, and judiciaries of their own.[121]

The federal government is limited to policymaking functions, whereas the execution of laws largely falls to the *Länder*.[122] There are also local governments (municipalities and counties) that have the right to regulate all matters

119 German Federal Constitutional Court. Bundesverfassungsgericht (BVerfG). *Beschluss der 1. Kammer des Ersten Senats vom 15. April 2020 - 1 BvR 828/20 -, Rn. 1–19.* Available at: https://www.bverfg.de/e/rk20200415_1bvr082820.html; *Beschluss der 1. Kammer des Ersten Senats vom 17. April 2020 - 1 BvQ 37/20 -, Rn. 1–32.* Available at: http://www.bverfg.de/e/qk20200417_1bvq003720.html; Bundesverfassungsgericht (BVerfG). *Beschluss der 2. Kammer des Ersten Senats vom 29. April 2020 - 1 BvQ 44/20 -, Rn. 1–19.* Available at: http://www.bverfg.de/e/qk20200429_1bvq004420.html.

120 Sturm, Roland. The federal system: Breaking through the barriers of interlocking federalism? In: Helms, Ludger (Ed.). *Institutions and institutional change in the Federal Republic of Germany.* London, UK: Palgrave Macmillan, 2000, p. 105–123.

121 Isensee, Josef. *Handbuch des Staatsrechts der Bundesrepublik Deutschland.* Heidelberg: CF Müller GmbH, 2003, *passim*; Bumke, Christian; Voßkuhle, Andreas. *German constitutional law: Introduction, cases, and principles.* Oxford: Oxford University Press, 2019, *passim.*

122 Kuhlmann, Sabine et al. Tracing divergence in crisis governance: Responses to the COVID-19 pandemic in France, Germany and Sweden compared. *International Review of Administrative Sciences*, v. 87, n. 3, 2021, p. 556–575.

relevant to the local community under their own responsibility, within the limits established by law. These subunits have strong administrative structures and a wide range of responsibilities, including public health issues.[123]

Regarding crises, the German Constitution ("Basic Law") regulates the "classical" emergencies, that is, internal insurrection, war, and natural disasters. In these cases, the Constitution does not allow the suspension of constitutional rights, but only their limitation. In the absence of an explicit provision on public health emergencies, the central instrument in the fight against COVID-19 was the Act on the Prevention and Control of Infectious Diseases in Humans (Infektionsschutzgesetz),[124] which was successively amended to adapt it to the crisis.[125]

In this context, the pandemic in Germany was fought through a multi-level system that activated various vertical and horizontal coordination mechanisms within its "unitary federalism". The main feature of German interlocking federalism is the administrative functional division of powers, whereby the *Länder* implements federal legislation on their own responsibility and at their own expense. Complex negotiations between the federal government and the *Länder* are common and often involve states governed by parties that are different from those in power at the federal level. As a result, there is a strong emphasis on coordination and cooperation.[126]

The political-administrative relationship between the federal government and the *Länder* during COVID-19 reflected the German tradition of this unitary federalism, characterized by a collaborative political culture. During non-crisis periods, coordination between the heads of the federal and *Länder* governments takes place through regular informal meetings. Although the agreements reached at these meetings are not binding, the federal and state governments usually abide by them. As a result, there is a high degree of

123 Kuhlmann, Sabine; Franzke, Jochen. Multi-level responses to COVID-19: Crisis coordination in Germany from an intergovernmental perspective. *Local Government Studies*, v. 48, n. 2, 2022, p. 316.

124 Germany. *Gesetz zur Verhütung und Bekämpfung von Infektionskrankheiten beim Menschen (Act on the Prevention and Control of Infectious Diseases in Humans)*. Available at: https://www.gesetze-im-internet.de/ifsg/index.html.

125 Kuhlmann, Sabine; Franzke, Jochen. Multi-level responses to COVID-19: Crisis coordination in Germany from an intergovernmental perspective. *Local Government Studies*, v. 48, n. 2, 2022, p. 312–334; Kuhlmann, Sabine et al. Tracing divergence in crisis governance: Responses to the COVID-19 pandemic in France, Germany and Sweden compared. *International Review of Administrative Sciences*, v. 87, n. 3, 2021, p. 556–575; Kuhn, Katharina; Morlino, Irene. Decentralisation in times of crisis: Asset or liability? The case of Germany and Italy during Covid-19. *Swiss Political Science Review*, v. 28, n. 1, 2022, p. 105–115.

126 Kropp, Sabine; Schnabel, Johanna. Germany's response to COVID-19: Federal coordination and executive politics. In: Chattopadhyay, Rupak et al. (Eds.). *Federalism and the response to COVID-19: A comparative analysis*. New York: Routledge, 2022, p. 158.

standardization and harmonization, even in areas that are the exclusive responsibility of the *Länder*.[127]

The constitutional distribution of powers in a public health crisis place most of the responsibility on the *Länder*, which decided to introduce or relax most of the measures during COVID.[128] The country's health system is highly decentralized and involves a variety of subnational and local institutional actors, autonomous bodies, and sub-state authorities. While the federal level is basically limited to monitoring, surveillance, research, and legislative functions, most health-related functions are assigned to the state and local governments. The *Länder* are responsible for public health protection and the supervision of health professionals and institutions. They were therefore primarily responsible for managing the crisis on their territory and for the horizontal coordination of the various crisis-related administrative units at the local level.[129]

In general terms, the *Länder* were responsible for (i) coordinating and developing plans for local pandemic response; (ii) collecting, evaluating, and disseminating all available information on the local pandemic situation to the federal unit; (iii) organizing temporary transfers of personnel and reallocation of resources within local administrations; (iv) informing local citizens about the management of the pandemic; and (v) recruiting new staff and procuring equipment for health units.[130] In short, subnational and local governments have been fundamental in the strategy to manage and contain the virus.

7.3.2 Coordination and decentralization

In March 2020, in response to the increase in coronavirus transmission and mortality rates, a national strategy was launched under the leadership of former chancellor Angela Merkel to standardize the containment of the pandemic. A series of agreements were reached between the federal government and the *Länder*, which, although not binding, sought to harmonize the restrictive measures. An agreement reached on March 16, 2020, defined the "Joint Guidelines for Slowing the Spread of the Coronavirus", in which state and

127 Kuhn, Katharina; Morlino, Irene. Decentralisation in times of crisis: Asset or liability? The case of Germany and Italy during Covid-19. *Op. cit.*

128 Kaiser, Anna-Bettina; Hensel, Roman. Federal Republic of Germany: Legal Response to Covid-19. In: *The Oxford compendium of national legal responses to Covid-19.* April 2021. Available at: https://oxcon.ouplaw.com/view/https://doi.org/10.1093/law-occ19/law-occ19-e2; Kaiser, Anna-Bettina. The state of exception under German law and the current pandemic: Comparative models and constitutional rights. *e-Pública*, v. 7, n. 3, 2020, p. 4–15.

129 Kaiser, Anna-Bettina. The state of exception under German law and the current pandemic: Comparative models and constitutional rights. *Op. cit.*

130 Kuhlmann, Sabine; Franzke, Jochen. Multi-level responses to COVID-19: Crisis coordination in Germany from an intergovernmental perspective. *Local Government Studies*, v. 48, n. 2, 2022, p. 322–325.

federal governments attempted to adopt a uniform procedure throughout the country, followed by a series of other intergovernmental agreements.[131] Despite its formally nonbinding nature, all *Länder* enacted a lockdown and no-contact orders were issued, with the possibility of heavy fines for noncompliance.[132]

However, these initial attempts to standardize the response began to lose their force in June 2020, when the management of the pandemic again became highly decentralized. For example, North Rhine-Westphalia and Bavaria represented two extremes, with the former adopting a more permissive approach with fewer restrictions and the latter adopting stricter restrictions with continuous lockdowns and high fines. Even the reopening of schools was treated quite differently across the country, with some *Länder* reopening earlier and others later. Thus, there was an increasing variation and diversity of approaches, as well as an increasing complexity of hygiene and protection regulations, which differed in detail from one *Länder* to another.[133]

In late October 2020, another national agreement was reached to implement a partial lockdown, but some *Länder* again decided to deviate from the joint resolution. For example, while some decided to reopen hotels over Christmas, other states, such as Bavaria and Berlin, reduced the number of people allowed to meet privately.[134] According to political scientists, these variations can be explained by regional differences in contamination rates and political preferences.[135]

In short, these multiple approaches show the importance of a plurality of decision-making bodies. Unlike in Brazil, most local governments in Germany had the resources and administrative efficiency to respond to the challenges. A fully centralized and uniform response by an "unbounded" central executive would probably not have been as effective. Despite the centrality and importance of Chancellor Angela Merkel during the pandemic, the plurality of decision-making poles certainly brought greater efficiency to the fight against

131 Germany. Federal Government Official Website. *The Federal Government informs. Agreement between the Federal Government and the federal states - Guidelines for the fight against the corona epidemic of 16.03.2020 (Die Bundesregierung informiert. Vereinbarung zwischen Bundesregierung und den Bundesländern - Leitlinien zum Kampf gegen die Corona-Epidemie vom 16.03.2020).* Available at: https://www.bundesregierung.de/breg-de/themen/coronavirus/leitlinien-zum-kampf-gegen-die-corona-epidemie-vom-16-03-2020-1730942.

132 Eckhard, Steffen; Lenz, Alexa. *Die öffentliche Wahrnehmung des Krisenmanagements in der Covid-19 Pandemie.* Konstanz: KOPS, 2020, p. 7.

133 Kuhlmann, Sabine; Franzke, Jochen. Multi-level responses to COVID-19: Crisis coordination in Germany from an intergovernmental perspective. *Local Government Studies*, v. 48, n. 2, 2022, p. 328.

134 Kropp, Sabine; Schnabel, Johanna. Germany's response to COVID-19: Federal coordination and executive politics. In: Chattopadhyay, Rupak et al. (Eds.). *Federalism and the response to COVID-19: A comparative analysis.* New York: Routledge, 2022, p. 162.

135 Kuhlmann, Sabine et al. Tracing divergence in crisis governance: Responses to the COVID-19 pandemic in France, Germany and Sweden compared. *International Review of Administrative Sciences*, v. 87, n. 3, 2021, p. 556–575.

the crisis. The pandemic revealed the importance of the *Länder* as providers of public policy.[136]

Moreover, the agreements reached between the central and state governments were very important in ensuring that all local governments were aware of the importance of the restrictive measures and the risks that the country as a whole was facing. As mentioned earlier, this kind of pluralistic and deliberative government is extremely important, especially in times of crisis. There was central coordination and attempts at standardization to prevent the response from becoming chaotic. This harmonization between local responses and central coordination was essential to the successful crisis management in Germany, which is the highest-ranked country in Europe for its COVID-19 response.[137]

7.3.3 *Delegated legislation: predefinition of the content, object, and scope of executive regulations*

Because of its dictatorial past, Germany's Constitution limits the legislative powers of the executive branch and is concerned about excessively strong chancellors.[138] In the case of delegation of normative power to the executive, article 80 of the Basic Law expressly states that the delegating statute must determine the content, object, and scope of the secondary legislation.[139] The

136 Kropp, Sabine; Schnabel, Johanna. Germany's response to COVID-19. Federal coordination and executive politics. *Op. cit.*, p. 166.

137 Euronews. *Germany is the highest-ranked country in Europe for its COVID-19 response, new survey reveals.* October 7, 2020. Available at: https://www.euronews.com/2020/10/07/germany-is-the-highest-ranked-country-in-europe-for-its-covid-19-response-new-survey-revea. *See also* Time Magazine. *The best global responses to the COVID-19 pandemic, 1 year later.* February 23, 2021. Available at: https://time.com/5851633/best-global-responses-covid-19/ and ISGlobal - Barcelona Institute for Global Health. *COVID-19: Scientific updates.* Available at: https://www.isglobal.org/en/archivo-novedades-cientificas-covid19.

138 Isensee, Josef. *Handbuch des Staatsrechts der Bundesrepublik Deutschland.* Heidelberg: CF Müller GmbH, 2003, *passim*; Bumke, Christian; Voßkuhle, Andreas. *German constitutional law: Introduction, cases, and principles.* Oxford University Press, 2019, *passim.*

139 Basic Law for the Federal Republic of Germany.

> Article 80 [Issuance of statutory instruments] (1) The Federal Government, a Federal Minister or the Land governments may be authorised by a law to issue statutory instruments. The content, purpose and scope of the authority conferred shall be specified in the law. Each statutory instrument shall contain a statement of its legal basis. If the law provides that such authority may be further delegated, such subdelegation shall be effected by statutory instrument. (2) Unless a federal law otherwise provides, the consent of the Bundesrat shall be required for statutory instruments issued by the Federal Government or a Federal Minister regarding fees or basic principles for the use of postal and telecommunication facilities, basic principles for levying of charges for the use of facilities of federal railways or the construction and operation of railways, as well as for statutory instruments issued pursuant to federal laws that require the consent of the Bundesrat or that are executed by the Länder on federal commission or in their own right. (3) The Bundesrat may submit to the Federal Government drafts of statutory instruments that require its consent. (4) Insofar as Land

legislator is obliged to indicate what purposes should be pursued by the government when using the legal authorization. There is a high level of requirements and "sufficiency" regarding a law's normative density. The executive's regulations must be as precise as possible.

The Constitution prohibits assigning "blank delegation" to the government: there is a "commandment of determinability" directed at the legislature when it comes to regulating or transferring normative power to the executive.[140] As already mentioned, according to the "materiality principle" (*Wesentlichkeitstheorie*), developed by the German Federal Constitutional Court, all relevant decisions, particularly those encroaching onto fundamental rights, must be made by parliament.

In other words, the federal government, the federal ministers, or the governments of the *Länder* may issue secondary regulations (*Rechtsverordnungen*) only if they have been expressly authorized to do so by a parliamentary act of delegation. In principle, parliaments are not involved in the enactment or review of regulations. However, there are specific situations in which the approval of the Federal Council (*Bundesrat*) is required for regulations issued by the federal executive, unless otherwise specified in the delegating statute.[141]

During the pandemic, the *Länder* governments gave concrete form to primary parliamentary legislation through secondary regulations. Sections 32 and 28 of the Infection Protection Act[142] gave the *Länder* executives the authority to enact regulations to combat the emergency. Initially, section 28 did not specifically describe the measures that the *Länder* were authorized to take, but instead spoke very broadly of "necessary protective measures".[143] Faced with this weak legal basis, German doctrine and jurisprudence began to criticize this excessively vague and imprecise delegation, stating that the law contained provisions that were not sufficiently specified. The local courts again and again overturned restrictions on the grounds that they were not well-founded in the rule of law. They also explicitly demanded a new legal

governments are authorised by or pursuant to federal laws to issue statutory instruments, the Länder shall also be entitled to regulate the matter by a law.

140 Pünder, Hermann. Democratic legitimation of delegated legislation – a comparative view on the American, British and German law. *International & Comparative Law Quarterly*, v. 58, n. 2, 2009, p. 353–378.

141 Kaiser, Anna-Bettina; Hensel, Roman. Federal Republic of Germany: Legal response to Covid-19. In: *The Oxford compendium of national legal responses to Covid-19*. April 2021. Available at: https://oxcon.ouplaw.com/view/https://doi.org/10.1093/law-occ19/law-occ19-e2.

142 Germany. *Gesetz zur Verhütung und Bekämpfung von Infektionskrankheiten beim Menschen (Act on the Prevention and Control of Infectious Diseases in Humans)*. Available at: https://www.gesetze-im-internet.de/ifsg/index.html.

143 Germany. *Gesetz zur Verhütung und Bekämpfung von Infektionskrankheiten beim Menschen (Act on the Prevention and Control of Infectious Diseases in Humans). Op. cit.*

basis from the legislature to clearly define and describe the "content, purpose and scope" of the measures.[144]

This debate led to the adoption of section 28a of the Infection Protection Act, which specifies the requirements and content of such regulations. This new provision, approved on November 18, 2020, finally provided an adequate legal basis for standard measures against the coronavirus, listing an extensive catalog of permissible measures to be implemented by the *Länder*. It defined the restrictive measures in detail, leaving little room for unconstitutional administrative creation. It also stipulated that this secondary legislation should contain a sunset clause limiting their validity to a specific date.[145] Indeed, the new section 28a of the Infection Protection Act specified that the *Länder* were allowed to take measures such as bans on events and gatherings, travel bans, the requirement to wear face masks, and the closure of shops and other premises. These measures were bound to specific thresholds and subject to further conditions, and *Länder's* orders were limited to a duration of four weeks.[146]

Section 28a established the following parameters to guide executive action: (i) the protective measures should not result in the complete isolation of individuals or groups, and a minimum of social contact should be ensured; (ii) executive authorities should take into account changes in the incidence of infection due to more contagious virus variants that place a greater burden on the health care system; and (iii) protective measures should take into account the respective regional and supra-regional incidence of infection, with the aim of avoiding imminent overburdening of regional and supra-regional health care systems.

The Infection Protection Act further stated that (iv) the main indicator for further protective measures should be the number of cases of coronavirus disease 2019 (COVID-19) per 100,000 population hospitalized within seven days; (v) the protective measures may be differentiated regionally within a *Länder*; and (vi) restrictive measures shall be accompanied by a general statement of reasons and shall be limited in time.[147]

144 Kropp, Sabine; Schnabel, Johanna. Germany's response to COVID-19: Federal coordination and executive politics. *Op. cit.*, p. 160.

145 Kaiser, Anna-Bettina. The state of exception under German law and the current pandemic: Comparative models and constitutional rights. *e-Pública*, v. 7, n. 3, 2020, p. 4–15.

146 Kropp, Sabine; Schnabel, Johanna. Germany's response to COVID-19: Federal coordination and executive politics. *Op. cit.*, p. 160.

147 German Infectious Diseases Protection Act (Infektionsschutzgesetz, IfSG). Section 5, § 28a.

> Special protective measures to prevent the spread of coronavirus disease 2019 (COVID-19) in the event of an epidemic situation of national significance (1) Necessary protective measures (. . .) to prevent the spread of the coronavirus disease 2019 (COVID-19) may be, in particular, for the duration of the declaration of an epidemic situation of national significance (. . .) 1. Arrangement of a distance requirement in public spaces, 2. Obligation to wear a mouth-nose cover (mask obligation), (. . .) shall be based in particular on the

These dialogues between parliament, courts, and jurists are extremely healthy and important in a democracy. The fact that the German parliament pushed for a reform of the Infection Protection Act after criticism of the lack of proper delegation shows a healthy openness to the other institutional actors. Although laws are not expected to exhaust all executive actions during a crisis, it is certain that they must contain a high normative density, as was the case with this November 2020 reform.

Moreover, the Infection Protection Act also delegated significant normative power to the central government's minister of health, who was empowered to issue unilateral regulations with restrictive measures without parliamentary approval and without consulting the states and their parliaments. This lack of prior control was also subject to much criticism by German jurists, who considered it unconstitutional for two reasons. First, they defended that the executive regulations couldn't deviate from parliamentary legislation. Second, according to the Basic Law, it is generally the *Länder* that applies federal law, not a federal authority.[148]

---

protection of life and health and the functioning of the health care system; foreseeable changes in the incidence of infection due to more contagious virus variants that place a greater burden on the health care system shall be taken into account. In particular, the protective measures referred to in points 1, 2, 3, 5 and 18 of paragraph 1 may be taken to prevent infection. Further protective measures shall be taken considering the respective regional and supra-regional incidence of infection with the aim of avoiding an imminent overload of regional and supra-regional inpatient care. The main indicator for further protective measures is the number of cases of coronavirus disease 2019 (COVID-19) per 100,000 population hospitalized within seven days. Other indicators, such as the number of new SARS-CoV-2 coronavirus infections per 100,000 population within seven days, differentiated according to aspects of the epidemiology of the infection, the available intensive care capacity and the number of persons vaccinated against coronavirus disease 2019 (COVID-19), should be taken into account when assessing the incidence of infection. When determining the protective measures, the Land governments may set threshold values for the indicators pursuant to sentences 4 and 5 in an ordinance pursuant to § 32, taking into account the respective inpatient treatment capacities; accordingly, the protective measures may be differentiated regionally within a Land. The Robert Koch Institute shall publish on the Internet at https://www.rki.de/ covid-19-trends daily data on the indicators pursuant to sentences 4 and 5, broken down by age group and relating at least to individual Länder and to the territory of the Federal Republic of Germany. The Länder may also use the indicators pursuant to sentences 4 and 5 as a benchmark for the Land or the respective region instead of in relation to 100,000 inhabitants, differentiated by Land or region. (4) When collecting contact data pursuant to subsection (1) no. 18, the data controllers may only collect and process personal data and information on the time and place of residence if this is absolutely necessary for contact tracing. The controllers shall ensure that the data collected are not accessible to unauthorized persons. The data may not be used for any other purpose than to provide them upon request to the authorities designated by state law (. . .) (5) Orders issued pursuant to *section 32* in conjunction with *section 28*(1) and *section 28a*(1) shall be accompanied by a general statement of reasons and shall be limited in time. The period of validity shall generally be four weeks; it may be extended.

148 Kaiser, Anna-Bettina; Hensel, Roman. Federal Republic of Germany: Legal response to Covid-19. In: *The Oxford compendium of national legal responses to Covid-19*. April 2021.

Also, it is interesting to comment briefly on the ways in which the legislature can participate in and control the issuance of executive regulations. The *Bundestag* can participate in the process of making *Rechtsverordnungen* (secondary legislation) in distinct ways. In the words of Hermann Pünder, the most important tools to ensure parliamentary influence are so-called *Zustimmungsverordnungen* (consent decrees) which "need the consent of parliament before they are promulgated. However, some subordinate legislation has only to be explained by the administration to the Bundestag. Parliament then has the chance to voice its opinion".[149] Also, there are the *Aufhebungsverordnungen* (cancellation regulations) which "can be vetoed by the Bundestag after their promulgation. The German Constitutional Court only requires a 'legitimate interest of the legislature' to maintain influence on the sub-legislative law-making".[150] Thus, it can be seen that a certain degree of legislative control over administrative regulations is possible in the German system.

7.3.4 Judicial oversight during the pandemic: balancing fundamental rights

Germany's Federal Constitutional Court has generally upheld the constitutionality of the coronavirus containment measures, rejecting hundreds of lawsuits seeking to overturn the restrictions. In some cases, however, the Court has intervened to limit executive action. It emphasized that despite the emergency scenario, fundamental rights should not be forgotten. In balancing rights, the Court sought to reconcile the right to life and public health with the freedoms of religion, assembly, and movement. Court justices analyzed whether the measures were in line with the principle of proportionality and whether they affected the essence of a basic right.

One of the most prominent cases decided by the Court during this period concerned a protest in Giessen, which the organizers called "Strengthening health instead of weakening basic rights – protection against viruses, not people". The organizers informed the City Council about the march that was to take place on April 17, 2020, with a limited participation of 30 people and the observance of the appropriate safety measures, such as wearing masks and

Available at: https://oxcon.ouplaw.com/view/https://doi.org/10.1093/law-occ19/law-occ19-e2, 2021; Thielbörger, P.; Behlert, B. *COVID-19 und das Grundgesetz. Verfassungsblog vom 19.03.2020.* Available at: https://verfassungsblog.de/covid-19-und-das-grundgesetz/; Kuhlmann, Sabine; Franzke, Jochen. Multi-level responses to COVID-19: Crisis coordination in Germany from an intergovernmental perspective. *Local Government Studies*, v. 48, n. 2, 2022, p. 328.

149 Pünder, Hermann. Democratic legitimation of delegated legislation – a comparative view on the American, British and German law. *International & Comparative Law Quarterly*, v. 58, n. 2, 2009, p. 353–378.

150 Pünder, Hermann. Democratic legitimation of delegated legislation – a comparative view on the American, British and German law. *Op. cit.*

maintaining a distance of 1.5 meters between participants, with markings on the ground indicating the positions.

The problem began when the local government banned the march on the grounds that a state decree on measures to fight the coronavirus prohibited the gathering in the street of more than two people who do not live in the same household. In addition, the City Council said that the organizers could not guarantee that the participants would respect the minimum distance rule, thus endangering public order and safety. One of the organizers then challenged the executive decision in the local courts. After court proceedings and appeals, the case reached the German Constitutional Court.

In the case, the Court recognized the undue restriction on freedom of assembly and demonstration and ruled that the protest could go ahead as planned. According to the ruling, the local government decree does not contain a general ban on assemblies of more than two people. It only states that contact with other people not living in the same building must be limited to the absolute minimum necessary. Thus, the analysis of the legality of the public demonstration must take into account all the circumstances of the concrete case. The Court stressed that the City Council simply banned the protest without taking into account all the circumstances of the case, including the fact that the demonstration would observe the protective measures ordered to prevent the spread of COVID-19, such as maintaining a minimum distance between participants and the use of appropriate masks. The Court then concluded that the local executive had violated the protesters' fundamental right to freedom of assembly.[151]

In the same vein, the Court analyzed another case on the constitutionality of public protests at the Schlossplatz in the center of Stuttgart, the capital of the state of Baden-Württemberg. The protest also aimed to draw attention to the impact of measures to combat the pandemic on the fundamental rights of citizens. The slogan of the demonstration in Stuttgart sent a very clear message to the parliament and the government: "We will not give up the first 20 articles of the constitution. We demand an end to the state of emergency". As in the previous case, the Court stressed that the local administrative authorities had failed to recognize that they had to take into account the freedom of assembly. The authorities should have considered, if possible together with the protest organizers, what alternative measures were available to balance freedom of assembly and protection against infectious diseases.[152]

In this case, the Court reaffirmed that restrictions on the right to freedom of assembly cannot be imposed by administrators or parliament in abstract

151 Germany. Bundesverfassungsgericht (BVerfG) (German Federal Constitutional Court). *Beschluss der 1. Kammer des Ersten Senats vom 15. April 2020 - 1 BvR 828/20 -, Rn. 1–19.* Available at: https://www.bverfg.de/e/rk20200415_1bvr082820.html.

152 Germany. Bundesverfassungsgericht (BVerfG) (German Federal Constitutional Court). *Beschluss der 1. Kammer des Ersten Senats vom 17. April 2020 - 1 BvQ 37/20 -, Rn. 1–32.* Available at: http://www.bverfg.de/e/qk20200417_1bvq003720.html.

terms, but only in concrete terms, taking into account all the circumstances of the particular case. It is the duty of the public authorities to adopt a cooperative attitude towards the organizers of demonstrations and, instead of simply prohibiting them, to try to take effective measures in each case to minimize the risk of contagion during demonstrations.

The third case decided by the Court concerned a request by a Muslim citizen to hold Friday prayers in the mosque during Ramadan, despite the ban on religious gatherings in Lower Saxony. The petitioner guaranteed a number of safeguards, including limiting the number of participants to 24 in a mosque with a capacity of 300 worshippers and maintaining a minimum distance of 1.5 meters. He argued that the mosque should be allowed to open under similar conditions as shops. The Court ruled that the risk of infection depended on several details, from the way the service itself was conducted to the size and construction of the mosque. Given the serious restriction of religious freedom that prohibiting Friday worship in mosques during Ramadan would entail, the policies to combat the pandemic do not justify a general ban without providing for the possibility of an exception. It should take into account all the circumstances of the case.[153]

Thus, it can be observed that the German Constitutional Court exercised attentive oversight of executive measures. Although it has generally recognized the constitutionality of the restrictions, in specific cases it has reaffirmed the importance of preserving the essence of fundamental rights. The Court has sent a clear message to the executive and parliament: it will not tolerate violations of fundamental rights that are not carefully justified by the facts of each case. In other words, fundamental rights cannot be limited in a broad and abstract way, but only within the limits that are strictly necessary in specific cases, always preserving the hard core of each right.

In summary, the German management of the COVID-19 pandemic demonstrates the importance of executive oversight by the legislature, the judiciary, and local governments. This "strong form review" approach is the optimal strategy for crisis management. Administrators should not act "unboundedly", especially in times of uncertainty when the optimal response is unclear. As happened in Germany, the judiciary can enforce constitutional principles, while local authorities can tailor policies to the specific interests of each location. Normative delegations should also have a very clear and specific legal basis and must specify the content, purpose, and scope of the secondary rule. This plural approach certainly provides for more effective and legitimate responses from a democratic and constitutional perspective.

153 Germany. Bundesverfassungsgericht (BVerfG) (German Federal Constitutional Court). Bundesverfassungsgericht (BVerfG). *Beschluss der 2. Kammer des Ersten Senats vom 29. April 2020 - 1 BvQ 44/20 -, Rn. 1–19.* Available at: http://www.bverfg.de/e/qk20200429_1bvq004420.html.

Bibliography

Bar-Siman-Tov, Ittai. Legislatures in the time of Covid-19. The *Theory and Practice of Legislation*, v. 8, n. 1–2, 2020, p. 8.

Beqiraj, Julinda. Italy's Coronavirus legislative response: Adjusting along the way. *Verfassungsblog*. April 8, 2020. Available at: https://verfassungsblog.de/italys-coronavirus-legislative- response-adjusting-along-the-way/.

Bickerton, Christopher J.; Accetti, Carlo Invernizzi. 'Techno-populism'as a new party family: The case of the five star movement and Podemos. *Contemporary Italian Politics*, v. 10, n. 2, 2018, p. 132–150.

Brazilian Supreme Federal Court (STF). ADI 6347 MC-Ref, Rel. Alexandre de Moraes, published on August 14, 2020; ADPF 690, Rel. Alexandre de Moraes, published on April 15, 2021.

Brazilian Supreme Federal Court (STF). ADI 6586 Rel. Ricardo Lewandowski, published on April 7, 2021.

Brazilian Supreme Federal Court (STF). ADPF 635 MC, Rel. Edson Fachin, published on December 15, 2021.

Brazilian Supreme Federal Court (STF). ADPF 668 Rel. Roberto Barroso, Monocratic Decision published on May 11, 2020.

Brazilian Supreme Federal Court (STF). ADPF 672 MC-Ref, Rel. Alexandre de Moraes, published on October 29, 2020; ADI 6341 MC-Ref, Rel. Marco Aurélio, Relator(a) p/ Acórdão: Edson Fachin, Tribunal Pleno, published on November 13, 2020.

Brazilian Supreme Federal Court (STF). ADPF 709 MC-Ref, Rel. Roberto Barroso, published on October 7, 2020.

Brazilian Supreme Federal Court (STF). ADPF 742 MC, Rel. Marco Aurélio, Relator(a) p/ Acórdão: Edson Fachin, published on April 29, 2021.

Brazilian Supreme Federal Court (STF). ADPF 754 TPI-segunda-Ref. Rel. Ricardo Lewandowski, published on March 11, 2021.

Brazilian Supreme Federal Court (STF). ADPF 756 TPI-Ref, Rel. Ricardo Lewandowski, published on March 30, 2021.

Brazilian Supreme Federal Court (STF). ADPF 770 MC-Ref, Rel. Min. Ricardo Lewandowski, published on February 24, 2021.

Carey, John M.; Shugart, Matthew Soberg. Calling out the tanks or filling out the forms? In: Carey, John M.; Shugart, Matthew Soberg (Org.). *Executive decree authority*. Cambridge: Cambridge University Press, 1998, p. 1–29.

Cavino, Massimo et al. Covid-19. Una prima lettura dei provvedimenti adottati dal Governo. *Op. cit.*

Claudiani, Simona. Brevi Note Sui DPCM: Tra Emergenza e Stabilizzazione. In: Morana, Donatella; Mabellini, Stefania (Eds.). *L'emergenza pandemica e l'impatto sul diritto pubblico: innovazione e prospettive future. Quaderni del Dottorato di Ricerca in Diritto Pubblico dell'Università degli Studi di Roma "Tor Vergata"*. Milan: Wolters Kluwer, 2022, p. 69.

Eckhard, Steffen; Lenz, Alexa. *Die öffentliche Wahrnehmung des Krisenmanagements in der Covid-19 Pandemie*. Konstanz: KOPS, 2020, p. 7.

Ferraz, Octávio Luiz Motta; Rached, Danielle; Ventura, Deisy; Hubner Mendes, Conrado; Alberto, Marco Antônio Moraes. Brazil: Legal response to Covid-19. In: King, Jeff et al. (Eds.). *The Oxford compendium of national legal responses to Covid-19*. 2021. Available at: https://oxcon.ouplaw.com/display/10.1093/law-occ19/law-occ19-e16.

Grogan, Joelle. Analyzing global use of emergency powers in response to COVID-19. *European Journal of Law Reform*, v. 4, 2020, p. 345.

Guzzetta, Giovanni. DPCM e Costituzione anche alla luce della sent. 198/2021 della Corte costituzionale. *Op. cit.*

Guzzetta, Giovanni. Le fonti dell'emergenza alla prova della pandemia. *Op. cit.*

Inácio, Magna; Recch, Filipe; Valencia, Carolina Guerrero. The power of the administrative decisions of Latin American presidents. In: Llanos, Mariana; Marsteintredet, Leiv (Eds.). *Latin America in Times of Turbulence: Presidentialism Under Stress.* New York: Routledge, 2023, p. 99–102.

Isensee, Josef. *Handbuch des Staatsrechts der Bundesrepublik Deutschland.* Heidelberg: CF Müller GmbH, 2003, *passim*; Bumke, Christian; Voßkuhle, Andreas. *German constitutional law: Introduction, cases, and principles.* Oxford: Oxford University Press, 2019, *passim.*

Kaiser, Anna-Bettina. The state of exception under German law and the current pandemic: Comparative models and constitutional rights. *e-Pública*, v. 7, n. 3, 2020, p. 4–15.

Kaiser, Anna-Bettina; Hensel, Roman. Federal Republic of Germany: Legal response to Covid-19. In: *The Oxford compendium of national legal responses to Covid-19.* May 2022. Available at: https://oxcon. ouplaw.com/view/https://doi.org/10.1093/law-occ19/law-occ19-e2.

Kropp, Sabine; Schnabel, Johanna. Germany's response to COVID-19: Federal coordination and executive politics. In: Chattopadhyay, Rupak et al. (Eds.). *Federalism and the response to COVID-19: A comparative analysis.* New York: Routledge, 2022, p. 158.

Kuhlmann, Sabine et al. Tracing divergence in crisis governance: Responses to the COVID-19 pandemic in France, Germany and Sweden compared. *International Review of Administrative Sciences*, v. 87, n. 3, 2021, p. 556–575.

Kuhn, Katharina; Morlino, Irene. Decentralisation in times of crisis: Asset or liability? The case of Germany and Italy during Covid-19. *Swiss Political Science Review*, v. 28, n. 1, 2022, p. 105–115.

Luciani, Massimo et al. Il sistema delle fonti del diritto alla prova dell'emergenza. *Rivista Aic*, v. 2020, n. 2, 2020, p. 109–141.

Lupo, Nicola et al. Come evitare l'auto-emarginazione del Parlamento nell'emergenza attuale. *Osservatorio Costituzionale*, n. 6, 2020, p. 7–28.

Matteucci, Stefano Civitarese et al. Italy: Legal response to Covid-19. In: *The Oxford compendium of national legal responses to Covid-19.* May 2022. Available at: https://oxcon.ouplaw.com/display/10.1093/law-occ19/law-occ19-e11.

Musella, Fortunato. I poteri di emergenza nella Repubblica dei Presidenti. *Op. cit.*

Pinheiro, Victor Marcel; Ilarraz, Marcelo; Mestriner, Melissa Terni. The impacts of the COVID-19 crisis on the Brazilian legal system–a report on the functioning of the branches of the government and on the legal scrutiny of their activities. *The Theory and Practice of Legislation*, v. 8, n. 1–2, 2020, p. 195.

Pozen, Davi; Scheppele, Kim L. Executive underreach, in pandemics and otherwise. *American Journal of International Law*, v. 114, 2020, p. 608–617.

Pünder, Hermann. Democratic legitimation of delegated legislation – a comparative view on the American, British and German law. *International & Comparative Law Quarterly*, v. 58, n. 2, 2009, p. 353–378.

Ramos, Edith Maria Barbosa; Ramos, Paulo Roberto Barbosa; Costa, Laísse Lima Silva. Pandemia e Federalismo: Reflexões sobre as decisões do Supremo Tribunal Federal na apreciação de conflitos de competência entre os entes federativos no enfrentamento à Covid-19. *Revista de Ciências Jurídicas e Sociais-IURJ*, v. 1, n. 1, 2020, p. 46–61.

Romanelli, Raffaele (Ed.). *Storia dello Stato italiano dall'Unità a oggi.* Roma: Donzelli editore, 1995, *passim.*

Rullo, Luigi. The COVID-19 pandemic crisis and the personalization of the government in Italy. *International Journal of Public Leadership*, v. 17, n. 2, 2021, p. 199.

Saurer, Johannes. Patterns of cooperative administrative federalism in the German response to COVID-19. *Administrative Law Review*, v. 73, n. 1, 2021, p. 139–163.

Sturm, Roland. The federal system: Breaking through the barriers of interlocking federalism? In: Helms, Ludger (Ed.). *Institutions and institutional change in the Federal Republic of Germany*. London, UK: Palgrave Macmillan, 2000, p. 105–123.
Teixeira, Carmen Fontes; Santos, Jamilli Silva. Análise estratégica da atuação do governo federal brasileiro na pandemia de COVID-19: 2020–2021. *Ciência & Saúde Coletiva*, v. 28, 2023, p. 1277–1286.
Trabucco, Daniele. Il "virus" nel sistema delle fonti: decreti-legge e dpcm al tempo del Covid-19: tra principio di legalità formale e principio di legalità sostanziale. *Op. cit.*
Vieira, Oscar Vilhena; Glezer, Rubens; Barbosa, Ana Laura Pereira. Supremocracia e Infralegalismo Autoritário: o comportamento do Supremo Tribunal Federal durante o governo Bolsonaro. *Novos estudos CEBRAP*, 2023, v. 41, p. 599.
Windholz, Eric L. Governing in a pandemic: From parliamentary sovereignty to autocratic technocracy. *The Theory and Practice of Legislation*, v. 8, n. 1–2, 2020, p. 93–113.

Conclusions

Executive dominance and unchecked regulatory activity are undesirable from a constitutional and democratic perspective, especially in times of crisis. Despite the need for speed and expertise in emergency management, parliamentary and judicial involvement remains important and necessary. The system of checks and balances should be even stronger and more active during crises. The legislature must play an active role in overseeing executive actions and in drafting new legislation to respond to problems that arise. It offers distinct advantages as an arena for political debate, and serves as the ultimate locus of democratic legitimacy. Courts, in turn, must provide substantive review of restrictions on rights and, in the case of omissions, require the government to take active steps to address the emergency. Finally, subnational governments can design policies that meet local needs and preferences.

Also, the need for speed and flexibility during crisis should not be used as a license for administrators to abuse their decree authority. Chief executives need to establish a dialogue with the legislature so that both can find cooperative solutions without the regulatory burden falling entirely on the executive. Technological communication tools and faster legislative processes allow legislators to participate in policymaking in emergencies, producing more democratic and responsive solutions to the different political forces that exist in society.

Indeed, the argument of the greater technical expertise of the public administration cannot be used as a trump card to approve exorbitant regulations that clearly go beyond the limits of the laws. Although the executive has broader technical and informational capacity to regulate certain matters, it should not use this institutional superiority to alienate the legislatures from issues that should clearly be the subject of broad democratic deliberation. It is important for the executive to share relevant technical information with the legislative bodies, rather than using it as a pretext for unilateral action. Armed with this relevant data, parliamentarians could engage in open and productive discussions, leading to greater publicity and increased popular participation.

During the COVID-19 pandemic, for example, the excessive use of executive decrees was widely criticized by constitutionalists and political scientists.

DOI: 10.4324/9781003610816-9

The monocratic and non-collegial nature of unilateral executive acts is reprehensible in light of the importance of democratic deliberation. The participation of parliament in important decisions is not a mere formality: the legislature is the place that best reflects the different political forces in society. Emergencies should not be an excuse to create an administrative leviathan. They do not justify a radical transfer of normative power from the legislature to the executive. In the future, crises must be addressed by collegial, pluralistic bodies, not by the pen of chief executives.

In several countries, the COVID-19 emergency has accelerated and deepened the growing presidentialization of parliamentary systems. It served as a favorable condition for presidents and prime ministers to introduce new practices and to expand their normative power. The pandemic led to a growing dominance of the executive and increased the verticalization and concentration of decision-making powers. In many democracies, it meant a consolidation of the dominance of presidents and prime ministers at the expense of parliaments.

In effect, jurists' concern about the legal instruments of anti-crisis measures does not reflect a mere formal concern or a legalistic caprice. On the contrary, the centrality of primary normative sources corresponds to an essential logic of constitutional design. Fundamental decisions in the public interest must originate in the choices made by the people's representatives, in the heart of the democratic circuit that is parliament. The principle of legality requires that normative instruments imposing restrictions on rights should follow a hierarchical system typical of the organization of a democratic state. Decrees cannot claim to regulate significant parts of citizens' lives in a preventive and general way without parliamentary control. Executive unilateral acts should not have been the instrument for fundamental political decisions during the COVID-19 emergency.

In this sense, in all anti-crisis measures, the legal basis for administrative action should include the circumstances under which an executive act can be taken, the forms of action that may be taken, time limits on both the use of power and the duration of measures adopted, and explicit provisions for the parliamentary scrutiny and judicial review. Legislatures must not give a "blank delegation" of normative authority to administrators. Governments should clearly identify the legal basis for their measures. Delegating laws should set explicit limits, conditions, and checks on administrative power.

In a comparative perspective, Italy, Brazil, and Germany provided significantly different legal responses to the COVID-19 pandemic, reflecting varying degrees of legislative and judicial involvement in managing the crisis. Italy's approach, characterized as a "weak-form review", highlighted the centralization of power in the executive branch through the extensive use of prime minister's decrees (DPCMs). This scenario raised constitutional concerns over the delegation of legislative power and the erosion of parliamentary oversight, illustrating the risks associated with concentrating authority without clear legal frameworks and robust checks and balances.

In contrast, Brazil's "mid-term review" revealed a complex interplay between federal, state, and municipal governments, exacerbated by a lack of coordination and conflicting policies. The National Congress and the judiciary played pivotal roles in attempting to mitigate the executive's inaction and denialist stance. However, the resulting regulatory chaos and federal omissions contributed to one of the worst humanitarian crises globally, underscoring the critical need for effective intergovernmental collaboration and adherence to scientific guidance during emergencies.

Germany's "strong-form review" exemplified an effective balance between executive action and oversight by legislative and judicial branches within a cooperative federalist system. The German response was characterized by detailed legislative frameworks, active involvement of the *Länder*, and vigilant judicial review that safeguarded fundamental rights while implementing necessary public health measures. This approach underscores the importance of clear constitutional provisions, precise delegation of powers, and the maintenance of democratic principles even in times of crisis.

The comparative analysis of these three countries reveals that a "strong-form review", involving comprehensive oversight and active participation of all branches of government, is optimal for managing emergencies. Such an approach ensures that executive actions are grounded in solid legal bases, respects the division of powers, and upholds constitutional safeguards. The experiences of Italy, Brazil, and Germany during the COVID-19 pandemic provide valuable lessons on the significance of constitutional design and federal structures in shaping effective and democratic responses to global crises. Emphasizing robust legislative and judicial engagement not only enhances the legitimacy of emergency measures but also contributes to more effective and balanced crisis management, ultimately safeguarding both public health and democratic integrity.

Furthermore, it is important to highlight that secondary legislation, such as decrees, ordinances, and regulations, is not only used for ordinary administrative matters of lesser political value. Presidents and prime ministers have resorted to these normative instruments to construct all sorts of public policies without the approval of parliament and to consolidate their political power. They are an easier alternative for chief executives than the legislative process, since they do not require the formation of coalitions, the cooperation of legislative committees, or the support of party leaders. Much more than administrative tools, they are effective legislative instruments containing general and abstract provisions and, in many cases, innovations in rights and obligations.

Chief executives can use decrees to (i) circumvent congressional opposition; (ii) develop public policy quickly and flexibly, especially in times of crisis; (iii) fulfill campaign promises and speak directly to their support base; (iv) fill regulatory gaps; (v) interpret laws according to their political-ideological guidelines; and, finally, (vi) relieve the legislature of the political burden of approving a particular policy.

The number and contours of decrees are explained not only by the personality of the executive, but also by the institutional arrangements defined by the constitution of each country and the political context of each period. The literature on the subject indicates that the frequency with which these acts are issued varies according to (i) the party composition of Congress, that is, whether or not the president has a legislative majority; (ii) the president's popularity; (iii) the length of his term; (iv) the proximity of the election period; and (v) the existence of an economic, political, or social crisis. Unilateral action in this context is the result of the president's interaction with Congress, the courts, the media, the public, and the business community in response to specific political strategies and motivations.

The abusive use of decrees violates the principle of separation of powers, because it is a way to bypass Congress and the ordinary legislative process; and bypass democracy itself, because the process of drafting these laws does not involve prior public deliberation and can be subject to review only after the fact. Allowing presidents and prime ministers to innovate in the legal order and to legislate on their own, creating rights and obligations, violates the principle of separation of powers and the framework that the Constitution creates for the executive branch. Certainly, concentrating the drafting of normative acts of broad political relevance in the hands of a unipersonal and non-deliberative body involves a high democratic risk. The executive's unilateral policymaking process should be carried out in a measured way, in specific situations and for specific purposes, within legal and constitutional limits, and should not be used as an excuse to circumvent political and partisan difficulties in Congress.

The top of the executive branch tends to be highly centralized, controlled by people from the same political party, or even by people with no party affiliation, who act in complete deference or subordination to the will of the president or prime minister. In the main executive bodies, there are usually no members of opposition parties or people with views clearly opposed to those of the chief executive. In this context, decrees are not the result of deliberations or compromises between clashing political forces, but the result of discussions and debates among people who generally think the same. Decrees of high political content, therefore, end up entering the legal scenario and producing all its effects without the healthy and necessary discussion and prior control of other political actors.

Decrees must comply with the following substantive limits: (i) the text of the law, (ii) the purpose of the law, and (iii) the constitutional-legislative system governing the matter regulated. In this sense, chief executives must adopt specific hermeneutical guidelines in legal regulation, such as grammatical, teleological, historical, or systematic interpretation, and not just take into account their political will to unilaterally fulfill a certain campaign promise.

In sum, the excessive and abusive use of unilateral executive action poses a threat to constitutionalism and to the principle of the separation of powers. Although decrees are necessary in certain circumstances, they can be a form of usurpation of legislative power and abuse of authority. It's not uncommon for presidents or prime ministers to opportunistically use their unilateral normative authority to expand their prerogatives and impose public policies against the will of the legislature. Unilateral acts can be evidence that legislatures are marginalized, and democratic institutions are ineffective. In this context, legislative and judicial oversight is not "undue interference" in executive actions – on the contrary, it is an important part of a constitutional democratic system. Decrees cannot – and should not – exceed or contradict legal provisions. Only the checks and balances of the courts, the legislature, local governments, the media, and civil society can prevent the spread and normalization of authoritarian "pen strokes".

Index

Bolsonaro, Jair 1, 9, 16, 32, 36, 47, 50, 63, 64, 78, 91, 102, 117, 125, 129
Brazil 1, 2, 8–11, 17–19, 21–24, 27, 31, 32, 34–36, 38, 39, 41, 43, 47, 48, 50, 51, 58, 63–65, 73–75, 78–80, 102, 103, 105, 107, 109, 111, 113, 115, 117, 119, 121, 123, 125–131, 133, 135, 137–139, 141, 143, 145–147, 150, 151
Brazilian Supreme Court 45, 78, 100, 102

checks and balances 6, 7, 19, 55, 61, 64, 65, 76, 81, 119, 134, 149, 150, 153
chief executive 3, 7, 11, 12, 15, 16, 19–21, 24–26, 28, 32, 33, 37, 40, 42, 48, 49, 53, 58, 59, 62, 79, 89–91, 111, 112, 121, 152
COVID-19, 2, 4, 5, 7–9, 11, 13, 14, 16, 25, 26, 29, 38, 40, 41, 43, 46, 55, 57, 63, 65–67, 69–71, 73–75, 77–84, 89, 91, 102–111, 113–117, 119–125, 127–131, 133–139, 141–151

decree-law 5, 89, 105, 106, 109–111, 113, 114, 116–118
decrees of the President of the Council of Ministers (DPCM) 4, 5, 8, 11, 13, 77, 83, 102, 104–108, 110, 111–113, 123, 124, 146

emergency 3–6, 8, 12, 13, 16, 24, 26, 29, 37, 38, 41, 56, 57, 65, 66, 69–81, 83–85, 87, 89, 91–93, 95–97, 99, 101, 102, 104–107, 109, 111, 114, 116, 118–121, 125–127, 134, 140, 144, 146, 149–151
executive dominance 5, 13, 15–17, 19, 21, 23, 25, 27, 29, 69, 72, 74, 82, 83
executive orders 2, 4, 13, 18, 26, 33–35, 38, 40, 42, 49, 50, 53, 54, 57, 58, 67
executive unbound 3, 14, 16, 17, 19, 23, 30, 39, 40, 42, 44, 55, 56, 65
executive underreach 63, 64, 67, 125, 147

German Constitutional Court 8, 46, 96–100, 143–145
German Infectious Diseases Protection Act 9, 77, 103, 114, 115, 141
Germany 6, 8–10, 13, 14, 46, 54, 71, 72, 75, 77–80, 83, 84, 86, 88, 94, 96, 102, 103, 105, 107, 109, 111, 113–117, 119, 121, 123–125, 127, 129, 131, 133–145, 147, 148, 150, 151
government ministers 11, 46, 55, 73, 85, 129

human rights 26, 66, 75, 76, 81, 82, 132
Hungary 7, 57, 59, 69, 70

Italian Constitutional Court 77, 102, 104–106, 113, 114, 117–120
Italy 4, 8, 10, 11, 14, 49, 57, 77, 79, 80, 84, 89, 102–105, 107, 109, 111, 113, 115, 117, 119–125, 127, 129, 131, 133–137, 139, 141, 143, 145–147, 150, 151

judicial oversight 7, 8, 16, 23, 61, 69, 76, 153

legislative delegation 4, 18, 22, 104, 106, 113, 114

legislative oversight 6, 19, 72, 102
legislative process 3, 15, 20, 38, 43, 48, 49, 52, 58, 81, 91, 94, 97, 108, 129, 151, 152

medidas provisórias 10, 11, 24, 35, 38, 58, 127

parliamentary systems 4, 10, 11, 33, 36, 150
populism 15, 30
presidentialism 5, 9, 14, 25, 37, 40, 72, 79, 82, 83, 126, 147
presidents 1, 4, 5, 7, 11, 13, 15–21, 24, 26, 31–37, 39–43, 46, 47, 49, 51, 52, 55, 57, 58, 59–61, 79, 83, 87, 126, 147, 150, 152, 153
primary legislation 2, 4, 10, 38, 50, 77, 87, 93, 94, 97, 98, 100, 104, 107, 109, 110, 113, 124
prime ministers 4, 5, 7, 8, 10, 11, 15, 19, 20, 24, 31–33, 35–37, 39–43, 46–48, 52, 55, 57, 59, 61, 87, 102, 117, 121, 150–153

restrictions on fundamental rights 8, 9, 76, 77, 93, 94, 98, 100, 114

secondary legislation 1, 4, 11, 39, 86, 87, 100, 103, 139, 143, 151
secondary regulation 11, 89, 96
subnational 6, 8, 12, 56, 65, 66, 71, 79–81, 126, 131, 134, 135, 137, 149

technical and scientific 12, 45, 86, 109, 117, 118
times of crisis 6, 7, 13, 24, 37, 43, 55, 57, 59, 61, 63, 65, 67, 70, 78–80, 82, 84, 110, 111, 112, 134, 136, 137, 139, 147, 149, 151
Trump, Donald 2, 63, 117
Turkey 7, 57, 69, 70

unilateral acts 3, 7, 8, 10, 11, 22, 26, 29, 35, 38, 42, 43, 49, 62, 110, 150
United States of America 2, 4, 19, 21, 27, 30, 34, 63, 65, 66, 76, 84, 117

For Product Safety Concerns and Information please contact our EU
representative GPSR@taylorandfrancis.com
Taylor & Francis Verlag GmbH, Kaufingerstraße 24, 80331 München, Germany

www.ingramcontent.com/pod-product-compliance
Ingram Content Group UK Ltd.
Pitfield, Milton Keynes, MK11 3LW, UK
UKHW022042061126
477531UK00009B/482

* 9 7 8 1 0 4 1 0 0 6 2 2 0 *